Behavioral Challenges
in Children with Autism
and Other Special Needs

Contents

Acknowledgments

I would like to express my gratitude to the many people who have taught me and encouraged my studies. In particular, Arthur H. Parmelee, MD, Stanley I. Greenspan, MD, and Serena Wieder, PhD. In addition, I extend my deepest respect for all my colleagues at Professional Child Development Associates, especially Mimi Winer, RN, MS, Julie Miller, MOT, OTR/L, SWC, Anne Davis, MS, MA, CCC-SLP, Brandt Chamberlain, PhD, LaJoi Johnson-Huff, PsyD, Betina Shain, MFT, Elaine Chen, NM, MT-BC, Denise Rugg, MA, and Jennifer Aceves, BA; and to my friends and fellow workers in the DIRFloortime Coalition of California, especially Joshua D. Feder, MD, Andrea Davis, PhD, Jonine Beisman, PsyD, APBdN, Pat Marquart, MFT, Mona Delahooke, PhD, Ben Zequeira Russell, PsyD, and Cherisse Sherin, MA.

I am truly grateful for all the professionals, parents, adults with autism, legislators, and advocates that have contributed to the great effort of advancing developmental principles for children throughout the country and the world. Sincere thanks to the children and families that have generously shared their journeys, challenges, and triumphs with us. And to my husband, Bill, and our children, Scott and Sara, I extend my unending gratitude for their patience and love.

Introduction

The way in which professionals work with children with special needs has changed dramatically over the past 50 years. Since the development and passage of the Education for All Handicapped Children Act in 1975, which later became the Individuals with Disabilities Education Act (IDEA), and the subsequent mandates to provide services to infants and young children, there has been an increased awareness and a sense of collective responsibility to care for infants and children with disabilities and at risk of disability. Initially, teachers and a few professional disciplines provided services, and now, a child may receive therapies from multiple specialists, and often from an integrated multidisciplinary team.

Although families are no longer isolated in their efforts to care for their child with special needs, there are still many questions regarding the best treatment approach, especially for a child with autism (Magiati, Tay, & Howlin, 2012; Weitlauf et al., 2014; Young, Corea, Kimani, & Mandell, 2010). During the past 50 years, there has also been an exponential increase in scientific advances in general, which has led to an expectation that precise empirical data should guide treatment choices, and a view that an objective attitude toward problem behavior is best. Applied behavioral analysis (ABA), which provides clear treatment goals and strategies and measureable quantitative data about behavior, has become a widely accepted practice.

ABA typically uses functional behavioral analysis for assessment with the premise that "problem behaviors are maintained by their functional effect" (Horner, Carr, Strain, Todd, & Reed, 2002). Intervention utilizes the construct of antecedents, behavior, and consequences, and manipulates the environment and responses in order to achieve targeted behavioral goals. ABA intervention has evolved from discrete trials done solely by a professional to a broader focus, including consideration of multiple behaviors across time, working in natural environments, and including parents and other adults. There is attention to creating environments to prevent behavior, offering choices, and implementing systems change (Carr et al., 2002; Horner et al., 2002). Many programs for children now incorporate developmental goals such as joint attention and imitation, and use strategies such as following the child's lead and emotion sharing to improve spontaneity, initiative, and generalization (Schreibman et al., 2015). Still, ABA programs operate within the behavioral paradigm of prompts and contingent reinforcers to achieve a desired measurable behavior (Carr et al., 2002; Horner et al., 2002; Rogers & Vismara, 2008; Schreibman et al., 2015).

Developmental approaches emanate from different theoretical roots and are concerned with a child's internal psychological processes, relationships, and individuality. Over the past 50 years, there have also been major advances in this field of study, including revelations about the capacities of infants to engage socially and the innate human drive to seek novelty (Brazelton & Nugent, 1973/1995; Mahler, 1975; Piaget, 1952). Others have added insights regarding the importance of affective interactions for learning (Fogel, 1993; Greenspan & Shanker, 2004; Vygotsky, 1978). For children with autism, there has been a new recognition of the desire to be connected in social relationships, despite appearances to the contrary (Bauminger & Kasari, 2000; Mazurek, 2014).

From a developmental perspective, affect is the guiding principle for behavior, and the pleasure derived from shared affect in relationships motivates developmental growth. Challenging behaviors are understood to be a manifestation of constrictions in the development of functional emotional capacities. A child with autism or other developmental challenges may have various barriers to successful social engagement including weaknesses in the underlying biology of emotional regulation itself (Greenspan, 2001; Mazefsky, Pelphrey, & Dahl, 2012). The remedy for a challenging behavior then becomes the use of increased affective interactions to strengthen a child's emotional development.

This book presents a developmental approach to behavioral challenges for children with autism and other disabilities, built upon the developmental, individual differences relationship (DIR) model (Greenspan & Wieder, 2006). This model emerged from the revolutionary insights of Stanley Greenspan, MD, and was elaborated by Serena Wieder, PhD. Their work revealed how affective interactions are the core organizing principle in development. This book applies the developmental framework to a full range of behavioral issues, for children of all ages and all abilities.

There are six basic functional emotional milestones in the DIR model. Deficits in each milestone correlate with behavioral challenges. A child that has difficulty with Milestone 1, basic regulation and shared attention, may withdraw and become self-absorbed, or escalate into fight-or-flight behaviors. A child that has constrictions in Milestone 2, the ability to form warm engagement with others, may have difficulty recovering from distress and become despondent or rigid and anxious. With deficits in the ability to engage in reciprocal interactions, Milestone 3, a child may remain isolated, may lack initiative, and may have a constricted range of emotional expression. A deficit in Milestone 4, sustained, coregulated interactions, results in a lack of persistence and inability to tolerate frustration or disappointment, and may result in defiant or oppositional behavior. A child who is not able to use symbolic and creative thinking, Milestone 5, may act out angry or anxious feelings, and a child that does not advance to logical thinking, Milestone 6, may have difficulty considering the perspective of others and discerning truth from fantasy.

A child's individual differences in sensory responses, language, movement, and cognition also contribute to a comprehensive understanding of behavioral challenges. For example, stubborn and defiant behavior may have roots in the frustration of a poor ability to sequence movements and a related weakness in the ability to connect affective gestures needed to engage in shared problem solving. Intervention would then focus on both improving sensory-motor processes and on strengthening the functional emotional developmental capacities needed for coregulated interactions. Developmental interventions are carefully tailored to the individual differences of each child.

The core of a developmental approach is an empathetic relationship, in which an adult attunes to a child's affective experience, and supports the child according to his or her developmental capacities, while also encouraging growth of those capacities. Progress occurs through stages of emotional transformation in the context of these relationships. Warm and trusting relationships can offer comfort during distress and lead to coregulated experiences wherein a child gains further self-regulation of emotion and behavior. At higher levels, affective relationships help a child to negotiate a wide range of emotional themes and the complex dynamics of emotional life.

This book is arranged in three parts: (1) understanding a child's behavior from a developmental perspective, (2) responding to a challenging behavior in the moment, and (3) making a long-term plan to support developmental and behavioral progress. The response in the moment is further divided into three steps: attune, help, and recover. By using this structured approach, an adult can be guided in interventions that logically follow a universal development progression.

When a child with a disability has a behavioral challenge, a clinician is confronted with the complexities of the child's developmental strengths and vulnerabilities, individual differences, and his or her unique pattern of interactions in personal relationships. Keeping all the variables in mind, the developmental approach provides a plan that supports growth to the child's highest potential. Not only will a child decrease specific unwanted behaviors, but he or she will also relate warmly to others, be caring, considerate, respectful, and may ultimately form personal values to guide independent ethical decisions.

This book is written for all adults who interact with a child with special needs, whether their work is directly focused on changing behavior, or if they simply provide support so that the child can participate in other endeavors. Teachers, educational assistants, developmental interventionists, speech and language pathologists, occupational therapists, physical therapists, music therapists, psychologists, marriage and family therapists, social workers, physicians, or any other professional that works with children may utilize the concepts presented here. Parents may follow these strategies as well, although parents are encouraged to partner with a professional to guide and support their efforts.

The developmental approach discussed here is applied to children with autism and other developmental challenges. The examples do not include children with emotional disturbance due to abuse, trauma, or primary issues related to parents that are physically or emotionally unavailable; however, the concepts may also be relevant to any of these situations. This book is not designed to provide guidance on in-depth psychotherapeutic understanding or strategies. Referral to specialists, including mental health specialists, may be needed. The book also does not discuss the use of medication to modify affect, mood, or behavior. Again, a professional is advised to utilize consultation and referral as appropriate. Clinicians must be aware of their own disciplinary boundaries and be able to recognize when further support is needed.

The examples used in this book are designed to illustrate specific concepts and do not represent actual cases. Many examples purposefully do not state a chronological age, as vignettes have been created to reflect developmental levels rather than age. The descriptions combine elements of different situations I have encountered over the past 30-plus years of work with children, and my role of providing supervision and consultation to professionals from many disciplines. Any similarity to an actual case is coincidental.

Behavioral Challenges
in Children with Autism
and Other Special Needs

Note to Readers: Standards of clinical practice and protocol change over time, and no technique or recommendation is guaranteed to be safe or effective in all circumstances. This volume is intended as a general information resource for professionals practicing in the field of psychotherapy and mental health; it is not a substitute for appropriate training, peer review, and/or clinical supervision. Neither the publisher nor the author(s) can guarantee the complete accuracy, efficacy, or appropriateness of any particular recommendation in every respect.

For information about permission to reproduce selections from this book, write to Permissions, W. W. Norton & Company, Inc., 500 Fifth Avenue, New York, NY 10110

For information about special discounts for bulk purchases, please contact W. W. Norton Special Sales at specialsales@wwnorton.com or 800-233-4830

Manufacturing by Edwards Brothers Malloy
Production manager: Christine Critelli

Library of Congress Cataloging-in-Publication Data

Names: Cullinane, Diane, author.
Title: Behavioral challenges in children with autism and other special needs
    : the developmental approach / Diane Cullinane.
Description: First edition. | New York : W. W. Norton & Company, [2016] |
    Series: A Norton professional book | Includes bibliographical references
    and index.
Identifiers: LCCN 2015049561 | ISBN 9780393709254 (hardcover)
Subjects: LCSH: Behavior disorders in children. | Autistic children—Behavior
    modification. | Developmentally disabled children—Behavior modification.
    | Children with disabilities—Psychology. | Behavior modification.
Classification: LCC RJ506.B44 C85 2016 | DDC 618.92/85882—dc23 LC record available at
http://lccn.loc.gov/2015049561

W. W. Norton & Company, Inc.
500 Fifth Avenue, New York, N.Y. 10110
www.wwnorton.com

W. W. Norton & Company Ltd.
Castle House, 75/76 Wells Street, London W1T 3QT

1 2 3 4 5 6 7 8 9 0

DIR®, DIRFloortime®, and Floortime® are registered trademarks of the Interdisciplinary Council on Development and Learning, Inc. (ICDL) in the United States and many other countries and are used in this book with the permission of ICDL.

Behavioral Challenges in Children with Autism and Other Special Needs

The Developmental Approach

Diane Cullinane, MD

W. W. Norton & Company
Indpendent Publishers Since 1923
New York • London

This book is dedicated to my husband,
Bill Cullinane,
for his love, encouragement and support.

PART I

UNDERSTANDING BEHAVIOR FROM A DEVELOPMENTAL PERSPECTIVE

The Developmental Approach

Ben, a husky 11-year-old nonverbal boy with autism, does not want to leave the building. He wants to continue his routine of counting all the doors. When urged to move toward the exit, he falls to the ground and resists all attempts to get him up. To make matters worse, he is screeching and blocking the path in a public place. This behavior happens almost every time he must leave a building. What can anyone do?

Parents, clinicians, and teachers face a multitude of similar situations, big and small, every day. There is no shortage of advice—often conflicting—coming from family, neighbors, friends, strangers, teachers, and a host of clinicians. An adult might demand, "Get up now, or you can't have your iPad," or try to entice with, "If you get up now, you can have ice cream," or simply give in: "Okay, let's go count the doors." Often, the adult in charge feels embarrassed, discouraged, and even desperate. Many of us would admit that we really don't know what to do.

The behavior of children with autism or other developmental disabilities can be perplexing. Both parents and professionals may seek help in understanding and managing challenging behaviors. Professionals in the behavioral or mental health field, such as those providing child and family counseling, address behaviors as a direct focus of their work.

Those in related fields whose focus is not directly related to behavior, such as speech and language therapy, occupational or physical therapy, music therapy, or education must respond to challenging behaviors that occur in their therapy sessions or classrooms simply to enable them to work on other goals. Both parents and professionals face these challenges, and the best success occurs when they collaborate to help children conquer their difficulties.

This book presents a developmental framework and practical steps for understanding and addressing behavioral challenges in children of all ages, especially those with autism or other developmental challenges. The developmental approach is a way of understanding and responding to behaviors in the context of a child's functional emotional developmental capacities, individual differences, and pattern of affective interactions in relationships. This approach is founded on universal principles and applied to fit the unique children and adults who are interacting together.

The History of the Developmental Approach

The developmental framework for understanding childhood behavior is the outgrowth of a rich history of the study of children and learning. Over the years, philosophers, psychologists, educators, and physicians have pondered the ideal way to parent, to educate, and to help children overcome immature, impulsive, self-centered behaviors and become productive citizens of the world. Theorists have debated the relative importance of experience versus the natural unfolding of biological maturational processes to account for volitional behavior, language, and complex thinking.

One early area of study was learning theory, in which behaviorists such as Ivan Pavlov (1927/2012), John B. Watson (1925), and B. F. Skinner (1953) focused on the power of environmental stimuli to shape behavior. They posited that human behavior could be understood as predictable responses to environmental signals.

The developmental psychologist, Jean Piaget (1952), viewed cognitive development as being internally motivated. He chronicled his observations of childrens' interactions with objects, and showed how children actively sought out novelty and learned from their own curiosity and initiative. Lev Vygotsky (1978) and Jerome Bruner (1990) also viewed children as active learners and emphasized the role of social interaction in cognitive development. Lawrence Kohlberg (1981, 1984) studied moral development in children using Piagetian constructs with further consideration of social interaction.

A separate field of study focused on psychodynamic development. Although Sigmund Freud (1923/1960) did not study children directly, he was one of the first to recognize the importance of childhood emotional experiences for the creation of the inner psychic life of adults, both conscious and unconscious. Anna Freud (1965), Erik Erikson (1963), and Margaret Mahler (1975) advanced the study of psychological development, particularly in regard to a child's relationship with his or her parents.

The field of humanistic psychology introduced a new perspective, valuing individuality, the development of the self as a comprehensive whole, creativity, and relationships. Major contributors to this area of thought were Carl Rogers (1961) and Abraham Maslow (1962/2014). Virginia Mae Axline (1947) built on these ideas and described play therapy for children using nondirective approaches.

Others extended insights into child development through their study of infants. Among these, John Bowlby (1951, 1969/1999), Mary Ainsworth (Ainsworth, Bell, & Stayton, 1974), T. Berry Brazelton (Brazelton & Nugent, 1973/1995), Alan Fogel (1993), Daniel Stern (1985/2000), Donald Winnicott (1971/2005), and others recognized the remarkable capacities of infants and young children to form emotional attachments and engage in complex social interactions with caregivers.

Two broad areas of study, cognitive-developmental psychology and affective psychodynamic psychology, were largely separate fields until relatively recently. Building on the values of humanistic psychology, Stanley I. Greenspan (1979) synthesized psychodynamic theory and cognitive developmental learning models into a comprehensive developmental framework. Greenspan was the first to put forward the idea that emotional or affective experience in social interactions paves the way for all learning, including cognition and language. This understanding creates a major paradigm shift in the approach to treatment of children with developmental challenges.

The DIR Approach and the
Role of Emotions in Development

Greenspan's insight was to recognize that emotion and reason are inextricably intertwined. Dr. Greenspan's (1979) seminal work, *Intelligence and Adaptation*, offers an integrated model of child development combining Piagetian cognitive stages and the Freudian psychoanalytic theoretical framework. This comprehensive model, now known as DIR and DIRFloortime, incorporates functional emotional developmental milestones (D) with each child's unique biological differences (I) and the patterns of affective interaction within key relationships (R).

The DIR model describes the integration of emotional experience and learning as predictable and consistent stages or milestones. The six milestones build from a foundation of shared attention, intimacy, and trust, to two-way gestural interaction, to shared problem solving, and then to higher levels of symbolic emotional ideas and logical thinking. These functional-emotional developmental milestones incorporate all the traditional domains of development, including movement, communication, social skills, and cognition. Greenspan's novel revelation is the primacy of emotional experiences and interactions in propelling development forward, even to higher capacities of logical and abstract thinking and communicating. Among a host of applications, this model has become the basis of developmentally based intervention for children with autism and other neurodevelopmental disorders. *Infancy and Early Childhood* (Greenspan, 1992) contains an in-depth description of the model for work in early childhood development. *Developmentally Based Psychotherapy* (Greenspan, 1997) provides guidance on the use of the DIR model in psychotherapy for mental health disorders. *Engaging Autism*, by Greenspan and Wieder (2006), describes the use of the DIR approach to support the development of children with autism.

The developmental approach is founded on an appreciation of the link between affective interactions and learning. Biology dictates that infants are immediately connected to a mother and father. Very quickly they are able to hold a memory of a caregiver, which importantly includes all of the associated sensory-motor-affective experiences—visual, auditory, tactile, kinesthetic, smell, taste. The bond created by shared experiences with a parent is the first step in learning. As children grow, they discover that they are able to cause things to happen, first through interaction with a caregiver: They can cry and be fed, raise their arms and be picked up, or smile to get a smile in return. Gradually, they learn to organize a sense of self through patterns in innumerable emotionally colored interactions.

The ability to attend, explore, and solve problems is based on an expanding capacity for emotional regulation. Through co-regulation with a parent, a child learns to work toward shared goals and to function during increasing levels of excitement, pleasure, and distress. Children can then independently concentrate, persist, and delay gratification. Through engagement with others, they learn to tolerate a broad range of feelings as they negotiate life's dramas.

> *"In order to develop symbols, we must transform our basic emotions into a series of succeedingly more complex emotional signals."*
> —Stanley Greenspan & Stuart Shanker

At higher levels of reasoning, emotional experiences continue to lead the way. The capacity for symbolic thinking emerges after many affectively laden experiences with people and sensations coalesce to form a free-standing symbol. A child can say, "I want it!" without grabbing, or "I hate you!" without acting aggressively. The child can then use ideas and imagination to create, plan, negotiate, and reason.

As children participate in more complex social interactions, they learn how multiple emotional factors intersect, and to weigh the variables of time, space, quantity, and degree by virtue of their emotional salience. Even the highest levels of reflective, comparative, and abstract thinking represent an underlying foundation of affective interaction with others. From an adult's casual conversation to high-level academic writing and study, emotion is an ever-present component. Conflict and controversy, joy and pride, disgust and fears, all permeate mature thinking and interaction. As emotional beings, adults continue to be dependent on one another for emotional and behavioral regulation.

The idea that affective or emotional experience underlies and organizes cognition is a revolutionary idea. The concept that emotional experience can support learning and, even more, can be the genesis of learning, is contrary to long-held assumptions that view emotion and reason as opposing forces. Many have considered emotions as corrupting influences on calm, rational thought. The developmental approach reformulates the relationship between emotion and reason and asserts that emotional experience and affectively based interactions are actually the context and motivation for cognition and achievement. It is a paradox that although strong emotions can reduce thinking capacities to lower levels and can be unpleasant or even painful, it is only through other counteracting emotions that reason can be elevated again.

The positive value of emotional experience is readily apparent in human endeavors and accomplishments. Children are naturally inquisitive and curious. They seek excitement and find pleasure in experiences of wonder and awe. Humans are drawn to social allegiance, fidelity, love, devotion, passion, and bravery. Sadness and loss, disappointment, frustration, anger, fear, pain, loneliness—all motivate constructive as well as regressive behavior. Creativity, ingenuity, courage, and loyalty have roots in evolutionary biology and reach new heights in human relations. Human character occurs not despite emotions, but because of emotions.

Connecting the Developmental Approach and Behavioral Goals

> The most important principle is to avoid focusing only on changing the behavior. The temptation is to institute a whole program just to curb the impulsivity, aggression, or moodiness and negativism. But if we do this without building the foundations for healthy behavior, the results are unsatisfactory.
> —Stanley Greenspan and Serena Wieder

Goals of the developmental approach include the ability of a child to engage in warm, trusting, and intimate relationships with others, to be curious and creative, and to have an ability to tolerate and function within a wide range of feelings. Functional emotional development includes the ability to consider the perspective of others and to be empathetic. Behavioral goals are the ability to act in ways that support both individual needs and contribute positively to a social community. A universal road map to achieving behavioral goals is provided when behavioral dramas are placed in the context of overall functional emotional development.

On the surface, the desired outcome for a child's behavioral challenge is often compliance with an adult directive: "Do what I say!" "Do it now!" or "Stop doing that!" All of life is replete with limits, rules, authority, and boundaries. Dealing with limits is one of the major themes of social development.

An infant and child learn limits of behavior through interactions with parents and other adults. A caregiver that communicates with emotional attunement, empathy, and compassion is both supporting emotional development and helping a child to gain behavioral control. In this way, a child develops the capacity to not only cope and comply with limits, but also to be internally motivated to want to behave in ways that are considerate and pleasing to others.

At higher levels, children may gain an ability to discuss, reflect, negotiate, and then to create their own limits based on their own internal value system. They can then grapple with complex social issues, balance conflicting values, and confront ethical dilemmas. A child may learn to discern rules of conduct that apply in different situations, and can use creative problem solving to adapt to novel situations.

Because the developmental approach follows this universal developmental progression, utilizing affectively based interactions, it is effective for all types of behavioral challenges and for all children. Complying with directions, respecting limits, and more complex expectations for behavior are addressed within a broader understanding of development and relationship.

Contrasting Developmental and Behavioral Approaches

The developmental approach is dramatically different than the behavioral approach. In general terms, the behavioral approach as described originally by Pavlov (1927/2012) and Skinner (1953), and later by O. Ivar Lovaas (1987) and others, describes how a particular behavior can be increased by positive outcomes and decreased by negative outcomes. The behavioral approach focuses on external, observable, and measurable behaviors, and is considered to be reductionist, as it proceeds by isolating and analyzing specific targeted behaviors and responses.

The basic sequence in the behavioral approach is antecedents, behavior, and consequences. Antecedents are the context or situation that motivates the behavior; behavior is the particular identified behavior; and consequences are the actions taken that reinforce, promote, or discourage the behavior. The behavioral approach examines the environment to discern motivations for behavior (for example, to seek tangibles, to gain attention, or avoidance) and then utilizes environmental manipulations to modify behavior and gradually attain compliance with behavioral directives (positive or negative reinforcements: reward, ignore, or punish).

It has been demonstrated that children, including those with autism, can learn and respond to structured behavioral teaching. Although the behavioral approach is conceptually attractive, the results are often disappointing. Learning in this way tends to be bound to environmental prompts and children may lack initiative as they wait for directions. Children can also become dependent on the reinforcer or consequence. They may always expect a reward for following commands, and may come to demand rewards as a condition of compliance. They may take advantage of opportunities to misbehave if they feel that they can avoid a negative consequence. It is also difficult to generalize structured teaching to a variety of novel situations. Even more concerning is that a child that learns to follow commands for rewards may be vulnerable to following malicious commands and become a victim of exploitation and abuse.

While recognizing the potency of conditioned behavioral learning for specific behaviors, such as routine procedures, a developmental approach considers behaviors within a broader scope and embraces the complexities of emotional development, individual differences, and interactions in relationships. Often, the developmental perspective offers radically different interpretations of behavior and leads to drastically different goals and intervention strategies.

> *The developmental approach does not negate or contradict dynamic and behavioral approaches; in fact, it would use specific components of these, but as a part of a larger developmental framework.*
>
> —Stanley Greenspan

In a behavioral approach, the preeminent goal is that a child becomes calm, attentive, and obedient. Intervention involves a consistent application of objective rules and consequences. Emotional experiences, particularly negative emotions, are discouraged and sometimes discounted. In contrast, the developmental approach is based on the idea that the sensitive and respectful mutual regulation of emotional experience, within a trusting relationship, is the catalyst for learning to function within an expanding range of emotional experience.

The behavioral approach teaches specific skills through adult-directed and controlled interaction. Children often rebel or withdraw when their natural desires are constrained in this way. By contrast, a developmental approach often uses play to build developmental capacities. Floortime play—which uses specific developmental strategies—follows a child's lead, takes advantage of the child's internal motivation, and then challenges the child to expand his or her developmental abilities.

Raul loved his little colored blocks. Persistently, he engaged in self-absorbed solitary and repetitive play. Everyone wanted Raul to interact. A behaviorist was teaching Raul to take turns by rolling a ball back and forth. When Raul successfully followed the command, "Roll the ball," and rolled the ball back to the behaviorist six times, he was given his blocks to play with for one minute. When they were taken away, he cried.

A developmental interventionist (DI) decided to join Raul with the blocks. She brought some similar blocks and began to play next to Raul. Slowly, Raul allowed the DI to get close. Then the DI placed a block in line with his. At first he just moved it away, but as she continued to playfully add to his design, he gradually allowed her blocks to mingle. After trust was built, Raul began to smile and communicate spontaneously with the DI, first with gestures, and then with words.

Using developmental principles, Raul not only achieved reciprocal interaction, but also experienced the enjoyment of a trusting relationship, and was motivated to initiate and continue the engagement.

The importance of developmental goals such as shared attention, pleasure in interactions, and initiative have been increasingly recognized as precursors for language and cognition. Unfortunately, behavioral strategies are sometimes used to attain behaviors that are only superficially associated with true development. For example, in pursuing a goal of shared attention, a child might be directed, "Look at me," and then told, "Good job," for looking toward an adult. Here, a child may respond behaviorally, but without understanding or genuine interest in the other person.

In contrast, a developmental interventionist would attune to a child's emotion and interests, even if subtle, and use natural affective gestures to create a mutual experience and connection: "Wow! That was a big one!" "Here, do you want another one?" These shared experiences might be acknowledged by a child's smile or movement, which may or may not include directly shared eye gaze. Genuine shared emotion, within a trusting relationship, lays a strong foundation for further growth. Later, that child may spontaneously look for the adult's facial expression for coregulatory cues as part of their natural interaction.

One behavioral strategy is targeted ignoring. The idea is to not provide attention as a reward for unwanted behavior.

Edward ran out of the room. He lay in the corner on the floor, loudly moaning and thrashing about. He said, "I want to go." His behavioral aid stood by, and followed his program which directed that she not intervene, as this would reward his behavior. After several minutes, he was told sternly, "Get up." He continued to moan, and say, "I want to go."

Investigation revealed that Edward was overwhelmed by the noise and commotion of the classroom activity. His schedule had changed recently, and he was tired. His pattern of expressing distress was occurring frequently, and an intensive behavioral program had been instituted with a new one-on-one aide that involved ignoring some behaviors and rewards for compliance involving time to use an iPad.

In contrast, a developmental approach would be based on attunement to Edward's feelings and intentions, and would use strategies both to help him attain behavioral regulation and to build a relationship of warmth and trust. An attitude of compassion and care would guide understanding and support. For example, a developmental interventionist would try to soothe his distress, help him to organize and express his feelings, and then provide the needed support for him to regain his composure and perhaps, with that sup-

port, rejoin his class. Strategies of giving directions, ignoring, and tangible rewards would not be used. A relationship of trust would create an expectation of kindness and support for subsequent episodes of distress.

In the moment of a behavioral challenge, and during ongoing therapy, a child is encouraged to continually expand the ability to function across a range of emotional experiences. Some parents and professionals may be concerned that challenging children to enlarge their emotional range, rather than seeking calm compliance, will lead to more behavioral problems. By understanding typical development, it becomes apparent that the opposite is true.

> *A complex problem calls for a complex approach.*
> —Stanley Greenspan and Serena Wieder

Developmental and behavioral approaches have distinct underlying principles, goals, and intervention methodologies. Directives and consequences for behavior are a regular part of daily life and behavioral strategies may be effective to achieve some behavioral goals, however a developmental approach considers behavior within a broader developmental framework. By using a developmental, relationship-based approach to behavioral challenges, a child not only improves specific behaviors but also advances on the pathway to higher cognitive, social, and communication skills.

Development, Learning, and Motivation

Development is a complex process of transformation, progress, and regression. Events are experienced at sensory, cognitive, and emotional levels, and occur in relationships with specific people. A growing child takes in information, incorporates that with previous experience, and generates new understanding. Knowledge is continuously reorganized as development advances.

Once an infant has achieved basic internal biological stability, he or she will actively attend to the environment and will seek out the excitement of novelty. An infant will naturally prefer the stimulus of humans over objects. This innate drive to explore and the desire for human connection is the motivation for looking, moving, communicating, and learning.

The desire for social relations continues as infant and caregiver engage in playful reciprocal interactions. These simple interactions are the harbingers of later creativity, invention, and discovery. Simple interactions are gradually expanded into longer and more complex dynamic interactions involving affective signaling around a range of emotions. With the help of caregivers, a child learns to tolerate negative emotions, and to be persistent as they engage in shared problem solving. From accumulated social experiences, with a broad range of emotional signaling, a child learns to understand the motivations of others, and to predict the consequences of behavior for themselves and for others. From the motivation of social relationships comes a desire to be accepted, to please others, and to share in the common good.

> "Long chains of reciprocal communication become pleasurable in their own right because they foster greater co-regulation of relationships and provide safe and secure ways to express and negotiate feelings and needs and therefore become an end in their own (rather than a means to some other gratification)."
> —Stanley Greenspan

The assumptions about what motivates children to learn have direct implications for how to teach acceptable behavior. If it is believed that children are motivated to learn primarily through feedback from tangible rewards in the environment, then teaching built on an organized and consistent reward system takes precedence. If, however, it is believed that children are motivated to learn by the joy of interaction in loving relationships, a desire for intimacy, acceptance, comfort, and the joy of cocreating, then expanded emotional experience with others becomes the primary means of learning.

In this later view, development cannot be directly taught. Rather, development evolves from internal motivation, opportunities for initiative, and accumulated experience of warmth and shared problem solving with others. Understanding what a child with autism or other developmental challenges is feeling or experiencing can be difficult, yet it is mandatory in order to harness the true motivations for learning.

From the perspective of a behavioral approach, a child's behavior may sometimes be determined to have the purpose of seeking attention, which is generally viewed as a selfish motivation that needs to be squelched by either ignoring or redirecting. In contrast, the developmental approach generally celebrates a child's desire for attention. Seeking attention is interpreted along the developmental continuum, with recognition that by strengthening social engagement, a child will eventually acquire greater ability to function independently.

For a child with developmental challenges, the drive to learn and to connect with others may seem limited. Some doubt whether these children possess the same capacity for internal motivation for relationship as other children. This doubt has contributed to programs with limited expectations and constricted opportunities for a child to gain the range of emotional experiences and relationships needed for growth. However, by adopting the view that a child may only have obstacles that obscure an underlying motivation for social connection, the possibility is opened for overcoming those barriers and tapping into a nascent force for learning.

Many adults with autism are now able to describe their intense childhood desire for friendship and how their behaviors were misunderstood. It may have seemed to others that they preferred to be alone, or that they were unable to understand, think, or use their imagination. Now, as adults, they have discovered ways to share their profound and sensitive insights and considerable talents. When the developmental approach is used, with a belief in the ability of children to learn through the motivation of deepening relationships, amazing capacities may be realized.

Relationship-Based Approach

A developmental approach is relationship based because it is concerned with the affective interaction between a child and others in his or her life, particularly the relationship between a child and his/her parents. It is impossible to understand children's behavior without reference to their relationships with their parents or other primary caregivers.

Interactions around behavior are shared experiences, occurring simultaneously in both parties through multiple modalities: words, actions, gestures, tone of voice, facial expressions, and internally with thoughts and feelings. These interactions form patterns in relationships from which a child forms a sense of self.

Children and caregivers develop their own way of communicating. Often a parent is able to interpret her child's body language, facial expressions, tone of voice, and gestures to gain an almost instantaneous understanding of the child's emotions and intent. In a similar way, a child learns to read the parent's cues. These nonverbal expressions are the basis of communication before a child learns to use words, and continue after a child has language, as a powerful and primary mode of communication.

Attunement to affective experience requires inferences about emotional life that extend beyond observable behavior. Emotion is highly personal and subjective. It is connected with internal biology, such as increasing heart rate, breathing, tightness in the stomach, sweating, and so on, that may or may not have external manifestations. At higher levels, symbolic ideas about emotions, wishes, and fears are also personal and internal.

To add complexity, an observable behavior may be associated with very different emotional experiences. A child may perform an action or obey a command and feel proud, or anxious, resentful, embarrassed, bored, or relieved. Some children are able to consciously inhibit emotional expression or feign emotion.

Emotional communication is inherently imprecise. It involves the constant use of inferences, guesses, and repair of miscommunications. While the multiplicity of variables involved in affective communication is daunting, it is also natural. Human biology provides capacities for reading emotional cues and empathizing with others' experience.

For a child with autism or other developmental challenge, the cues about feelings and intentions may be absent, misleading, or confusing. A child may have only a limited range of facial expressions and a limited repertoire of vocalizations and gestures. A child's emotional state may not be well organized. A vocalization may not differentiate between angry, sad, or scared. Emotional signals and actions may not be congruent. A child may be smiling or giggling while hitting, or suddenly walk away in the midst of a fun interaction.

A focus on accurately interpreting a child's subtle or idiosyncratic way of conveying his or her internal affective state provides the foundation for advancing emotional development. A professional can assist parents by drawing attention to a child's cues, proposing a different interpretation for a child's expressions or gestures, and supporting a child to clarify his or her intent.

A successful communicative partner encourages emotional expression and supports children to organize their feelings. Success with an interested and sensitive adult brings satisfaction and enjoyment, which leads a child to seek out more interaction. Development then advances as a child achieves greater coregulation of emotion and behavior.

Inquiry into parent-child communication is not standard practice for some professionals. There may be many barriers to working with parents, including dilemmas about professional boundaries and the appropriate relationship to have with parents. There may be legitimate issues about finding time and the occasion to be together. These are serious and significant questions, and are answered differently for different professionals and in different contexts. However, the fundamental principle remains that helping a child with behaviors requires an appreciation of the parent-child relationship, and collaboration between parents and professionals in the process of change.

Dependence and Independence

Parenting involves two seemingly opposing forces: (1) the caring and nurturance of a dependent child, and (2) promoting and celebrating a child's increasing autonomy, initiative, and assertiveness. Paradoxically, these two divergent roles support each other. A foundation of strong attachment, gaining pleasure, comfort, and regulation through interactions and the ability to form and rely on relationships enables a child to achieve greater independence.

The support received from others is not simply to obtain a tangible item, but is, more importantly, to transform a feeling. A child may also receive support from a relationship when experiencing happiness: sharing the experience can heighten the joy while also modulating the excitement. Feelings might also be confusion, fear, sadness, frustration, loneliness, anger, jealousy, surprise, or disappointment. Relationships provide comfort, a context to explore feelings more deeply, and to organize thoughts and feelings.

The dynamic balance of parenting is carried out through increasing refinement in affective communication and shared understanding. Parents set limits to teach and protect their child: Parents limit the amount of indulgence and the range of allowed independence. As development proceeds, a child's growing autonomy includes the ability to internalize limits and develop self-control.

The ultimate goal for a child with challenging behaviors is to manage emotions in an adaptive way, and build a strong capacity to problem solve independently. By knowing how to ask for and use help, a child forms a confident attitude that help will be available if needed. The security of this knowledge allows a child the liberty to tolerate negative feelings longer and to persist in finding solutions without collapsing into despair or abandoning the effort.

A strategic plan to build a capacity for independence calls for first strengthening a healthy dependence on others and then gradually challenging the child to take more ownership through his or her own abilities. The strength of the foundational capacities for engagement is critical for success at the higher levels. When a child is helped to use relationships successfully in a functional dependency, they grow in their capacity to function independently.

Parenting and Limits

Parents have the awesome responsibility of helping their children to advance up the developmental hierarchy. This includes helping children to gain control of their emotions and impulses so that they can interact successfully with others. The process of parents helping a child to regulate emotions begins at birth with basic physiological regulation. Parents soothe crying babies, feed them when they are hungry, keep them warm, and rock them to help them go to sleep. Parents kiss and caress their babies, building a strong bond of intimacy and love.

Through the childhood years, parents encourage children to be brave as they try new experiences, shelter them when afraid, comfort their sadness, and limit their outbursts of anger. It is a complex emotional process carried out in daily interactions with mothers and fathers, and always with variations. Success is achieved in greater or lesser degrees with no universal standard for perfection. Typically, by adulthood, all have mastered the basic skills of emotional and behavioral control, so that they can function in a variety of relationships and contexts, within society's parameters of acceptable behavior.

Setting limits on behavior is an integral part of parenting from birth. Typically limits are set within a relationship of love and caring. For example, a parent must decide when an infant's cry means a need for more milk, or simply that the baby is tired and needs to be soothed to sleep. A parent may determine how much milk to offer, help set the pace of eating, and choose how much to hold the infant or let him or her fall asleep independently. Each infant has a personal temperament and responses that combine with each parent's personality to form unique patterns of interaction. Even at this early stage, a relationship begins to manifest a tone that is more or less sensitive and attuned, with greater or lesser degrees of closeness or autonomy for the infant.

As infants grow, parents decide whether to pick them up at the first cry, wait for them to self-soothe, or utilize communication at a distance to help them regulate while waiting. Parents may find success in responding to a fussing infant with a gentle voice and touch, or by placing a pacifier and walking away. Infants learn the limits of their body versus a parent's body, distinguish their own voice from others', and begin to appreciate a growing sense of time, action, and space based on these richly affective experiences.

Parents and infants may quickly settle into comfortable routines, including warm and playful interactions, or their signals and responses may be inconsistent or unsuccessful. With more time, parents and infants generally find their way to a dance in which there is a gradually increasing sense of mutual regulation, autonomy, and the precursors of boundaries and limits.

Over time, the limits on behavior become more definite: "You can't poke my nose"; "No throwing food"; "Don't grab the dog's tail." The way parent and child interact around these limits already conveys a expanding range of emotional communication.

At 9 months, as an infant reaches for the electric outlet, Mom uses a warning and gentle tone as she says "no" while moving the infant's hand away. Through repeated similar experiences, the child learns to distinguish looks, vocal tones, and the behavioral meaning of "no." Gradually a range of tones is connected with the word "no" reflecting different levels of urgency, danger, or anger. A child begins to learn what is acceptable and what is not, and can begin to anticipate the escalation of "no" that might be forthcoming. An infant can even read Mom's facial expressions or gestures before she utters a word.

Parents help their children to learn limits with the expectation that more help will be needed initially, and then gradually less support will be required. For a 9-month-old, the word "no" must be accompanied by physically moving the child's hand away from the outlet. Additionally, a parent may support children through distraction, moving them away and offering another toy. There are higher expectations for self-control as children grow, and confidence in their ability to gradually accept more responsibility.

In the second year of life, the way a child and parents negotiate limit setting becomes a part of the child's developing sense of self. For example, a child wants her brother's toy. How is this wish acknowledged? Does a child develop a sense of being respected or belittled? Is she powerful or ignored? Is she usually accepted and cherished or shamed and rejected? Even at this early age, children engage in complex affective interactions. The 2-year-old dramas with willfulness and tantrums are evidence of a process of psychological development as a child learns to internalize the limits on desires and ideas.

Consistent and clear limit setting by a parent actually contributes to a child's sense of security and trust. Many games and even pretend play are built around self-imposed limits. For example, a child's pretend play character may only have certain powers, or must follow certain rules and consequences. Children enjoy the mastery of controlling their impulses within this pretend world. A developmental approach helps a child form their own limits and eventually their own personal values through warm interactions in spontaneous play.

Over time, a child learns to tolerate disappointment and loss, to wait, to inhibit desires, and most importantly gains a foundation for respect and empathy for others. A parent that can provide limits with patience, consistency, respect, kindness, and a capacity for forgiveness enables the child to gain the same qualities.

For a parent of a child with autism or other developmental challenges, the process of setting limits becomes exponentially more complex. Problematic behaviors occur that are often intense, pervasive, and disruptive. It becomes much harder for parents to know how to balance their efforts between nurturing and encouraging self-sufficiency. Often parents are left on their own to sort through a tumult of feelings around how to help their child control behavior, and also hold on to the loving relationship with their child.

While many professionals may take part in helping a child learn to accept limits, comply with rules, and manage behavior, ultimately it is the parents who are the primary force to guide their child to adulthood. Therefore, parents are partners in this work, whether present or not, and should always be a major part of understanding behavior and creating treatment plans.

The developmental approach utilizes the pattern of development that is universal. An attitude of caring, respect, compassion, empathy, and patience is used to help children develop the capacities to manage their behavior. The same attitudes are used in the relationship of professional to parent. Relationships are based on trust and knowledge of each other, built over time.

Individual Differences

The developmental approach recognizes and tailors interactions to the individual differences of each child. Every child has special interests and ways of responding to the world. For children with autism and other developmental challenges this is especially true. It is important to consider how a child perceives and processes information in each of the sensory modalities, and how the combination contributes to an overall emotional regulatory pattern.

Some children are very sensitive and aware of their surroundings, while others have relatively low awareness. A child may be aware of the larger environment or may be distracted and overfocused on details. Children also differ in their motor skills, visual-motor coordination, stamina, and strength. In language, children vary greatly in their ability to identify sounds, tolerate noise, and understand and produce language.

Often there are differences in perception between sensory channels, creating a mixed pattern of responsiveness. A child may be highly attuned visually and able to track, focus, find, and understand the world more easily through vision. For other children, the auditory channel is stronger: They listen, imitate sounds, and understand language more readily. As adults, it is easier to understand the experience of children that is more similar to our own particular profile, but other sensory experiences such as synesthesia (when one type of sensory experience evokes the sensation of another) may be difficult to imagine.

Children often select interests that align with their sensory-motor preferences. Through awareness of a child's unique profile, interactions can take advantage of areas of strengths and bolster areas of relative weakness. For example, limits might be set with visual cues for one child and auditory cues for another.

Experience always has both sensory and affective aspects, and both dimensions need to be considered together in understanding behavior. Sensory, motor, and language differences contribute to the disposition of a child to be obstinate and angry, or sad, frustrated, resilient, brave, or anxious. The overall pattern of behavior can be more effectively addressed through a detailed understanding of how individual differences contribute to a child's temperament.

The abilities of a child may be a confusing scatter of higher and lower skills that fluctuate from day to day. To avoid misperceptions about the motivations for behavior, it is necessary to consider not only a child's individual differences but also emotional developmental capacities, and how the two dimensions interrelate. Specialists can help others to appreciate a child's individual sensory, motor, and language differences, and together a team can integrate how these differences impact development and behavior.

The consideration of unique individual differences and shifting developmental capacities contribute to a holistic understanding of a child. This complexity is compounded with the additional layer of interaction patterns between multiple adults in a child's life and the adults' own unique individual differences. Despite the multiple factors involved, it is possible to help a child with behavior by utilizing an adult's natural abilities to be emotionally attuned and by trusting in a child's underlying abilities. In fact, it is the only way to help children achieve their true potential.

The Structure of the Developmental Approach

The developmental approach provides a systematic organization for both responding in the moment of a difficult behavior and for creating a long-term plan. It is based on the developmental milestones described originally by Dr. Stanley Greenspan (1992) and later elaborated by Greenspan and Wieder (1998, 2006). An adult estimates the child's developmental capacities in a moment of distress and, starting where the child is, supports him or her to use gradually higher-level abilities.

A child's competencies are expected to fluctuate during any interaction. By knowing the universal sequence of development, an adult is able to provide a flexible response that moves up and down the hierarchy to match a child in the moment, with the goal of moving to the highest levels possible. By following the steps of (1) attune and organize, (2) help, and (3) recover, an adult not only can diffuse a problematic situation but can help a child to build new skills.

In this approach, a long-term plan is developed, together with the parents and other professionals, based upon a comprehensive understanding of a child's developmental capacities, areas of constriction or delay, individual differences, and patterns of interaction. A child can then utilize these skills independently or with others, and in familiar or new situations and relationships.

An important aspect of the developmental approach is that all interactions throughout the day are understood using the same framework. A child's day is full of adventure, excitement, and drama. Each experience is an opportunity for interaction with genuine emotion. Based on developmental goals, adults can utilize specific strategies to help children increase their abilities in these daily interactions.

The long-term plan may include specific types of activities to provide more practice dealing with certain types of emotional challenges. Still, the developmental approach to behavioral challenges relies on spontaneous and genuine emotional experiences on the part of both a child and key adults. Through the use of natural experiences and providing a wide range of opportunities, a child increases the ability to be flexible and to adapt successfully to new and unpredictable situations.

Free play time is particularly important for children. During the course of the day, a child learns that some behaviors are acceptable at times but not acceptable at other times. It is during free play that children can explore, be loud and rambunctious, run, jump, test their strength, and expend youthful energy. Even then, certain limits must apply to keep themselves and others safe, and to follow basic social etiquette.

Free play time is also a time for a child to build relationships and to practice emotional interactions around limits. Limits may be negotiated around various aspects of physical self-control—not pushing too hard, jumping from too high, or yelling too loudly. Children may practice frustration tolerance and persistence in attempting physical feats. They may experience a mixture of sadness and frustration when their play tower collapses or the balloon pops. Emotions rapidly flow and change in typical play, from anticipation, excitement, and surprise to anger, disappointment, anxiety, and sadness.

Pretend play allows children to know that they will survive hard feelings, because they can pretend to experience events that evoke those difficult feelings, and even more intense emotions derived from fantasy and magical thinking. Children set their own limits within play; they create a structure with roles, rules, and limits. An important aspect of an overall plan for behavioral challenges is dedicated time for free play.

Thus, the developmental approach to behavioral challenges utilizes the three core components of functional emotional developmental milestones, individual differences, and affective interactions in relationships to construct a plan for behavioral intervention. The plan includes responses in the moment of the behavior, and a longer term plan with an emphasis on opportunities in daily interactions and free interactive play.

Qualities of Developmental Intervention

Developmentally oriented interventions have the qualities of being fluid, affectively rich and spontaneous, even as a child is being challenged to new levels of ability. Bonds of trust and affection are created and strengthened through deepening familiarity with another person. The feelings reciprocated in the interaction help a child to define a growing knowledge of self. A child gains a sense of safety, respect, pride, and competency through the interaction. Moreover, a child develops a sense of the world, and expectations for acceptance and pleasure from interaction with others, known and unknown.

Emotional development is built on an appreciation of the nuanced and complex affective exchanges of social communication. During intervention, a child participates in a dynamic exchange, with coregulation of multiple emotions with varying degrees of intensity. Through a diversity of experiences, children expand the capacity to understand the perspective of others. As they contribute to shared goals, children join in the creation of a shared identity. As a result, they form a desire to help others and a concern that others accept and value them.

Developmental intervention during a challenging behavior also has the quality of flexibly interacting in the moment, with a continuous respect for the child's experience. Using the framework of developmental milestones, interactions are founded on mutual regulation and a relationship of trust. As a child is able, the interactions advance to higher levels of reciprocal communication and shared problem solving. Throughout the interaction, there is a focus on supporting a child's development of a positive sense of self and warm regard for others.

Kevin is having a bad day. He is irritable, and for some inscrutable reason he is becoming aggressive and destructive. As the behavior escalates, he seems to spiral more out of control.

Dad is at a loss to understand what is happening for Kevin. Dad becomes anxious, as he must protect himself, keep Kevin safe, and be sure that Kevin doesn't injure anyone nearby. Dad reacts instinctively to block Kevin's path and prevent further harm.

Dad remembers that it helps to act calmly. He repeats in a soothing tone, "It's okay, Kevin." He turns off the lights since he knows lights sometimes bother Kevin. "Let me know when you are ready to talk." Dad's support helps Kevin to regain some level of composure. Now, Dad asks Kevin, "What happened?" and Kevin is able to tell him some of the things that were troubling him.

Later that evening, Dad reviews what happened with Kevin, and they discuss his behavior. Dad also speaks with a therapist, to reflect, analyze, and plan ways to help avoid these outbursts of distress in the future.

Marianne often rebuffs attempts to engage her with warmth and interest. Most offers are met with, "Go away!" and conversation is countered with, "Be quiet!" It is difficult to avoid feelings of anger from her constant negativity and rejection. An empathetic approach would lead an adult to consider what challenges underlie this behavior. Further evaluation revealed that Marianne was very anxious, and had many challenges in understanding sensory input.

In the moments of her hostile rebukes, an adult endeavored to establish a calm interaction. It was possible through patient persistence and supporting her need to be in control. The adult could begin by asking, "How long do I need to wait?" "Where do you think I should go?" "My little friend (a puppet) would like to watch you. He thinks your tower looks like fun." Then, a long term plan was designed to address her need for safety, boundaries, and trusting relationships.

The developmental approach provides both guidance in the moment of behavioral challenge and a framework for analyzing behavior and creating a plan to help build the needed skills to avoid these upsets. These two components are not separate. The larger understanding of a child's abilities supports the strategies used in the moment of distress. With an appreciation of a child's development and individual differences, an adult is able to focus on the child's perspective and respond with sympathetic support in moments of heightened emotion for all.

Even in moments of distress, an adult is helping a child to gain new skills. A child is supported to organize feelings and modulate reactions. Through that interaction, child is gaining experience of how an adult can help him or her to recover from distress. Trust is strengthened, and the child gains a sense of the world as a place of warm, kind, and caring people.

By helping a child to find answers, rather than providing them, adults encourage him or her to gradually move up to higher levels of thinking and reflecting. An adult projects patient interest and acceptance as a child discovers new ways of thinking and new abilities to connect feelings, ideas, and expressions. A child may learn to problem solve with others, and to negotiate and compromise, or how to repair a hurt relationship or express remorse and regret.

While an adult's response of care and comfort may seem indulgent, a child is also being challenged to move up the developmental hierarchy. The intermediate range of emotional arousal is the context for developmental growth. Through interaction, a child is helped to gain the skills to function across a gradually broader range of emotional experiences. Always, a child is treated with respect and kindness. A child's capacity for warmth, trust, and care toward others is ultimately a reflection of how he or she is treated.

Progress Over Time

The developmental approach invests time into creating trusting relationships and understanding between a child and an adult. Changes in behavior may or may not occur quickly, but the focus on systematically building underlying skills leads to the possibility of rich capacities at higher levels. A priority is placed on dedicating time to build these relationships both in the moment of distress and in the long-term plan.

Success is measured not only in decreasing behaviors, but also by the strength of relationships, the ability of a child to be comforted by an adult, and the shared pleasure in their interactions. It is from the fund of positive feelings in this relationship that a child will learn to coregulate a wide range of emotions, engage in shared problem solving, and ultimately be successful in a wide range of interactions.

Punishments, threats, or promises of rewards can sometimes cause a child to stop an unwanted behavior quickly; however, an opportunity for advancement in social skills and emotional development may be missed. Rewards cannot provide the satisfaction needed to negotiate all of life's challenges. Of course, belittling, shaming, and spanking never succeed in building the skills of self-control and self-respect. Ultimately, the acquisition of socially responsible behavior is built on a parent-child relationship of security, trust, caring, and respect that conveys confidence in a child's potential.

A slow process may not always be practical; in some situations, it is wise to distract the child or even give in to demands just to keep the child safe or attend to other priorities. For example, if a parent needs to fasten the seat belt in a car with an upset child, a distracter or a promise of a treat may be expedient. Still, a long-term plan will identify other opportunities for helping a child learn to manage feelings of disappointment, sadness, or frustration, so that distracters are no longer needed.

A child's behavior may engender strong emotions in a parent or other adult, including anger, fear, disappointment, rejection, guilt, embarrassment, or humiliation. A parent may want to be kind, patient, and empathetic, but have very real concerns that a child's behavior is dangerous or destructive. A child may physically hurt a parent, professional, peer, or sibling. These traumas may undermine a relationship to the point that a parent is drained of warm and loving feelings toward the child. Because of exhaustion and anxiety, an adult may not utilize the highest level of logical and reflective thinking and may resort to a more didactic and rigid response.

With the help of a professional, an adult can gain a better understanding of a child's developmental capacities and individual differences, and become more aware of their pattern of interacting. Together a plan can be devised with strategies to help a child in the moment of distress, and a treatment plan to increase the relationship of warmth and engagement. Through the process of planning and reflection, a parent or other adult is then prepared to take the time needed to support a child through a troubling behavior with patience and compassion.

Culture, Values, and Goals

The goal of the developmental approach is to help a child acquire the skills to live fully, to manage a broad array of emotions in life, and develop relationships with others in which emotions are shared and mutually negotiated. Children can be supported to advance in the sophistication of their emotional and social development, to communicate complex emotions, to think reflectively about emotion, and to develop a rich and positive sense of self.

These goals are based on values that resonate within a cultural perspective that encourages individual initiative, creativity, and assertiveness. These values are balanced by respect for others, an ability to engage in reciprocal shared problem solving, and exchange of symbolic ideas. A high value is placed on flexibility, exploration, and change through cooperation of individuals. In this way, there can be harmonious and productive interactions between both individuals and groups.

Not all cultures, however, place the same emphasis on these values. Some cultures hold group identity and allegiance, self-sacrifice, obedience, dependency, and deference to authority as preeminent. There may be a greater interest in conformity and tradition. Acceptable behavior and morality may be defined differently in diverse cultures. Nevertheless, when limits are crossed, and challenging behavior occurs, developmental principles founded on the universal stages of human development can be useful to help support the child's ability to comply with expectations.

Behavioral Outcomes Using the Developmental Approach

The outcomes for a child using a developmental approach are profound. Interventions are founded on the recognition of every child's potential to be socially connected in warm, trusting relationships, to achieve self-regulation and an ability to function while experiencing a wide range of emotions. A child with neurodevelopmental challenges often experiences barriers to effective social interaction, and the corresponding development may be delayed or incomplete. However, at any chronological age, nascent developmental capacities can be evoked and expanded through robust affective interactions and relationships with others.

By following a natural sequence of development, a child increases the capacity for regulation, initiative, flexibility, resiliency, and creativity. The confidence derived from the ability to seek and utilize help from others enables children to function independently and to challenge themselves with persistence and determination.

Children are then prepared to grow into happy adults, capable of true friendship and loving relationships. They can reach the maximum of their potential to engage in shared problem solving, to innovate, discover, and think intuitively about others. At the highest levels, behavior is based on their own ethical values and in accordance with the values of a larger social group.

The developmental approach offers hope as it does not assume limits on a child's potential to grow and learn. Interactions are informed by a systematic hierarchy of functional emotional milestones and tailored to a child's individual differences in the context of unique patterns of interaction in specific relationships. Through an empathetic perspective, an adult is able to support a child to overcome behavioral challenges, as well as advancing overall functional development.

A Comment Regarding Research

> *Not everything that counts can be counted and not everything that is counted counts.*
> —W. B. Cameron (1963, p. 13)

Currently, there is an urgent interest in confirming that treatments for a whole range of conditions are empirically "evidence based." Unease with the rapidly changing world of diagnoses and treatments and a growing insecurity about claims of effectiveness have prompted a movement toward new standards of proof. There is a desire for efforts, time, and money to be directed wisely.

In disorders such as autism and other neurodevelopmental disabilities, where so much is still unknown, the fervent wish for definitive answers is profound. Unfortunately, even with burgeoning knowledge comes the uncomfortable awareness of the depth of our ignorance. In this setting, equivocal studies are sometimes consumed as absolute assurances, and old-fashioned clinical experience is eschewed with disdain. Strident voices often outweigh those who more humbly acknowledge the frontier ahead.

One area of attraction for those who seek evidence is quantitative measure. The developmental approach, however, does not lend itself easily to concrete measurement. By its very nature, the developmental approach is interested in the internal world of thoughts and feelings, and individual patterns of interaction within relationships, over long spans of time. For children with autism and other neurodevelopmental disorders, individual differences are particularly apparent and defy quantification.

Evidence-based practice is defined by three components: research evidence, clinical expertise, and consideration of patient preferences and values. (American Psychological Association, 2005; American Speech-Language-Hearing Association, 2005; Buysse, Winton, Rous, Epstein, & Lim, 2012; Prizant, 2011). Despite the challenges in measuring developmental goals, a growing number of well-conducted scientific studies are providing solid support for the developmental approach (Aldred, Green, & Adams, 2004; Casenhiser, Binns, McGill, Morderer, & Shanker, 2014; Casenhiser, Shanker, & Stieben, 2011; Green et al., 2010; Liao et al., 2014; Mahoney & Perales, 2003, 2005; Pajareya & Nopmaneejumruslers, 2011; Salt et al., 2002; Siller & Sigman, 2002; Siller, Hutman, & Sigman, 2013; Siller, Swanson, Gerber, Hutman, & Sigman, 2014; Solomon, Necheles, Ferch, & Bruckman, 2007; Solomon, Van Egeren, Mahoney, Quon-Huber, & Zimmerman, 2014). Effectiveness is also documented for elements of clinical practice in the mental health field that overlap directly with developmental principles (Shedler, 2010).

The developmental approach to behavioral challenges is based on an optimistic view of the potential of children with developmental differences. Greenspan and Weider (1997, 2005) were the first to describe the capacities of infants and children at risk, along with those with autism, to reach the highest levels of relating, thinking, and communicating. These goals were achieved through the strength of human relations and the power of affect. In the future, more sophisticated means of measuring human behavior will undoubtedly provide further evidence to inform the efforts of teachers, parents, and clinicians as they help children to achieve their highest potential.

—

Chapter 2

Developmental Capacities

Helping a child to overcome a behavioral challenge begins with an understanding of his or her overall development, individual differences, and relationships. The DIR model provides a hierarchy of universal milestones of functional emotional development, the (D) component of the model. The milestones do not describe a child's motor, language, or cognitive skills separately, but rather reflect how a child utilizes all of these skills to engage with others, along with increasingly complex levels of social relationship, communication, cognition, and behavior.

The six basic developmental milestones (or capacities) of the DIR model are:

1. Basic regulation and shared attention
2. Engagement and forming relationships
3. Two-way communication
4. Coregulation and shared problem solving
5. Use of emotional and symbolic ideas
6. Bridging ideas and emotional thinking

There are three additional higher milestones in childhood, which are continuing transformations of milestone 6:

7. Multicausal, comparative, and triangular thinking
8. Gray-area thinking
9. Reflective thinking

In *The First Idea*, Greenspan and Shanker (2004) outline additional milestones that cover the entire life span.

Each of the six basic levels of functional emotional development reflects a different dimension of development. They build from one to the next up the developmental ladder, with each milestone providing the prerequisite skills for advancement to the subsequent level (Figure 1). As a child acquires new capacities, he also continues to strengthen his underlying abilities. In typical development, these milestones begin at birth and progress quickly, with skills at Milestone 6 first appearing around 4 years of age. However, the milestones can be reached at any age.

Each milestone continues to broaden throughout life, so that an individual can manifest the capacities corresponding to each milestone during an increasing range and depth of emotional experience, and with more stability and quicker recovery. A child may have relative strengths

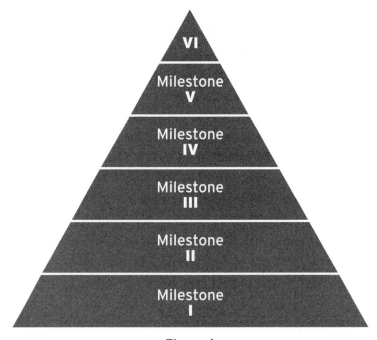

Figure I

or constrictions in any of the milestones. Ideally, a child forms a strong base to support expansion of the higher levels.

Milestone 1: Regulation and Shared Attention

The foundation of development and all behavior is a child's ability to regulate his or her own nervous system and achieve physiological homeostasis. A primary level of self-control involves the organization of sleep-wake cycles and arousal, development of regular patterns of hunger, eating, and elimination, the perception and discrimination of muscular movement, the coordination of breathing and swallowing, and the modulation of heart rate, blood pressure, and so on. Regulation is accomplished through the neurological, immunological, and endocrine systems and involves continuous feedback between internal and external sensory input. The experience of the physical body is the root of affective experience.

A child who is able to achieve a calm, regulated state can show an active interest in the environment. He or she is curious and explores for the enjoyment of finding familiar and novel stimuli. A child will seek out and find caregivers and connect with shared attention, gaze, and interest. With an ability to maintain a stable internal state, a child will expand exploration and respond to new environments with pleasure.

An infant gradually develops an increasing capacity to function across a broader range of arousal. The breadth of this capacity is a result of both physiological and neurological maturity and the support of affectively attuned interactions with caregivers. Alan Fogel (1993) eloquently described the process of mutual regulation of mother-infant dyads and the resultant development of regulation in infants. Development is supported when a parent soothes a crying infant, rocks a baby to sleep, covers them when they are cold, presents a new toy or game, or entices them to eat a new food. Through innumerable nuanced interactions, parents help children regulate through excitement, distress, discomfort, and pleasure.

Infants and young children learn ways to increase or decrease input so that they can modulate the intensity of a stimulus. An infant may momentarily look away during an excited play interaction, or pull a hand away from a startling or uncomfortable touch. When stressed, a child will attempt to regain an optimal level of functioning, or homeostasis. Children may seek out soothing input by sucking their fingers, or stroking their mother's hair. If overwhelmed, children may withdraw and become detached, or even more profoundly dissociated, from their physical experience. Such infants may develop rumination or failure to thrive.

All children adapt to perturbations in their environment and differences from expectations. Some children are easily stressed by lights, sound, movement, touch, smell, and taste, as well as by internal sensations. Generally, a certain level of novelty and change is a source of pleasure and excitement. However, for some children, the range of change that is tolerated can be quite narrow. They may then quickly fall into profound distress and have great difficulty regaining their composure.

Problematic behaviors may occur as children respond and attempt to recover. Responses tend toward either of two extremes: shutting down and withdrawing, or escalating to a fight-or-flight response. Children shut down by closing their eyes, burying their heads, ignoring or disregarding a stimulus, or perhaps slumping to the ground in an unresponsive heap. A child may engage in self-distraction by humming or overfocusing on a visual or auditory stimulus or even going to sleep. Dysregulation and the resulting break in shared attention can also be more subtle. A child might simply go to the bathroom frequently, aimlessly shift through papers in his desk, or daydream.

In primitive fight-or-flight reactions a child may experience extreme fear or rage, with behaviors including biting, hitting, spitting, scratching, kicking, grabbing, or running away. These behavioral patterns are part of evolutionary biology, and similar behaviors can be witnessed in other animal species.

Children may try to regulate themselves in ways that are even more disruptive. They may create other strong stimulus, like hitting their heads or biting their hands. Attempts to physically restrain a child in this state may heighten the struggle as a child escalates due to being held and fights back in panic.

Often parents have discovered ways to help their child in this state of distress to be soothed, such as blowing a fan, playing a favorite song, or letting the child go to a quiet room alone. While these responses are helpful, the key to developmental progress is to strive for a process of soothing and comforting that also builds shared attention and mutual regulation. Higher developmental milestones require increasing levels of communication and interaction. Beginning with strategies where a caregiver can support regulation at this basic level provides the foundation for progress to higher capacities.

Most children are able to join in shared attention, even if fleetingly with preferred adults, in familiar settings. When a child's capacity for basic regulation is weak, it is difficult to move beyond momentary connection to sustained shared attention, especially in new environments or with change. A child may become self-absorbed and seem to be disinterested, or may be easily panicked and resistant to engagement. It is imperative to address the barriers to this social connection. The developmental approach does not view the deficits in shared attention as fixed, but rather as indications that a child requires more intensive support to enable increased capacities at this level.

Assessment of Milestone 1 involves inquiry into a child's ability to maintain a sense of calm and show an attentive interest in the environment. The capacity for basic regulation results in shared attention with another, particularly an adult who is available, nonthreatening, and shares in a child's focus of interest. Through success in mutual regulation with a caregiver, and then expanding to other relationships and situations, a child increases the ability to accommodate to change. Over time, a child develops expectations for pleasure and safety in new experiences and will have fewer primitive behavioral responses generated from a sense of danger and fear.

In the developmental approach, an assessor observes a child to determine what factors contribute to the ability to reach a state of equanimity, and what factors might be disruptive. He or she would inquire about how frequently a child achieves a regulated state and the duration and stability of shared attention. A survey of sensory responses provides valuable insight about underlying factors that contribute to a child's ability to organize a calm, alert state. A review of events, particularly video review, can be enlightening, as subtle cues may be noted that presage behavioral events. If adults can recognize the early signs of impending dysregulation, they can better understand the root causes, as well as provide support to help avoid or mitigate the intensity of these episodes.

Health is an important aspect of assessment at Milestone 1. A child's behavior may be a response to some type of pain or internal discomfort.

An inventory of health conditions would include the child's ability to signal hunger and satiety, need for toileting, evidence of allergies, constipation, seizures, and any type of pain, including headaches, toothaches, muscle and joint pain, stomachaches, rashes, reactions to medications or dietary supplements, or other illness. Some children may respond strongly to fatigue and need rest, especially if they are not sleeping well at night. A child's diet may not provide adequate nutrition for well-being. While it may be difficult to assess all of these experiences, especially in a nonverbal child, patterns of behavior may lead to possible sources of discomfort for further investigation.

Observations of interactions include a caregiver's ability to attune to a child's level of stress, and the ability to modulate interactions to support the child's regulation. Therapeutic interactions also contribute to ongoing assessment of basic regulation. A therapist strives to find the just-right level of challenge, moment by moment, and to minimize the instances when a child becomes overwhelmed. A basic tenet of the DIR developmental approach is that a child is always supported at the primary level of safety and security. Since a therapist is also encouraging expansion of skills, there are times when the limit of tolerance may be breached; however, the goal is to hold a child within a functional capacity, to respectfully support engagement, trust, and security in the relationship.

Assessment also includes an examination of the process of recovery from distress. How does recovery occur? What strategies are employed by the child and by those trying to help? How long does it take? Is the child able to fully recover to a sense of relaxation and calm, or is there a lingering sense of sadness, frustration, or irritability? What is the pattern of interaction and recovery with different adults or caregivers? This information will be very useful in knowing how to respond to a child in distress, and in planning for building new strengths in this milestone. The goal is that an adult will be the instrument of soothing and an integral part of recovery so that a child maintains shared attention and begins the process of developing trust.

Episodes of extreme behavioral dysregulation are very difficult for both a child and the caregivers. Similarly, a child that is aloof or detached can be extremely discouraging. Parents will often make great accommodations to avoid instances of dysregulation for their child; however, both child and family may become fixed in routines that, while avoiding some distress, do not enable a child to move forward in the ability to manage disappointment, sadness, or frustration. The developmental approach can help parents and caregivers to create a plan to help a child gradually expand capacities for basic regulation and shared attention.

It is helpful to maintain an attitude of empathy toward children's experience when they are overwhelmed. A compassionate perspective can be difficult when children are rigid or aggressive; however, an objective appraisal would conclude that they would not choose to experience such distress if they possessed more effective strategies for managing their feelings.

Many children, even those with higher-level capacities, continue to have challenges in maintaining a basic sense of safety and security in multiple environments, and achieving shared attention with others. Over time, a child with such challenges may develop a chronic pattern of stress, hypervigilance, and anxiety, or a pattern of withdrawal and self-absorption. With success at Milestone 1, children demonstrate calm interest and pleasure in people and the environment around them.

> Mark enjoyed going outside to pick up leaves. He enjoyed filling a particular bag with two of each type. On some days, there were few colored leaves to be found. Mom said, "I'm sorry. I don't think there are any red leaves today." Mark suddenly kicked her. In fact, Mark was very rigid in his expectations, and when disappointed he often would kick or pinch.
>
> Although Mark had a scattering of abilities at different levels, he had deficits in Milestone 1, basic regulation. He was often on the verge of declining into primitive fight behavior. His anxiety was just below the surface. Intervention goals were focused on increasing his sense of security throughout the day and on strengthening the connection between Mark and his parents and caregivers. Opportunities were created for warm engagement. In this way, Mark was able to expand the range of distress that he could tolerate, and he was able to be comforted through the support of caring adults.

Milestone 2: Engagement

A child who notices and shares attention with another person, begins to know that person, remembering and anticipating both sensory and affective components of their interaction. The doctor's white coat is associated with pain, or Grandma's gray hair and cheerful voice are associated with warmth and pleasure. Each experience adds to a pattern that forms a relationship. If interactions bring pleasure and joy, a child will form special, warm feelings toward that person.

Usually parents are able to find moments when they feel truly connected with their child, and share a special bond and enjoyment of being together. Often these special times involve private games, like a dad growling and pretending in a play ambush, or a mom who makes a funny sound at a particular point in a story. Activities at this level involve shared experiences such as reading a book, singing a song, dancing together, running or jumping or splashing, or any other activity done in a mutually shared and pleasurable way.

There is a rhythm to joyful shared experience, built on anticipation, expectation, and then completion of the interaction. Positive feelings are derived from the microdynamics of the exchange, involving a rise of tension and then release of stress. The quick release of tension results in a pleasurable feeling. This pattern of stress and release is present in many children's early infant games. Songs and rhythms contain these patterns in timing as well as harmonic structure. Examples in universal games include "Ready, set, go" or "One, two, three . . . " to build anticipation. Similarly, "I'm gonna get you," which precedes a tickling or chase game, or "Here it comes" before the water pours or the puppet tickles.

In addition to microdynamics and rhythm, repetition is an important element in shared pleasure. Repetition allows for expectation, and builds anticipation. Consider the old nursery rhyme:

Hickory, dickory, dock,
The mouse ran up the clock.
The clock struck one,
The mouse ran down,
Hickory, dickory, dock. (Opie, 1997)

There is rhyme in the sounds, repetition, and dynamic flow. These simple elements are present in various forms in many early childhood favorites.

The pattern of eliciting pleasure from the microdynamics of emotional exchange may be varied in pace to be slow or fast, more or less intense in excitement, and have infinite variations. Emotions range from positive interest, relaxed pleasure, and patient anticipation, to joy, delight and elation. Bonds of affection grow from the ability to create and share these experiences together, and frequent experiences of shared pleasure lead to a positive and stable mood.

Intimacy is derived from the knowledge of each other's expressions, actions, and rhythms gained through shared experiences. A child can anticipate the good feelings from the interaction, and associates the pleasure with a particular person. A child increases a sense of anticipation and protests when expectations are not met. Over time, a child develops a sense of approval and feeling worthy of love through these warm, affectionate interactions. A foundational attitude is created that pleasure is possible and available in interaction with others.

A relationship built on a sense of trust is a source of comfort and security. Warmth and closeness create a trove of strength that is then used to counter the pain of negative emotions. A child that experiences intimacy and trust will increase tolerance for waiting for that person, holding the memory, and will build the capacity to self-soothe. Not only will children seek out comfort from the special persons in their life, but they will begin to form confidence that others are also capable of providing comfort.

An assessment of Milestone 2 probes the depth and quality of relationships. Questions may include: With whom does the child have fun and enjoy playful interactions? What is the activity that they do together? Is there a range of people and activities that bring pleasure? How often does the child experience genuine pleasure throughout the day? Are there experiences that reliably bring pleasure, or is the response highly variable? Is the person that brings pleasure also able to soothe the child when distressed? Is the response consistent and predictable?

Some children and their parents find it difficult to gauge the right level of pacing, intonation, arousal, and repetition to create a fun, mutually pleasurable experience. It may seem that a parent and child are continually missing each other, misreading cues, and not experiencing a close sense of connection. Patterns of interaction may veer off into more rote or isolated activities to accomplish the necessary tasks of the day.

Without the expectation of pleasure and comfort from another person, children may become withdrawn, self-absorbed, flat, or avoidant. They may experience loneliness, sadness, and even depression. In children, depression may manifest as agitation, an inability to focus, or other disruptive behavior.

A paucity of intimate, warm relationships also leaves children with few resources for comfort during distress and when worried, anxious, sad, or angry. They are then vulnerable to being overwhelmed by these feelings, and may act out with more desperate behaviors. Over time, they may try to avoid anything that may arouse strong feelings, and become isolated or resistant to new experiences.

A common misperception is that children who isolate themselves actually prefer to be alone; however, adults with autism are often able to reflect on their childhood and reveal that they always held a deep longing for friendship, but did not know how to begin to form relationships. The ability to participate in warm, intimate relationships is necessary for success at higher-level skills, as well as critical for basic quality of life for everyone.

A different challenge occurs when a child forms a very close relationship, but with only one person.

Marcia is 6 years old and has been home schooled. Mother virtually never leaves Marcia alone. When another adult approaches, she clings to Mom and refuses to talk.

While a parent is the key person in a child's life, it is also important for the child to form trusting relationships with others. Sometimes, due to health, behavior, or other needs, the child is always cared for by a single adult. Other times, a parent may contribute to the isolation because of his or her own concerns, fears, or needs. A goal would be to help a child to feel safe and form trusting relationships with others. A plan can be created to fully understand the background, and then to gradually provide the needed experiences for a child to form warm relationships with others, and eventually be able to rely on those experiences to function independently.

Milestone 2 reflects the extent to which a child is able to form intimate and pleasurable relationships, and the ability to be comforted by these trusting relationships. An assessment of the child's capacities for engagement with others contributes to an understanding of the root causes of behavioral challenges and how to plan strategies for intervention that not only alter specific behaviors but also build capacities for friendship, warmth, and positive disposition.

Milestone 3: Two-Way Communication

At a very young age, children discover that their actions and sounds cause things to happen. A parent reads and responds to the child's actions and gestures as communication. "Oh, you wanted that!" "He said, 'Daddy'!" And the child begins to read the meaning of a parent's gestures and words. Now they are engaged in back-and-forth communication, with sounds, words, and gestures. The child initiates communication, such as sharing his discoveries by saying, "Ah!" while looking at Dad and pointing. The child also responds to a parent's overtures, by reaching when a parent offers a cookie, or rejecting a shirt by pushing it away. Over time, a child becomes more purposeful, and the interactions develop a rhythmic, reciprocal flow.

At Milestone 3, a child engages in "circles of communication." The child may initiate an interaction by showing interest. A parent then responds contingently, and the child responds back again. These circles begin around pleasurable activities, such as those described in Milestone 2. A child is now expressing intentionality and being an equal partner in a back-and-forth flow of interaction. Over time, a child is able to sustain these interactions, playing fun games with many circles of interaction in a row.

Through such exchanges, a child begins to distinguish different emotional experiences and the corresponding expressions. With an attuned adult, communication assumes a variety of different emotional tones—happy, mad/frustrated, sad, anxious, surprised, and so on. A child is then engaged in back-and-forth emotional signaling using differentiated emotions.

In the course of development, a child's emotion and intent are not always clear or organized. He or she may portray a mixture or confusion of feelings. Through an insightful approach to understanding the child's experience, a parent makes a best guess at the child's emotion and intent and responds in a contingent way, which actually helps to shape and organize the child's experience and helps to modulate his or her feelings.

If a parent's assessment is that the child is afraid, an attuned parent might respond with, "Oh! That was a big sound! I think it was just the trash cans banging." By their facial expressions and tone of voice, parents help to organize a congruent emotional expression, and then help to soothe and diminish the response, with voice, movement, words, and cognitive support. In a myriad of experiences, parents support children to organize emotional experience and interact in ways that are comforting and productive.

An assessment for Milestone 3 includes an inventory of the organization and range of a child's repertoire of emotional life with key figures. How does he or she interact around pleasure and excitement? Anger and frustration? Sadness and loss? Fear and surprise? Does he or she engage in purposeful reciprocal interactions? Can he or she interact in a variety of situations and across space? Does the child initiate interaction?

A robust capacity at Milestone 3 would be manifested in a child's ability to purposefully interact while feeling different emotions. For example, pushing or pulling Mom's hand to indicate a choice, bringing Grandma a favorite book to read for comfort when feeling sad, or giving Mom her keys to show a desire to leave when feeling anxious. A child begins to use differentiated and congruent expressions with vocal tones, sounds, words, gestures, and actions that communicate intent. Circles of communication are formed as an adult responds with attunement to the child's intent, and the child responds back to close the circle.

Deficits at this level will be apparent if the child only intermittently responds to social overtures and rarely initiates interaction. He or she may use language to request an object or action, but not to play with another person. In pretend play, a parent may offer a block. The child takes it, but then turns around to continue stacking, without looking back. Engagement may have an in-and-out quality and it may take extra effort to get a flow of interaction.

Constrictions at this level are also manifested in a lack of range in emotional expressions. A child may engage in a game of rolling a car or ball, or play a game of chase, but the range of emotion only extends from neutral to happy or excited. Once there is frustration or a distraction, the child disengages. The strength of the engagement is weak and intermittent.

When not modulated by a flow of interaction and affect cueing with a sensitive and responsive adult, emotional experiences and behaviors can be extreme. A child may only display the polarities of happiness and distress, and these expressions may shift suddenly without a range of other types and intensities of emotions. A child may go from content to screaming, without differentiated expressions of moderate frustration or other unhappiness. A more gradual and fluid flow of emotion and behavior is possible when tempered by interaction.

A child with deficits in two-way communication often displays odd and incongruent expressions of emotion, reflecting a disorganized emotional state. If a toy is taken away, the child may respond with both a cry and a smile, and perhaps be unable to organize a purposeful response. An adult may react to the smile and be unaware of the inner confusion behind such a mixed expression. A skillful therapist would help the child to perceive the meaning of this experience and help to clarify the turmoil of feelings, using not only words but clear affective signaling.

Another aspect of learning to organize emotional experiences is that children can have an emotional reaction to their own emotion. For example, a child may become angry, and then become fearful of the feelings of anger. Or feelings of sadness may provoke anger. A child's ability to organize these feelings and to tolerate and accept them is created by the support and attitude of caregiving adults.

In sensitive affective interchanges with a trusted adult, children learn how to distinguish and modulate their feelings. They experience acceptance of their emotions, and learn whether their corresponding behaviors are approved or disapproved. This exchange is not based on neutral directives from an adult to a child about correct behavior, but is rather a reciprocal flow of mutual affective signaling. The developmental approach has an appreciation for the importance of children's emotional experience and the power of a caregiver's attuned response to help them build developmental capacities related to intentionality, initiative, and emotional organization.

Milestone 4: Complex Communication: Coregulation and Shared Problem Solving

> We all want children who are well regulated or modulated, that is, who can be active and explorative some of the time, concentrate and be thoughtful and cautious other times, joyful yet other times. We all want children who can regulate their emotions in a way that is appropriate to the situation and also regulate their behavior in a way that is appropriate to the situation.
> —Stanley Greenspan (2001)

Complex communication occurs when a child can sustain a back-and-forth interaction, connecting many different emotional experiences and affective signals, and enter into a coregulated experience. "Coregulation" refers to a dynamic interaction in which there is simultaneous attunement of feelings and intentional adjustment of actions and attitudes between two people.

With capacities at Milestone 4, children will respond when a partner looks confused, surprised, disappointed, or sad. They will ask for help, give help, and work toward a common goal with others. Communication begins with gestures, but as children develop more language, they may use words to express ideas related to the immediate experience. For example, two children might dialogue as they work together to build a moat in the sand. They may gesture, ask and answer questions, and comment aloud about what they are doing and thinking. They will try a number of strategies to communicate, and will repair communication to ensure that they are understood. They both initiate communication and respond to others' emotional signals in a continuous flow.

At this Milestone, play is highly reliant on the manipulation of objects that are tangible and inherently meaningful. The ability to coordinate movement, to manipulate objects, plan and sequencing multiple steps, is important for the capacity for sustained interaction. In representational play, such as filling or emptying a dump truck, constructing a tower, or drawing a picture, children are able to practice working toward a goal, and experience a range of emotions engendered in pursuit of that goal. Children enjoy games with simple rules, and invent rules to support their play. Trucks have to stay on the right road to deliver their payload, or the play clothes have to be divided according to set parameters among the dolls. Without adequate motor-planning abilities, children may wander aimlessly or their actions may become repetitive and constricted.

Shared problem solving requires patience and persistence through times of frustration, worry, and elation and the ability to maintain communication through trials, success and failure. A child must be able to hold a certain degree of tension in order to allow time to experiment and find an effective solution, to consider another's idea, and to make decisions without falling into dysregulation. The stronger the ability to maneuver through a range of feelings, the more successful a child will be in participating in a process of trial and error, and share in teamwork for a common goal.

In developing capacities at Milestone 4, children will test limits and learn consequences. From patterns of interaction with others, children begin to develop expectations about how they will be treated. When negative emotions of anger, fear, or sadness are not recognized, a child may become trapped and overwhelmed with their feelings or they may simply ignore or deny them. An expectation may be formed that their feelings will not be valued and that they will not be understood or helped. Children that are not supported to persist through negative emotions, may abandon their intent and develop an identity of being ineffective. Alternatively, children may learn to expect shame and disapproval and develop an identity of being unworthy of love. When children and parents sustain an interaction through anger, recovery, and closeness, children learn that their feelings will be accepted, and develop a sense of resilience and positive self-esteem.

> *Children acquire patterns of action and thought that work for them in particular real-life situations, when alone and in the company of others. Children discover those patterns of acting and thinking via their own activity with others; they are not explicitly learning, nor are they following rules.*
>
> —A. Fogel

Assessment of a child's capacities at Milestone 4 includes inquiries such as: Does the child sustain interaction, using multiple gestures in a row, through multiple emotional states such as worry, confusion surprise and relief, or anticipation, frustration and sadness? Can she tolerate urgency and waiting through a dynamic interaction with others? Does the child seek and give help? Does the child understand and respond to others' emotional expressions while engaged in sustained interaction? Does the child look for social cues or ask permission before acting? What patterns of interaction are forming? Is the child developing a positive sense of self and self-esteem?

Ernie ran into the room and kicked over the board game. Everyone yelled at him to stop and go away. Ernie smiled and ran away. When he got the chance he did it again. He seemed to find it amusing that everyone turned to pay attention to him.

Such misbehavior might be understandable in a 2-year-old; however, Ernie was 9. His parents were concerned that he was purposefully being mean. In truth, Ernie was simply excited and wanted to join the game. He did not know another way to join, and was not yet able to recognize others' expressions of anger.

Intervention goals focused on helping Ernie to interpret others' cues, as well as building many successful shared experiences of play. Throughout the day, an adult responded to his actions with simple, clear differentiated gradations of affect to help him understand their meaning. A plan was made to help Ernie to gradually increase his capacity for sustained coregulated interactions, reading and responding to social cues. Eventually, Ernie was able to interact more successfully, and the other children accepted him and appreciated his excitement and playfulness.

A child with weakness at Milestone 4 will often not persevere through a challenge that arouses strong feelings. When confronted with a difficulty, a child may give up and walk away, abruptly change their goal, or act out angrily. An older child with more language skills may suddenly change the topic of conversation if an idea evokes an uncomfortable emotion. A child may avoid competition, disappointment, and loss. With these deficits, a child will likely have difficulty in spontaneous play and conversation with peers.

When feelings are not linked through sustained interaction, each feeling can become overwhelming. A child that is angry and does not experience a counterbalancing interaction may become fearful of conflict, or perhaps develop a false sense of power to control and intimidate others. Without the capacity to work through negative feelings with others, a child may feel easily embarrassed, ashamed, or unworthy or friendship. A reliable relationship contributes to a stable sense of self, and further supports the ability to modulate emotions and to recover from distress.

Milestone 4 is important for understanding behavioral challenges. The skills at this level allow a child to successfully navigate through problem solving with others and the myriad of associated emotions. The process of coregulation develops gradually and requires a solid foundation of the earlier milestones. With practice and support to connect failures and successes, joys and sorrows, a child develops an integrated and positive sense of self.

Milestone 5: Symbolic Ideas

Milestone 5 describes a child's capacity to use words and objects as symbols to represent a wish, feeling, intention, or idea. This uniquely human capacity allows a child to express and consider ideas separately from immediate experience, and use symbols in place of actions. A child can say, "That's mine. Give it to me!" without grabbing. A child can express fear by bravely growling using a toy lion rather than retreating. A child can deal with guilty feelings after spilling the milk by saying, "The dinosaur did it." Increasingly, a child is able to employ symbolic ideas to negotiate a wide range of feelings.

Pretend play is a hallmark of symbolic thinking. A child moves from the mechanics of functional play such as pushing, pulling, or dumping to representations of familiar activities, like eating, sleeping, or other imitations of daily life, to symbolically pretending about emotional ideas such as dolls hugging, animals fighting, or hiding from scary monsters. She can now imagine that an arrangement of blocks is a castle or a fort or a house. Eventually, a child can pretend about a whole scenario such as being on an airplane that is going on a big trip, a policeman directing traffic, or a hero battling a fierce alligator. A child can act out a past experience or a fantasy.

At Milestone 5, a child begins to connect their symbolic ideas, but with loose associations rather than causality. A child may be playing with boats in the bathtub that float and move about, and may then introduce an idea that they are sinking and need to be rescued, and then become tankers that battle each other. Over time, these ideas become more elaborate and are linked into connected sequences of ideas and feelings.

Pretend play is a safe zone for children to explore a myriad of concerns and dramas of life. Here they can pretend about being vulnerable or brave, aggressive or meek, mean or kind, broken or whole, lost or found, victor or defeated. They can enact hellos and goodbyes, control and loss of control, devastation and rescue.

The joy of symbolic play is derived from the ability to share meanings with others. Now a parent, sibling or peer can respond to the child's ideas in words and play, and introduce more ideas in a shared drama. The child can then interact around those ideas as well. There is a pleasure and excitement in the discovery of a new way to connect to a loved one through mutual understanding and acceptance of a wide range of emotional ideas.

Along with imaginative play, language is used to express intentions, wishes, ideas, and feelings, moving from immediate perceptions to true symbols. Feelings may initially be described as urgent physical sensations, such as, "I feel like I'm going to explode." Gradually feelings become labeled, "I want to scream. I am so mad." Then, a child is able to use words to describe feelings abstractly. A child shifts from saying, "I'm scared" to "I feel scared when it's dark." An emotional label, such as mad, sad, or scared, becomes meaningful as it is associated with a variety of different experiences, including the feelings aroused in reading about an experience, or watching a video. It is generally not helpful to teach emotion words in a rote way.

Children may also express emotions symbolically by employing a phrase from a favorite character: "I'm the mightiest on earth" or "Never cross the Badger." A child can also communicate emotion using nonverbal symbols, for example, making a stuffed elephant trumpet to show anger, or pretending to be a baby to show neediness.

Gradually, a child can use language to express a wish for the future, such as, "Go swimming?" or to make a plan: "I'm going to win!" In pretend play, children can ascribe feelings such as, "She is sad" when acting out a mother leaving or "He is scared of the tiger" while having their character run and hide. They may give a character attributes, such as, "He's mean" or "She's always nice."

Use of Symbols and Behavior

The capacity for symbolic thinking is vital for advancing emotional and behavioral regulation. A child progresses from using words together with an action, such as, "Stop!" while pushing another child, to using words alone. The ability to consider feelings in a symbolic way creates distance between feelings and actions.

Behavior benefits from a child's ability to use symbols to explore, communicate and modulate feelings. A child can use symbols to deal with fears and other distress. A favorite character may help support a feeling of bravery, strength, or beauty. In pretend play, a child can pretend to protest or do the thing that was not allowed in real life. Rules within play become more abstract. Instead of, "Everyone gets two" a child may determine, "Everyone should have the same amount." Rules are not necessarily logical, and a child may suddenly change the rules to their advantage.

As children develop the capacity for imagination, they may begin to expand their thinking to a wide range of "what if" scenarios. They can become frightened of the possibility of a monster under the bed, or encountering a big dog, or getting lost. Fears may lead to regressions in other areas of development at this time, such as an increase in clinginess, loss of toilet training, or increased difficulties with tantrums or negative behaviors.

Assessment capacities at Milestone 5 focuses on the ability to engage in pretend play and to use language or other symbols to express wishes, feelings, and ideas. Further assessment would examine the content of those ideas. What emotional themes are represented? Does the child restrict symbolic thinking to one theme such as fearful ideas, aggression and fighting, loss and sadness, bodily injury, or limits and control? Strength at this level would be manifested in the ability to use imagination and creativity about a broad range of emotional themes and to elaborate on those ideas in multiple ways, as well as to use symbolic thinking to recover from distress.

The power to think creatively allows a child to fill a blank page with a drawing, make up a song, or answer an open-ended question with reference to another time. By recognizing the feelings represented in these expressions, or in the choice of symbols chosen in play, the adult is offered an insight into the child's concerns, wishes, and emotional life. By sharing meanings, an adult encourages and motivates the child to continue to explore and elaborate ideas, leading to higher levels of logical thinking and reflection.

When children have deficits at Milestone 5, their behaviors are closely tied to the perceptions of the moment. Language, especially under stress, would not be available to convey their ideas and feelings independently of action. They would have difficulty thinking into the future or the past. The safe world of pretend would not be available to explore and help them gain an understanding of emotions, and they could not use symbols to cope with distress.

For a child with behavioral challenges, the capacity to express ideas with words and enact them symbolically is very helpful. When children are able to communicate about their feelings, adults are able to respectfully reciprocate symbolically in a way which helps them succeed in meeting the demands of the moment. Gradually, they learn to postpone satisfaction, cope with disappointment, and adapt to unexpected change. Capacities at Milestone 5 are a major advance in this developmental progress.

Milestone 6: Logical Thinking

Milestone 6 is the capacity to bridge symbolic ideas, eventually using logical connections and reasoning. With this ability, children are now able to distinguish more clearly between ideas generated in their own mind and the outer real world, and can better distinguish their feelings from another's feelings. They develop a keen interest in why things occur, and further understand motivations and consequences for behavior.

Development occurs as a child begins to organize ideas, grouping and connecting them. For example, he may associate "all my favorite things," "things that are scary," "things that make me mad," "things I want to do at camp," and "things we need to take to the beach." A child can then make connections between ideas and feelings: "I need my big red shovel because I want to make a super high sand castle." "I get mad when Mark takes my toys." "I feel sad when you yell at me." She may abstract a general principle, such as, "You shouldn't break other people's toys."

With the capacity to link ideas, a child may state, "I'm scared and I want to run away *because* then I wouldn't have to read in front of everyone." Without needing to act on an idea immediately, he has the opportunity to reflect and plan.

In play, a child expands the capacity for symbolic thinking by linking one idea to the next, in gradually more complex ways. She can exchange ideas with another player, and incorporate others' ideas into a shared story. She may pretend about elaborate fantasy: dragons, witches, dinosaurs, princesses, and kings. The stories gain in complexity of design and detail. As emotional challenges arise, she may counter with another emotional idea. A dragon steals the princess, and now the princess turns into a warrior to fight back.

As a child relates one idea to the next, pretend play begins to take on the characteristics of a story. Initially it is a story without end; the plot meanders and evolves, with characters changing and both logical and illogical connections. Bad guys and good guys may be identified, but then through various actions, the good guys end up in jail, and are now being punished. It is difficult for an adult to sort out the jumble of ideas, yet the child is eager and enthusiastic to continue adding more and embellishing each idea that tumbles forth.

Over time, as he explores various feelings and ideas, not only do characters become more complex, but plot lines begin to emerge that are more discernible as one event and emotional idea leads logically to another. Eventually he can even plan ahead, saying, "Today let's pretend that there are two armies that fight each other, and the leader of this army is going to steal all the tanks, and then he is going to win. You be the red ones."

In play, emotions are genuinely felt. A child may aggressively hit to rebuff a scary stuffed snake even though she has never had any previous experience with a snake. At times, the emotions envisioned may be so strong that the child cannot allow them in play. She might say, "That scary lion is not going to come out." Of course, this utterance provides a clinician with an idea to later gradually challenge the child to confront this fear. Magic is often used as an expedient and powerful solution to strong feelings. Gradually, as a child is able to tolerate the intense feelings, she can expand to a wider range of symbolic and then more realistic solutions.

In pretend play, children practice symbolic thinking around all of the themes of life, including dependency and autonomy, power, winning, losing, limits, jealousy, bravery, and so on. As they have more experience with pretending, they are more secure in the difference between play and reality. This safety allows them to explore even stronger emotions. They might imagine a storm without being terrified, or pretend to be naughty, knowing that they will not really be punished, or pretend that their mother was banished to a distant island, knowing that she is really safe. A new level of distance between an idea and reality broadens the safety zone for fantasizing about potentially devastating feelings.

Symbolic thinking and logical connections now support understanding in daily life. A child can consider emotional motivations and consequences for behavior, such as, "He will be mad if I take the last cookie" or "I will be sad if I lose again." He can answer "why" questions, and connect "if . . . then," especially as related to feelings.

A hierarchy of questions reveals emerging abilities in logical thinking: What? Where? When? How long? Why? Gradually, children can apply logical reasoning to these questions. They may wonder about what they can really do, and may consider how others will respond to their actions.

Dr. Greenspan, in his description of the development of reasoning, asserts that emotional experiences pave the way for logical thinking. For example, in pretend play with a car, "What will happen . . . ?" means, "What feeling will direct what happens?" "Where will it go?" becomes, "Where will it feel fun/exciting/daring to go?" or "Where will it be safe to escape?" "When will it get there?" means, "How will it feel to wait or to be first?" and "Why are you going?" becomes "What feeling motivates your actions?"

Similarly, a child forms concepts of quantity based on emotionally lived experience. For example, the idea of quantity, the meaning of more or less, may come from wanting more treats or from getting less than was expected. In play, a child may grapple with how much money it would take to get out of jail, and how much more would be needed if the character does not have enough.

Logical thinking also extends to connections made across time and space. A child may consider, "If I finish all my homework this week, Dad might be proud of me when he gets home from his trip." Or "It must take a long time to get to the moon, but I would never be able to wait as long as it takes to go to Mars." With the advent of these logical skills, a child gains a greater sense of reality versus fantasy. In play, he becomes more interested in facts, such as which fire truck has the ladder and how high it can go, and in playing about what really can happen.

The ability to connect ideas logically enables children to play games with more complex rules. All start a game with hope of winning, and fear of losing. In playing a game with rules, children learn to tolerate waiting for their turn, deal with setbacks in the game, and modulate their feelings around winning. For some children, the anxiety is too great to play without cheating, or even to start.

During a rule-based game, children may be corrected when they transgress the rules, which arouses feelings of anger, sadness, or shame. They may observe and empathize with others experiencing similar events and feelings. They learn to anticipate consequences of their actions. With a variety of similar experiences, they can develop a concept of fairness. A child may say, "He can't take two turns—that's not fair!" Fairness is not a rule that can be taught in isolation, but is the outcome of the organization of a collection of emotional experiences.

Through the ability to connect ideas, children begin to understand the perspective of others. "If I bring my shovel and bucket, and if Mary brings hers too, we can make a super-high castle together. Mary is going to like that." As they connect their ideas with others' ideas, they also combine or contrast feelings. "Mary likes to build castles like me, but Mark only wants to make tunnels."

As skills advance, children become able to connect two different ideas regarding feelings and actions: "I am sad because you broke my crayon and because you beat me in the race." They may also be able to identify their feelings and give reasons for them: "I am so happy because we are going to the zoo. I love to see the elephants." And they begin to recognize and label more nuanced feelings such as annoyance, loneliness, nervousness, or embarrassment.

They are now able to share ideas and build on another person's ideas. The discovery that connections exist between one's ideas and the ideas of others causes children to search for those connections, and to begin to guess what others might be thinking or feeling. The process of searching for and considering the perspective of others lengthens the process of thinking, weighing different options, and making conclusions. The maturity of thinking is evident in a decrease in impulsive decisions and actions. With the abilities of Milestone 6, buttressed by skills at the lower milestones, children now achieve a more stable regulation of mood.

Assessment at Milestone 6 includes observations of the use of symbolic thinking in play, art, and conversations about feelings and ideas. An inventory of themes explored by a child might include warmth, dependency, pleasure, excitement, assertiveness, anger, curiosity, limit setting, empathy, love, being admired, respect, shame, and humiliation. The ideas represented in play, as well as those missing from play, provide insight regarding current development and can guide intervention. A child may have different capacities for expansion and elaboration for different themes.

When children can communicate using words to express their feelings, and can connect their feelings with others to predict and understand behavior, they are equipped to establish and sustain friendships. When there are deficits in the ability to understand motivations and consequences, it is difficult to feel truly connected with the social world. Some individuals are able to do so within a narrow set of circumstances, but struggle to understand more complex social interactions. Humor, irony, deception, and malicious intent may be missed or misunderstood.

Assessment also probes a child's ability to distinguish fantasy and reality. He may have a hard time shifting between thinking about a wish or feeling and an actual experience. Thomas was playing with a friend and told a tall tale about how he had three puppies at home. While this was clearly untrue, Thomas was sharing an idea that he had vividly imagined. His strong desire for the puppies had overwhelmed his ability to separate internal and external experience.

With constrictions in Milestone 6, children may attempt to rationalize a behavior or argue their point, but get tied up in convoluted, irrelevant reasons and unproductive conversations. Arguments might be as unsuccessful as a parent trying to explain to a 3-year-old why the toy in the plain box is as good as the toy in the fancy box. Children who have difficulty with logical thinking tend to make black-or-white, all-or-nothing determinations. It becomes difficult to convince them of alternatives or to negotiate compromises.

> *Reggie is an energetic 8-year-old boy who loves to push elevator buttons and talk incessantly about elevators. Mother has high expectations for Reggie, but unfortunately their interactions often result in confrontations, arguments, threats, and punishments. Mother tries to reason with Reggie, but he argues back with circuitous and illogical reasoning.*
>
> *Although Reggie may be able to use logical reasoning in some situations, particularly when calm, he does not yet have the capacity to think symbolically or logically while experiencing heightened emotions. With practice broadening the capacity for coregulated emotional exchanges including gestural affective cueing, he can develop the necessary foundation for higher-level logical thinking.*

Children who have not yet attained the ability to link ideas have difficulty identifying broad categories. A child may rely on narrow and specific characteristics to identify an object, a person, or a feeling, which can lead to rigid thinking and behavior. Reggie likes the surprise and excitement of elevator doors opening and closing, but only associates these feelings with elevators. Children begin to conceptualize what others know or may not know, and what others might know or not know about them. Misperception about the distinction between internal thoughts and feelings and others' internal thoughts and feelings can be a great source of confusion and a barrier to developing relationships.

> Raymond cheerfully approaches a friendly adult. However, as usual, he starts the conversation with, "What color car do you drive?" He would happily continue a conversation detailing facts about cars, and would not recognize the listener's signals of boredom or annoyance.

A child with deficits in logical thinking may misinterpret the meaning of others' behavior and may be unable to accurately distinguish reality from an internal thought.

> Myra is a teenager with low self-esteem. She is bright and very aware of her challenges with social interactions. She longs for friends but is extremely anxious about approaching her peers. Often she will complain that others are saying critical things about her. In fact, this is usually not true, but rather a confused projection of her fears.

Children who fail to see the logical connection between their actions and ideas, and the actions and ideas of others, operate in a lonely and isolated way. They may then act without regard for others, and with no sense of awareness or remorse for the harm or hurt that they may be causing.

> Parker liked toy cars, and there were always shiny model cars by the checkout of the local store. He was easily able to pick one up and carry it out without paying. Although Parker knew the rules, he did not readily link his actions to how others would feel or even potential consequences for himself.

While taking an item without paying can be deconstructed to clear rules, unfortunately much of life is not clearly logical. Is it acceptable to pick the flowers at the park? Is it okay to leave the empty cups on the ground, when the trash bin is full? Adaptive behavior requires flexibility and the ability to use inferential thinking. Practice with spontaneous and varied interactions, including forming hypotheses, making informed guesses, and forming suppositions, challenge a child to move beyond concrete thinking to abstract reasoning.

Skills at Milestone 6 enable children to connect ideas, use logic to understand the motivations and consequences of both their own behavior and the behavior of others, and to begin to think with greater complexity. They can confront the realities of feelings and behavior, rather than escaping into imaginary and wishful thinking. These capacities enable them to advance to even higher levels of abstract and reflective thinking, and ultimately navigate the highly irregular and complex social world.

Milestone 7: Multicausal, Comparative, and Triangular Thinking

There are three higher milestones in the DIR framework that further describe developmental advances in childhood, relating to increasing abilities to manipulate symbolic ideas. Milestone 7 is the capacity to use multicausal, comparative, and triangular thinking. This level of thinking typically emerges around 4½ to 7 years of age, as children begin to consider multiple perspectives and indirect influences on a situation.

A child who has difficulty considering more than one cause or perspective may make decisions in a black-and-white, rapid and concrete fashion based on a single more superficial reason. Estimations of another's character may take the form of good guy, bad guy, rather than something like, "He is generally my friend, but was in a bad mood today."

With the capacity for multicausal thinking, children consider more than one reason for an event or feeling, for themselves and for others, for example:

- Yolanda supposed that, "Ana is sad because she tore her dress and also because she lost her favorite doll yesterday."
- "Pierre was sure awesome today in the game. I think he really practiced a lot because he was worried he was going to lose his spot on the team."

- "I was glad my mother was there, but also disappointed that my dad couldn't come."
- "I was proud that I got up on stage, but embarrassed when I messed up."

Using triangular thinking, a child considers multiple viewpoints and may strategize for a preferred outcome.

- In planning a party, Joey considers that Mark may want to play softball, but Jason probably won't because he only likes soccer. He decides to go swimming, since they all like the water.
- "I will take my water gun over to Mike's house because then Mike's mother will let us play outside."

It is at this level that children may become truly manipulative. They may scheme to get Mom to agree when Dad said no. While being manipulative is generally considered a negative attribute, it represents a growth in mental prowess and can be used for productive ends.

Social interactions become more complex as children consider multiple viewpoints. They must learn to weigh their own ideas against others' opinions.

Vincent reflects, "I was thinking about being friends with Julia, because she looks like she is all alone, but then people will think I'm weird for talking to her."

When children can consider multiple reasons for feelings and actions, they become more tolerant, flexible, and understanding. The capacity to consider multiple perspectives and possible influences, even when strong feelings are aroused, is a skill that is acquired gradually and expands throughout life.

Milestone 8: Gray-Area Thinking

Milestone 8 is the capacity to use gray-area thinking, or the ability to consider a range of intensity of emotional experience. Children who advance to this level will be able to describe shades or gradations of different feelings, such as being more or less nervous, a lot or a little discouraged. They can make subtle distinctions in type and intensity of their emotional state. They are more able to consider the big picture, rather than discrete relationships.

Children with the capacity for gray-area thinking will be able to reflect on the degree of relative influence between different feelings.

- "I was sort of excited, but a lot more nervous."
- "I was a little sad, but mostly angry."
- "My whole class was really excited, especially John and Stacy."

They may express these mixtures of feelings in charts and graphs, and also in art, music, and creative writing.

The capacity at this level typically begins to emerge around 7–10 years of age. Peer pressure can become intense as children judge themselves in comparison to others. Hierarchies and pecking orders may be applied to a host of activities. Children at this level may be highly competitive, rigid about rules, and concerned about losing, loss of respect, and humiliation. They may also show increasing sensitivity to others, as they are able to sensitively empathize with others' feelings.

A child who has difficulty with gray-area thinking is prone to black-and-white judgments and may not be able to understand or be successful with complex social dynamics and moral conundrums. With increasing ability to use comparative thinking within a range of intensity of emotions, he will have a greater ability to modulate feelings and behavior.

Milestone 9: Reflective Thinking

Milestone 9 is the stage of development when a child develops their own personal value system. Typically this begins around 10–13 years of age. Through accumulated affective experiences, children begin to form their own standards for values such as beauty, fairness, quality of effort, justice, and ethics. The ability to abstract values from reflective thinking enables them to think independently and frees them to a large extent from peer pressure.

Those who have the ability to think and judge relative to an internal standard will evaluate their behaviors and feelings, as well as others', in relation to their personal ideal. Comments that reflect this type of appraisal might include, "I was not as nervous as I thought I would be." "My painting was not as good as it usually is." "I know I get irritable when I'm tired." "My friends thought it was okay, but I didn't." "He should have given her the book."

A child may struggle with how to adapt values in social situations that are not necessarily logical or standard. A boy might say, "My dad tells me to always try my best. But, in sports, my coach says, 'Take it easy on the girls.'" Through an appreciation of the feelings of all involved and a child's own affect and values, he can determine the appropriate action for himself.

Self-identity continues to develop through symbolic and reflective thinking. Children may initially consider themselves in extreme terms: "I'm right and everyone else is wrong," or "There is something wrong with me." By increasing accuracy in understanding the perspective of others, and the compass of a personal value system, a child can gain a positive and moderated sense of self-esteem.

The ability to abstract meaning and judgments about one's own actions, feelings, and values enables children to take ownership of personal change. The ability to have insight into the values reflected in behavior and to evaluate behaviors based on concepts of ethics and morality enables children to perceive the social world in increasing levels of complexity and sophistication.

Using the Developmental Capacities Framework

The functional emotional developmental milestones form a framework for understanding a child's capacities to interact across a range of emotional experience. Prior to an analysis of a particular behavioral challenge, it is imperative to consider a child's capacities in each of these milestones. What are a child's developmental capacities? What are areas of relative strength? In what context are strengths apparent? Where are areas of relative weakness? And what factors are associated with deficits or constrictions of abilities?

It is expected that a child's abilities will fluctuate throughout the day, in familiar or novel contexts, and even moment to moment. Some children's abilities are more vulnerable to being tired, hungry, or sick. If they have certain capacities when calm, they may lose them when feeling a strong emotion. In order to get an accurate assessment, it is necessary to consider the child's interactions in multiple contexts, with multiple partners (parents, other adults, and peers), and in structured activities and free spontaneous play.

Information about a child's abilities is obtained from both history and observation. Capacities can be described qualitatively or by using a rating scale, such as the Functional Emotional Assessment Scale (Greenspan, Wieder, & DeGangi, 2001) or the Social-Emotional Subtest of the Bayley Scales of Infant Development Part III (Greenspan, 2005). The parameters for measurement include how frequently a skill is observed, the level of support that is needed, and the child's ability to expand or elaborate abilities across a full range of emotional experiences.

Behavioral challenges usually arise from delays or deficits in functional emotional development; however, some behavioral challenges may actually reflect developmental growth that is atypical for the chronological age. For example, strong-willed, obstinate, or defiant behavior , may occur in a typical 2-year-old as they create goals and have the capacity to sustain interaction even during intense emotions. Similar behavior may present many years later for a child with developmental differences as they reach capacities at Milestone 4. The process of advancing through these stages and coming to new states of equanimity and balance can be intense and prolonged in children with developmental challenges. By referencing typical developmental stages, an adult is able to recognize weaknesses in underlying abilities and evidence of developmental growth in these struggles.

The developmental framework is a powerful tool for gaining an understanding of functional emotional development. With an appreciation for a child's skills, strengths, and deficits, the meaning of behavior becomes more apparent. By considering developmental capacities, as well as individual differences, and patterns of interaction in relationships, a plan for intervention can be created that is not only effective in addressing a particular behavior, but does so by promoting the underlying functional emotional development.

Chapter 3

Individual Differences

Each child with autism or other developmental challenges has a unique way of responding to sensory experiences. Each child also has unique capacities for language, cognition, attention, memory, and movement. These differences, along with a child's health, are a biological inheritance and evolve with time and experience. The (I) in the DIRFloortime approach refers to these "individual differences."

To help children with behavioral challenges, it is essential to understand their profile of individual differences and how they contribute to overall development, relationships, and behavior. An adult can then tailor interactions with a child to support behavioral goals. A parent, teacher, or clinician can help a child take advantage of areas of individual difference that are strong, and provide support to improve areas that are less developed.

A pattern of sensory, motor, and cognitive responses often leads directly to a child's interests. He will often seek out sensory-motor experiences that are pleasurable and avoid those that are not. Strengths may lie in individual sensory systems for perception and memory, motor or language skills, or more broadly in curiosity, intelligence, knowledge, creativity, honesty, humor, or sensitivity to others. The pleasurable activities engender initiative and are motivators for problem solving and creativity. Ultimately, pleasurable activities may lead to acquisition of skills, and lifelong sources of pleasure in hobbies or vocations.

Sensory responses and individual differences can also become problematic behaviors. It is natural to avoid experiences that are uncomfortable or frustrating, and to persist in experiences that bring pleasure. Developmental progress is dependent on the ability to tolerate uncomfortable feelings, such as uncertainty, disappointment, surprise, frustration, or waiting, and balance those with pleasure derived from novelty, discovery, and accomplishment. Extremes in individual responses can alter this delicate balance.

All learning begins with sensory experience. Children develop a sense of their physical being in relation to others and the environment, and then learn to connect sensory input with motor output, while developing cognitive skills. The processes involved in sensory processing include perception, attention, discrimination, identification, affective arousal, and motor response. The field is indebted to the pioneering work of Jean Ayres (1970) for building awareness of this important aspect of child behavior.

Sensory systems are highly complex. Each sensory channel provides overlapping information and is integrated with other sensory information and with memory, language and other cognitive functions. Sensory systems change and develop, along with other aspects of development. Development proceeds from primitive reflexive responses to conscious self-control. Sensory information contributes to inhibition or facilitation of responses, associations with previous learning, and the ability to plan and predict the future.

Sensations are perceived and recognized with associated emotional tones and in a particular context. The emotional arousal is a critical factor in directing the response. A light touch may be perceived as pleasant in the context of a parent at bedtime, and lead to a look, hug, and relaxation. Or a light touch from a mosquito in the park may cause quite a different response.

To understand behaviors, it is particularly important to discern the emotional experience that is connected to a sensory experience. More than simple, linear connection between pleasure-causing seeking and displeasure-causing avoidance, a behavior may be related to a more complex, dynamic flow of feelings. For example, a child may move from a feeling of curiosity and interest, to excitement and pleasure, to becoming overwhelmed, irritated, and anxious. She may have difficulty knowing how to start and stop or modulate the intensity of a sensory experience, or the experience may trigger memories tied to yet other feelings.

Children with autism and other neurodevelopmental differences may have unusual ways of responding to sensory experience, as well as atypical cognitive, language, and motor functions. Some of the complex ways in which information is received and processed for these children are not well understood. Differences that might occur include an inability to synchronize sensory information such as sound and vision, or touch and movement. Difficulties may arise in any aspect of sensory processing or in the overall organization and integration of sensory input, motor output, memory, or concept formation.

The ability to perceive, discriminate, identify, and then respond to sensory experience changes as a child grows and learns. The development of visual, auditory, motor, and other cognitive systems is therefore amenable to the influences of experience, including therapeutic interventions. Within a developmental approach to behavioral challenges, supporting the development of individual sensory-motor-cognitive capacities and understanding their contribution to behavior is a major component of intervention.

Assessment of Individual Differences

Assessment of a child's individual differences requires a thorough history, careful observation, and curiosity on the part of the assessor. A history can include information about how a child responds to each of the sensory systems and about his ability to move, communicate, remember, and problem solve. A clinician would want to know about current functioning and past development in each of these areas. Information may be direct or inferred from narratives about a child's choices, preferred activities, and patterns of behavior. For more verbal children, an assessor might ask what they like to do, why they like a certain favorite figure, or why they have chosen a particular poster to decorate their notebook or lunch box.

Observation of a child in free play and in different environments will provide further information about individual differences. With the history and observations, an assessor can then form impressions about the child's unique individual profile. During the assessment process, a clinician may also be forming impressions about the parents' sensory-motor-language and cognitive profiles, which may be useful in the course of intervention. Standardized sensory profile surveys may support gathering historical information but are not sufficient by themselves. An assessment is focused on the individuality of the child, and how the array of her particular differences is manifested in her interests, relationships, and behavior.

The most dramatic features of individual differences are often sensory responses. For children with autism and related disorders, differences in sensory reactivity can be extreme. Many children have mixed sensory reactivity, with heightened and decreased responses in different sensory systems. Many children have a predominant pattern of either sensory seeking, underreactive, or overreactive profiles. However, behaviors occur as a result of the complex interplay of sensory systems, often with mixed patterns of response. Some responses are more subtle and difficult to discern. If a child is underreactive, it may be difficult to know what he perceives and what sensory stimulus may be causing distress or avoidance. A child may seek out a sensation such as touch, smell, or movement, and then become overwhelmed by it. Responses and intensity of response may also be variable from day to day, or even moment to moment.

It is not sufficient to attribute a behavior to a sensory response alone. All sensory experience has an emotional aspect that contributes to behavior, and an assessment is not complete without a consideration of the corresponding emotional experience. Every sensory experience is processed or understood in context: as a perception that is noticed, identified, evaluated, and perhaps associated with a motor response. Each sensory experience is also tied to an emotional experience, creating meaning and contributing to a memory.

The processing of sensory input happens at both a conscious and unconscious or automatic level. Some children with autism and other sensory processing challenges have difficulty automatically habituating to a stimulus. Typically, there is a response to a stimulus, and over time the response decreases as the same stimulus continues. For example, if the heater is making a clicking sound, a child might notice and attend to it, but if the sound continues, the child can gradually ignore it and attend to other things. For a child with sensory challenges, each clicking sound may elicit the same level of response as the initial sound. A decreased ability to habituate to an irrelevant stimulus can be a major challenge.

Some individuals describe strong cross-modal sensory experiences, or synesthesia, such as when hearing a certain note will produce an experience of seeing a certain color. These experiences may include symbolic ideas linked to sensations as well. Thinking about dates on a calendar may induce a specific visual-spatial image. Children with neurodevelopmental differences may have such conscious perceptions but be unable to describe them in words.

The emotion or affective tone that is associated with a sensory perception is fundamental in determining its significance and contribution to thought and action. Some sensations may be soothing, others exciting, others frightening or irritating. Sensations can trigger emotions, and conversely, emotions initially generated by thoughts can change perception and interpretation of sensory experience. In this way, sensory experience and emotion are tightly coupled. A child with behavioral challenges may have increased or decreased sensitivity to sensory perceptions with either positive or negative emotional associations.

To add even more complexity, sensory information is received through multiple sensory systems at the same time. A child filters the vast array of sensory inputs, and salient information is registered and then combined from different sensory systems to create meaning and corresponding responses. Although assessment may be directed to each sensory, motor, language, and cognitive system independently, it is equally important to consider patterns of behavior that result from the interaction of these various facets of individual difference.

Justin, age 6, was perplexing to his parents and teachers. At times, he would be nicely cooperative, would respond to requests, and was calm and patient. More often, he was disobedient and confrontational, and seemed not to listen or respond to his parents or teacher.

An assessment revealed that Justin had very poor fine motor skills, poor visual-spatial skills, poor sense of rhythm, and at the same time had excellent auditory and language skills. He was bright and curious, but was often lonely, confused, and frustrated. By understanding both his sensory differences and how they impacted him emotionally, his parents and teachers were able to approach his behaviors with compassion. Therapists that were sensitively attuned to his challenges were able to provide graded experiences to help improve the sensory-motor weaknesses and their emotional ramifications.

Careful observation and consideration of multiple possibilities can help to accurately identify the factors that contribute to a particular child's pattern of behavior. Although a skilled observer can appreciate many individual differences, no one professional can be an expert in all areas. Collaboration between teachers, clinicians, and parents is the best way to gain a thorough assessment of a child's individual differences, and then to create an appropriate treatment plan.

Health

A child's health is perhaps the first factor to consider when there are behavioral challenges. The ability to attend, focus, move with strength and stamina, be persistent, have patience, energy and regulation may all be impacted by how he feels. Past history of health issues and experiences with health care may also be a factor for some behavioral challenges, such as a history of pain with eating, fear of separation after a hospitalization, or anger and mistrust after a traumatic procedure. Rather than leaving health issues to be managed solely by health care professionals, everyone can consider how a child's health and related experiences may be affecting behavior and performance.

Some children with neurodevelopmental disorders have chronic medical conditions, and others have frequent intermittent illnesses. Some conditions are well defined, or symptoms may occur without a clear medical diagnosis. Children with autism have an increased incidence of gastrointestinal difficulties such as gastroesophageal reflux and constipation. They also have an increased risk of sleep disorders and seizures. Some seem to have altered immunity, with multiple allergies and frequent infections. Many have feeding difficulties affecting nutrition. Children with a genetic syndrome such as Down syndrome may have associated medical conditions. And all children are subject to the routine illnesses of childhood.

An illness or injury may be more difficult to identify in a child with a developmental disability. She may have difficulty perceiving and localizing pain or discomfort, and may have difficulty communicating how she is feeling. When there is a sudden or dramatic change in a child's behavior, it is crucial to consider if an underlying health or dental problem might be contributing to the change.

While children have different potentials for cognitive, motor, and language skills, the goal for all children is to function successfully across a full range of emotions and continually advance in development. For most children, behavioral regulation can be accomplished without the use of medication. However, if a child's behavior creates danger to themselves or others, if they have seizures, sleep disturbance, a secondary mental health condition, or tremendous difficulty with basic regulation, medication may be needed as additional support. A neurologist, psychiatrist, or developmental pediatrician can provide the needed assessment and monitoring of medical treatment. When medication is used, it is helpful for all professionals working with the child to have open and regular communication with the prescribing physician.

Suzy had a pattern of waking in the middle of the night, crying and thrashing about for 30 minutes before falling back asleep. If she became stressed during the day, she would have violent tantrums that could last for almost an hour. She would scratch herself, or anyone that approached, hit her head on the ground, and bite her hands. Everyone tried to comfort her, but to no avail.

A neurologist performed a complete assessment and subsequently prescribed a medication that helped her sleep better and calmed her enough to eliminate the episodes of complete dysregulation during the day.

If a child is receiving medications, including vitamins and dietary supplements, it is important to consider their effectiveness as well as the possibility of unwanted side effects. It is often difficult for children to say when they are experiencing an upset stomach, a headache, a funny taste in their mouth, or increased sensitivity to sounds. Adults must be vigilant to the possibility of secondary effects for all medications.

Sleep, exercise, and diet all contribute to well-being. A comprehensive developmental approach to behavioral challenges includes a complete health history and monitoring of health issues to consider how they may impact behavior. Children with chronic allergies, frequent ear infections, poor sleep, or stomach pains may not be functioning at their best. The normal hormonal changes of adolescence, with a characteristic pattern of strong emotions, increased appetite, and rapid growth, can contribute to behavioral challenges for teenagers.

It is important that all children receive the medical care, including specialized care, required for their particular needs. All clinicians can help by noting changes in health or changes in behavior that may be related to health issues. Communicating these observations to parents and health care providers can be extremely helpful in detecting and monitoring a health-related condition. Everyone who cares for a child has a responsibility to consider how her health may be affecting her behavior.

Auditory System

There is sound in almost all environments, and often children have little control over the sounds that they hear. If children are overly reactive to sound, it may be evident in their reactions. They may startle, panic, wince in pain, or cover their ears. Or a child may be overly sensitive, but without any signs. When a wall clock was removed from the room, a child commented, "Now I don't have to hear the ticking." Up to that time, no one was aware that the sound of the clock was disturbing to her.

Auditory skills involve passive and active listening, discrimination, identification, localization of sound in direction and distance, and auditory memory, as well as skills involved with the flow of sound through time: sequencing, blending, and closure. Sound has qualities of pitch and timbre, and occurs in time with possible rhythm or dynamic patterns. Multiple sounds interact, creating harmony or dissonance. Sound, like all sensory experience, is remembered and associated with feelings and context. In addition, sound and rhythm are closely connected with movement, and can support initiation and patterns of movement.

It is difficult to assess all of the components of hearing, listening, and understanding of sound. A child may be thinking about sound experiences, drawn from memory, or other associations that are difficult to explain. One child said, "The music in my head is too loud; I can't turn it down." While not clearly sound hallucinations, a child may be experiencing phenomena that are atypical in some way.

An exquisitely sensitive sense of hearing can create both pleasing and disturbing experiences. A child with perfect pitch can derive great joy from music, but may be equally disturbed by music that is out of true pitch. A child that remembers a song in a certain way may be upset with even a slight change that few would notice.

Children may have particular strengths or deficits in any of the components of auditory processing. One may have obvious difficulty in identifying and localizing sounds. Another may seem to have little awareness or perception of sounds. Of course, it is important to ensure that a child does not have a true hearing loss; however, many children with normal hearing may still show little awareness of the sound environment.

Some children have particular strengths in auditory processing. They may take great pleasure in creating sound, either with their voice, singing, tapping on the ground or an object, or playing an instrument. A child may derive a sense of space and distance from sound more than sight. Some types of echolalia may simply be a child's enjoyment of saying a pleasing word or phrase. An interest in creating sound can be a gateway for gaining shared pleasure in an interaction.

Sound and music easily evoke strong emotion. Because of this, music can be a powerful medium for supporting social-emotional development. Even without words, the dynamic flow of music can support regulation and shared attention, reciprocal two-way communication, and coregulated interactions. With the addition of words in songs, a child can express ideas and strong sentiments. Music therapy utilizes the power of music to support advancement in many areas of development.

By considering how sound may be influencing a child's development and behavior, an adult can apply strategies using sound that support developmental goals. Like all skills, auditory processes can improve with practice. Strategies can be directed at accommodating to deficits or helping a child to learn new skills. If necessary, a child can avoid certain sounds or wear headphones. At the same time, a child might learn to gradually tolerate more sounds through exposure, or be supported by explanations about the source and meaning of the sound.

> *Cecilia is an 8-year-old girl who was extremely frightened by the loud sounds of a nearby factory, and was very resistant to leaving the house. She had relative strengths in language skills and would describe her fears and why she felt she needed to always stay inside. Cecilia asked repeatedly about the factory and the noise.*
>
> *Through a trusting relationship, Cecilia's therapist provided information and dispelled misconceptions about the meaning of the sounds. She convinced her to visit the factory, viewing it from a distance. She learned about the sounds and the work being done. They drew pictures to show the distance between the house and the factory. She learned about the work schedule to help anticipate the noise. This information helped her to feel more secure, and eliminated her disabling fear of leaving the house.*
>
> *At the same time, Cecilia was very anxious about separation from Mom. Her poor sense of distance and space affected many areas of her life. Occupational therapy helped Cecilia to improve her visual-spatial abilities. She now enjoys going outside, and has made steady progress as she gains more confidence in her ability localize sounds, objects, and people in her world.*

Language

Language is the use of a symbolic system to represent and communicate ideas. Nonverbal gestural communication, including facial expression, eye gaze, and body language, is the precursor to language and continues to be very important for shared understanding even as symbolic language develops. Language ability includes both the understanding of language, or receptive language, and the formulation and production of expressive language.

Language is not synonymous with speech. Speech refers to the oral (or synthesized voice) production of expressive language. As in other areas of development, the ability to use speech and language may be compromised in children with autism and other developmental disorders. A child may have challenges with the understanding of language, formulation of language, speech, and/or use of nonverbal gestures. A child may have difficulties with voice modulation or lack the skills needed for social conversation.

Even when children have strengths in some areas of language, they may have significant deficits in other areas. They may use language but have a flat facial expression and a monotone voice. The voice may always be loud or have a sing-song quality. Many children have difficulty reading others' nonverbal cues in conversation, and interrupt or fail to take natural turns in a dialogue. Some children have difficulty understanding and using figures of speech or other idioms. Although a child may have strong auditory memory and use language with a large vocabulary, they may lack understanding the meaning of the words they are using.

Some children have facility with language but cannot speak. Some of these children can write, and others can communicate with augmentative and alternative communication (AAC). For children who have challenges with movement and oral-motor control needed for speech, and with limited abilities to express themselves through nonverbal gestures or writing, it may be difficult to discern their true level of cognitive and language ability. If children have limited ways to communicate, it is important to begin with the assumption that they do have awareness of language and can generate their own thoughts. Many nonverbal children have been given the ability to communicate through AAC and have then demonstrated the depth of cognition and language ability that they were previously unable to share.

Some children engage in echolalia, repeating what they have just heard, or scripting, reciting words, phrases, or lines heard previously. There are many possible reasons for echolalia and scripting. Sometimes children simply enjoy the sound of the word or the feel of the word in the mouth. They may say the word when happy, bored, or stressed. Sometimes, a child recites a phrase from a favorite video or story because the words correlate with a particular idea or feeling, such as being frustrated and stuck, or afraid. It is useful to investigate the possible meanings and associations of words used by a child as these may be used for two-way communication.

> *At odd times Paula would repeat softly, "In the bucket it goes. In the bucket it goes." Her family knew the exact source of this script—it was said at a pivotal moment in a favorite movie, as an evil witch hid a prized key. Paula said the words with the exact same intonation as the character. While most listeners were puzzled by her recitation, her mother knew it was Paula's way of saying that she was feeling nervous.*

A child that has challenges in understanding language, or discerning language when there is background sound, may appear to be inattentive. Eliminating background noise, using language that is simpler or slower, or adding visual cues or sound amplification may be helpful. For children that have difficulty understanding and responding, it may be helpful to provide extra time to respond.

Language abilities may vary dramatically at different times. Under emotional stress, the ability to use full language capacity may diminish dramatically. When children are agitated or afraid, they may have difficulty not only finding the words to use, but also in understanding the language they are hearing. It may take them longer to understand and to answer. For some children, movement may either help or hinder their ability to use language. In supporting a child with behavioral challenges, it is important to tailor language to the ability of the child in that moment.

When children that usually have the capacity to express themselves with language are having difficulty because of heightened emotion, an adult may be able to provide a cue to help them get started.

> *Michael was playing happily with his brother with the train set. Then his brother sent a train head-on toward his. The two trains collided and both fell off the track. Michael was so distressed that he literally started spitting. Dad rushed to his side and said, "Oh! The trains crashed! Michael, you can tell Sam, 'No crashing!'" Michael stopped spitting, and repeated, "No crashing!" to his brother.*

Helping a child by providing the needed words can convert a physical act to a symbolic communication. Using a strong emotional tone helps children connect their experience with the words. They may then be able to repeat and use those words to facilitate a productive interaction. For all children, attunement to the emotional meaning of their sounds, words, and gestures can support two-way communication.

Sometimes using any language can be too much. If a child is overwhelmed by sensory experiences and emotion, and auditory processing is not an area of strength, an adult might choose to not speak at all. Instead, the adult may offer support simply through their presence, adding touch or movement to nonverbal expressions of comfort and care. Through a nonverbal interaction, adults may become more aware of their own nonverbal communication, and an adult and child may find that they are more successful in forming shared engagement and reciprocal communication, and even advance to shared problem solving with a sustained flow of affective gestures. Language skills are built from success in these nonverbal affective gestures.

Touch

The tactile system registers light touch, temperature, vibration, and pain. Children may have increased or decreased awareness and responses, may seek or avoid tactile experiences, or may shift from enjoyment to becoming overwhelmed and distressed. Children with autism or other developmental challenges often have strong responses to touch. Some are terribly bothered by the feel of clothing, brushing teeth, combing hair, or holding hands. A child may insist on taking off his clothes if there is a wet spot on them. Walking barefoot in the grass or sand can seem painful. Or a child may react violently to the touch of another child.

Carl was sitting next to his brother on the couch. Mom, Dad, and the boys crowded together to look at a book. Suddenly Carl kicked his brother. It was so unexpected. Mom said, "Why did you do that? Don't kick your brother!"

Mom realized that Carl was sensitive to touch. The light touch of his brother's pants against his skin led to a reflexive kick. His parents learned they could help Carl by providing a soft blanket that he could drape over his legs when they snuggled together.

While some tactile experiences may be avoided, it is helpful to gradually expose a child to a range of experiences connected with daily life. By building on a trusting relationship, a child can learn to tolerate more touch experiences and can recover more quickly from those which cause distress.

Strategies that may help a child to tolerate uncomfortable touch experiences include overriding the discomfort of light touch by providing a deep touch, and allowing a child to have some control, such as using an adult's hand over a child's hand. An adult can also provide a warning before touching, with a clear time frame for touch. For example, Mom always let Angel know before she wiped his face, and counted aloud to 10 so that he could anticipate its ending.

Marcos hated having his nails cut. It seemed both the tactile experience and the sounds were difficult. With utmost patience, Dad helped Marcos to learn a routine, where Marcos would extend his hand, one finger at a time, while Dad told him a story of a brave little bear. The story was full of sound effects, paired to the sound of the nail trimmer. Dad sensitively noticed when Marcos was ready, gently held his hand, and together they negotiated the process together.

In contrast to children that are overly sensitive, other children show little awareness of touch experiences. These children have difficulty finding or identifying an object by touch, unless it is visible. They may not notice water or food on their clothes, skin, or face. Some children overstuff their mouth while eating to increase awareness of the food. Others have decreased responses to pain. All can benefit from practice that draws attention to touch.

Even though he was a bit clumsy, Julian loved to run and play outdoors. Mom watched in amazement as he would crash and fall and just get up and keep going. He seemed not to notice what must surely be painful. Together with their therapist, they decided to help Julian develop more awareness of his body. When he fell, Mom would come and say, "Ooo! You hurt your knee!" using the matching tone of voice and facial expression. She would rub his knee and draw attention to it. After a while, Julian started to respond to an accident by looking to Mom and saying "Ouch!" Now, Mom could add, "I see, you fell and hit your knee. But it's okay." helping him to recover and resume play.

Some children seek tactile experiences. They may want to feel their favorite things—Mom's hair or skin, ladies' hosiery, the girl sitting in front of them, or their favorite little stuffed toy. They show great joy with a tub of beans or playing with water. A child may have both aversive reactions to some things and seeking behaviors toward others.

Seeking behavior for touch, when it involves touching other people, is usually a problematic behavior. A child may need help to learn appropriate limits around touch. A direct command, such as "hands down" or "no touching," can provide a clear limit; however, it does not fulfill the sensory craving or help a child to connect their behavior with the social meaning of personal touch. A more comprehensive approach would focus on other ways to fulfill the sensory craving and build the child's capacity for two-way communication and reading social cues.

All children need to learn the social boundaries about appropriate and inappropriate touching, especially as they approach the teenage years. As they undergo the hormonal changes of adolescence, teens are naturally curious about sexuality and may be interested in how affection is expressed through touch. It is important that all children receive information appropriate to their development and are provided with clear parameters for intimate behavior.

Depending on the child's developmental capacities, pleasure derived from touch experience can be used to support new skills. A child might be engaged in activities that utilize tactile experiences to develop shared attention and reciprocal, coregulated interactions. For example, a child who relishes playing in a tub of beans, rice, or water can build skills in reciprocal interaction and shared problem solving with some simple tactile experiences. An older child might enjoy making bread, creating art with clay, or gardening with others.

Tickling

Tickling is a fairly reliable way to get some children to smile. It is not surprising then that parents may tickle their child to get a predictable smile and laugh. The trouble with tickling is that a child is a relatively passive recipient of the tickling, and it does not present a clear avenue to expand into a two-way interaction. In addition, tickling can easily move a child to a disorganized state that is no longer clearly pleasurable, but instead is a disorganized mixture of excitement, irritation, and pleasure. Some parents use tickling in a sensitive, interactive way, waiting for a child to indicate a desire to be tickled, and continuing at a pace that allows the child a measure of control. At best, tickling should be used cautiously, while expanding play to other forms of pleasurable interaction.

Proprioception

Proprioception is the sense of body position gained through receptors in the joints and muscles. Some children seem to seek out proprioceptive input by pounding, pulling, pushing, heavy lifting, squeezing, jumping, and crashing. They love roughhouse play. Such a child may bite and chew on clothes or love crunchy foods. With this form of input, the children seem to become more regulated, calm, and focused. Without it, they may have great difficulty sitting still, focusing, or being cooperative.

> Melissa had a hard time at circle time. She was always leaning against the wall or the teacher, or squeezing between two peers. When the teacher suggested that the children spread out, Melissa started grabbing and squeezing the sweater of the child next to her. On a daily basis, Melissa was called out for bothering others.

Children that seek proprioceptive input often have challenging behavior. In addition to being very active, they may respond to distress by biting or may even engage in self-injurious behavior. With recognition of a child's need for proprioceptive input, activities can be provided that support regulation.

Once it was recognized that Melissa craved proprioceptive input, she was allowed to lean against a bookcase at circle time. In addition, she was given the task of moving the chairs to the side before she sat down. Similar proprioceptive activities were given immediately before more sedentary activities, such as helping to carry pitchers of water before snack time.

"Do You Need a Hug?"

When a child who enjoys proprioceptive input is distressed, an adult might say, "Do you need a hug?" A child who responds "Yes," or comes toward the adult, would receive a tight squeeze. Some children are greatly calmed by such a hug, or pressure on the head or shoulders. A child might learn to say, "I want a hug," and the pattern evolves that when she feels worried or anxious, she asks for a hug. While a hug can be effective to help a child to relax, it is not an adaptive long-term solution for distress. It would not be appropriate for an older child to ask his teacher for a hug. A clinician must always be thinking toward the future, and to higher levels of skill, including the ability for self-regulation.

If children need adult support for regulation, the adult could squeeze their hands, pull them by the hands, or perhaps use a stretchy fabric to pull together, moving toward an interactive experience. As children are better able to signal their needs, they can be encouraged to find ways to provide proprioceptive input themselves. A child might tighten her muscles, do deep knee bends or wall push-ups, or push against a table or chair. Many children and adults have found their own way to obtain a squeeze that they can control themselves. At the same time, an adult can help a child to improve overall regulation and advance from sensory supports to symbolic-affective support, such as a verbal exchange of problem solving, encouragement, or reassurance.

In contrast, some children have low arousal overall, and do not seem to seek out or respond to sensory stimulation. Although they may not initiate proprioceptive input on their own, they may be calmed when distressed by an activity that provides strong input.

Marion, age 8, was lying on the ground and whining in distress for over 10 minutes. He was nonverbal and couldn't say what was bothering him. It seemed he had had a series of changes and disappointments that day and was overwhelmed. Mom grabbed his ankles firmly and gave each leg a brisk tug as she softly chanted a familiar verse about climbing up a hill. With that, he quieted a little. Then she gestured for his hands. He reached for her, and she pulled him up to a sitting position. Together they continued the chant as she pulled on his arms in big up-and-down movements. Gradually, he became more composed, as he listened and watched Mom intently. When the chant ended, he gestured for her to do it again.

Vestibular System

The vestibular system senses movement of the body in relation to gravity and guides actions and balance. The vestibular, tactile, and proprioceptive systems work together, along with vision and sound, to help children develop a sense of their body in space.

Some children seem to crave vestibular stimulation and are always moving. They like to rock, run, twirl, hang upside down, and swing. After lots of movement, they seem calmer and more organized. Without an opportunity to move, they can become irritable and have difficult focusing attention.

On the other hand, some children avoid movement. They prefer to sit in one place and dislike going on a swing or seesaw, or stepping up on a stool. These children may have poor balance reactions, and may easily feel uncomfortable, dizzy, or nauseous with movement. Being asked to sit on a chair where their feet do not touch the floor or on a moving platform can cause them to become anxious.

Recognizing that a child does best when he has time for active play and movement can help in planning a daily schedule. Ideally, he would have ample opportunities for movement on a regular basis, and in anticipation of more sedentary activities. For children that are always on the move, it is necessary to provide clear boundaries to ensure safety. Games can help them practice stopping and returning, as well as going slow or fast, marching, or jumping, so that they gain greater awareness and control of their body.

It often becomes difficult to find appropriate opportunities for vigorous movement as children become older, and especially in the teen years. Teens often benefit from a 30- or 60-minute workout several times a week, and not simply a 3-minute break to run across the yard and back. Therapy gyms are often not designed for older children, and the exercise equipment in adult gyms may not offer the kinds of activities that would interest an older child with developmental differences. Keeping children safe in large open spaces can be a challenge. If possible, they can participate in sports, or adapted sports activities, or simply engage in physical activities with a peer or adult. For some children, it is very helpful to arrange a vigorous workout several times a week.

Therapists often use swinging as an activity for children who love it because they become happy, regulated, and often have their best abilities to talk and interact. A swing provides a relatively passive and easy way to receive strong vestibular input. However, it is important to advance to other forms of movement, such as running or jumping, where children more actively participate in generating and controlling their own movement.

For children that are more sedentary, and perhaps have generally low arousal, an assessment may indicate how the introduction of activities with gradually increasing movement may support arousal, attention, and engagement, without being overwhelming. Pairing those activities with preferred sensory modalities such as vision, sound, or touch may increase tolerance for vestibular input.

Vision

The visual system is a large component of overall development. Vision develops from infancy through childhood, and visual skills continue to be refined throughout life. Skills include perception of line, shape, color, form, and movement, the ability to focus near and far, to alternate gaze, to follow another person's gaze, to shift visual attention, to discriminate figure and ground, discern detailed parts from whole, and visual memory. Vision is employed with cognitive skills in the use of visual symbols and with movement for searching. Visual skills support social interaction, especially joint attention and nonverbal communication.

The visual system is extremely complex, and differences in visual function may manifest in a myriad of ways. Some children have particularly keen abilities to notice and remember visual information. A child may notice small details, even at a distance. Others are enthralled by colors, lines, angles, shapes, or watching movement. A highly sensitive visual system can create both benefits and challenges for development.

The ability to recognize numbers and letters and read at an early age may benefit a child. But a child may also be distracted by objects or detail that might be irrelevant to a larger goal. By recognizing a child's pattern of visual response, an adult can adjust the environment and tailor interactions to take advantage of strengths and minimize challenges, in order to support behavior and development.

Visual memory, an ability to remember what is seen, can be a strength or a barrier to function. A child may remember the exact placement of furniture, or the route taken to the store, and be upset when things are different. At the same time, strong visual memory can be a useful asset for learning facts, problem solving, or creating art.

While some children have incredibly acute visual abilities, other children seem to have limited visual awareness, even with apparently normal vision. They may only respond to visual information that is directly in front of them at close range or, conversely, only respond to visual information in the distance, or only particular types of stimuli such as a moving fan or spinning object. They may constantly step or sit on their playthings, have difficulty finding a nearby object, or almost run into walls or poles. These children often respond much more to auditory input.

A particular challenge can be lack of shared eye gaze, or eye contact. Children with autism usually have difficulty sharing eye gaze for communication. Adults with autism often remark that it is too difficult to both look and listen at the same time, or that looking directly at someone can be so intense that it is described as painful. They may tend to use peripheral vision or look away. A sensitive awareness of visual processing differences can help an adult to elicit true shared attention and social referencing without a demand for eye contact.

Various strategies can support development, according to each child's unique visual system. It may be possible to eliminate or avoid the more challenging visual environments, or provide visual aids to diminish the challenge. A child who is bothered by bright lights may be able to wear tinted glasses, or a hat with a visor, or simply dim the lights. For children that are particularly distracted by visual information, it may be possible to support their attention by creating an uncluttered visual space or visual barriers. In play, select toys that have less detail and help maintain an organized play area. For eating, dressing, and other routines, it may be possible to support focus by simplifying the visual environment. Gradually, a child may learn to tolerate more intense light, improve the ability to search and focus, and then require fewer supports.

Therapy may directly focus on strengthening weaker visual skills. It may be possible to take advantage of stronger aspects of visual skills to support other areas of development. Any visual preference, such as looking at lines, angles, or movement, can be incorporated into fun, shared play experiences. If a child is motivated by colors, then colorful materials may support shared attention and interaction. For children that attend best to stable visual images, pictures or labels may support understanding of language. If a child has a fascination and visual recognition of particular signs, logos, car models, and such, this interest can be the genesis of developing other skills, such as graphic design or engineering.

Two-dimensional moving images, such as video games that appear on relatively small screens, can be particularly appealing. A form of eye-hand coordination and visual-spatial reasoning is involved in such games, and skills may translate to other areas of learning and even vocations.

If children flick their fingers or shake a little string or other object in front of their eyes, it may be assumed that they are deriving some pleasure from that stimulus. However, they may also be stuck in a response to emotional arousal and know no other ways to achieve a sense of safety and regulation. In order to create a plan to draw them into shared attention and engagement, it is necessary to have a hypothesis about their sensory profile, including all of their visual preferences. Then, an adult may try to find an activity that would take advantage of their visual interest, while simultaneously making it more fun by their participation. Perhaps the adult could introduce a game that involved playing with strings together. In some cases, a child may resist any attempt to join his activity. If playfully joining is unsuccessful, another strategy may be to interest the child in engagement through another activity that has similar sensory properties.

Sometimes, visual preferences can be so intense that a child becomes locked onto the stimulus. Rather than having a pleasurable experience, the child seems to be aroused to the point of dysregulation. By noting the type of visual stimulus that creates such a strong response, an adult can help by decreasing or limiting exposure to that particular stimulus. For example, if a child is fascinated by lines on the tile floor and is unable to switch attention to anything else, the family may cover the floor with a rug. Through practice, a child can be supported to gradually modulate the level of arousal derived from a particular type of sensory stimulus.

Visual-Spatial Skills

The visual system, along with awareness of the body, contributes to visual-motor and visual-spatial skills. Some children have excellent visual-spatial skills and can apply those abilities to problem solving, physical activities, or art. Other children have significant deficits in visual-spatial skills. They may have trouble searching for things in the environment, finding their way, or spatial problem solving. At a symbolic level they may have difficulty using maps or understanding prepositional concepts like under, over, inside, and behind.

Children that have a poor sense of distance and space can become anxious in new environments. They may worry that Mom is gone when she is out of sight. They may hear a sound in the distance and think that it is close. They may often feel lost. At a higher level, they may be concerned that news events such as a war or hurricane may be happening close by, rather than on the other side of the world.

An adult can compensate for weaknesses in visual-spatial skills so that a child can focus on other goals. For example, a child may be exploring a frightening theme in play. An adult can help create a location for the monster to live, and a wall to protect the princess, so that the child can continue to explore the theme.

Play can also be used to strengthen skills. A child can practice visual searching through games of hide and seek, or scavenger hunts. Drawing diagrams can be incorporated in play such as making a map to find pirate treasure. Maps and diagrams, especially when tied to tangible experience, can help a child to perceive relationships in space and distance.

Adapted art lessons may help a child learn about two-dimensional and three-dimensional perspective. Optometrists that specialize in functional vision assessment and vision therapy also offer specific forms of therapy to improve visual abilities.

Motor System

The motor system refers to the work of muscles in voluntary movement. Voluntary, learned movement is built upon underlying muscle tone and posture. Sensory feedback from all of the sensory systems contributes to muscle tone, posture, body awareness, and movement. Differences in the motor system may be related to the central or peripheral nervous system, the muscles themselves, or the process of sensory feedback and control. In any case, a child's posture, tone, and movement have significant impact on arousal, attention, and organization of purposeful actions.

At the park, Tommy, 4 years old, was always leaning against Dad or lying on the ground. It was difficult to convince him to do anything on his own. He seemed to collapse in a heap wherever he happened to be, or he wanted to be carried. Dad devised a game that involved Tommy falling into Dad's arms, followed by a bit of roughhouse play, combined with a rhythmic chant. After a few minutes, Dad stood for Tommy to run to him to continue the game. Dad gradually moved farther away, and then inserted other obstacles for Tommy to navigate on his way to Dad. In this way, Tommy increased his strength, stamina, and confidence to move on his own.

Motor skills have a typical developmental progression from infancy through childhood, and more refined skills can be acquired throughout life through active learning and practice. Children with developmental challenges often have atypical motor development, movement patterns, and motor skills. Motor differences are most apparent in a disorder such as cerebral palsy, which directly affects the nervous system controlling movement, or in neuromuscular disorders. The motor differences in autism are less appreciated but also important. Strengths and challenges in coordination and movement can occur to a greater or lesser degree for all children and are an important aspect of individual differences.

The ability to move with control and coordination is generally described in categories of fine motor skills, gross motor skills, and motor planning. Fine motor skills relate to small muscles, such as hand movements. Gross motor skills refer to large movements, such as walking, climbing, and jumping.

Motor planning refers to the process of creating an idea of movement (ideation), formulating a movement plan for action (praxis), and carrying out a sequence of steps and adapting the movements as needed (execution). Motor planning may be a particular area of challenge. A child that has difficulty with ideation may see a toy on the top shelf but may not realize that it could come down. Another child may have the idea of getting it down, but not be able to create a plan such as moving the chair to climb and reach it. Another child may have the idea to move the chair and climb, but would not be able to perform the movements. That child may talk about the idea or direct others to do it.

Children with poor motor planning may fail to act or initiate play, and seem to be dull or uninterested. A child with limited ability to plan a sequence of movements to achieve a goal may engage in extraneous movements and may seem to have poor attention. A child with poor ability to carry out ideas may quickly become frustrated and lack persistence.

Ironically, once children have learned a motor pattern or habitual movement pattern, such as riding a tricycle, they may do it well. They may persist in the one thing they know how to do and appear to have good coordination. But such a child may have difficulty planning or learning new movements.

Children with poor visual-spatial awareness combined with poor motor planning are often anxious. They may have difficulty anticipating movement, judging if something is near or far, or if something is coming toward them or moving away. They may not be able to respond quickly or effectively to protect themselves. In addition, they may have limited ideas for play. These children often roam the periphery of the play yard or touch the walls and floor to gain more information about their location in space, and avoid crowds and movement.

Initiating movement can be a challenge for some children and they may benefit from a verbal or physical cue to start a movement. This concept has been particularly important for some children who use augmentative and alternative communication. Here, an adult may provide a tactile or physical cue to help a child to start a movement.

Other children have difficulty ending a movement pattern and may need visual, auditory, or physical cues to help them interrupt a repetitive action. Another form of motor challenge is difficulty imitating movements. Some children have particular difficulty in copying others' movements and reversing those movements to orient to themselves. Other children have the opposite challenge and repeat others' movements automatically.

Some children have challenges in modulating movements and may always perform them with a particular level of force or distance, without modifying them depending on the circumstances. Generally, children gradually learn to modulate the speed and intensity of their actions. They learn to speak not only loudly and softly, but at in-between volumes depending on the distance of the listener. They learn to push a little or a lot depending on the force needed to move the object. They learn how hard to push down on a pencil or scissors, or how far to lift their leg to climb up a big step or a little step.

Catatonia, a particular form of movement disorder can occur is adolescents and adults with autism. In this condition, a child will have a decline from previous abilities and have greater difficulties with initiating movement. They may have very slow movements, odd stiff postures, as well as diminished speech. If this condition is suspected, the child (or adult) should be referred for medical evaluation and treatment.

Unfortunately, motor challenges often lead to patterns of interaction with behaviors that are rigid, negative, obstinate, or defiant. All of these types of motor challenges can be improved with support and practice, and interaction patterns can be improved with greater understanding of a child's individual strengths and challenges. Exceptionally strong abilities in motor skills and motor planning can lead to great sources of pleasure, success, pride, and long-term occupation.

Taste, Smell, and Eating

Some children with autism or other neurodevelopmental disorders have extremely acute senses of smell and taste. As with other sensory differences, this ability may interfere with adaptive function. A child may be distracted or disturbed by a whole variety of environmental smells, or may use smell and taste to explore objects or food by sniffing or licking.

Children may be particularly sensitive to the smell or flavor of foods. They may be highly selective and reject food if it is slightly changed or unfamiliar.

> Rosie was so sensitive to smells that she could tell if a peanut butter sandwich, wrapped in plastic, was buried in Mom's purse across the room. When the store ran out of the brand of milk Mom usually purchased, and Mom bought a different brand, Rosie noticed immediately and was reluctant to accept it.

Or a child may have low sensitivity to smell and taste and have a strong preference for sour or spicy flavored foods.

> Christopher liked the hot variety of potato chips and strong flavors. He was generally uninterested in the school's lunch foods, so his mom prepared his lunch each day.

Eating is a complex process that involves many sensory and motor processes. In addition, mealtimes are typically social events involving relationships, conversation, social expectations, and routine. Many challenging behaviors can arise around eating. Challenges can include highly selective diets: selecting foods based on the appearance of the food or the packaging, only eating in certain environments, or requiring particular distractions. Children may only accept foods of a certain texture, taste, or change of texture in the mouth. They may want to be fed, or only use their hands. They may only drink from a bottle. Other problem behaviors include pocketing or holding food in the mouth, throwing food, spitting, vomiting, rumination, overstuffing the mouth, pica, and overeating. Some children have poor oral-motor control, resulting in coughing, gagging, and aspiration.

Ideally, an interdisciplinary team is involved with the evaluation of eating problems, including a specialist in oral-motor skills, swallowing, diet, health, and mental health. Areas to consider include:

1. Health issues: general health, medications, sleep, and gastrointestinal issues such as reflux, food allergies, constipation, or bowel habits
2. Eating and growth history, including previous interventions
3. Current diet and nutritional status
4. Evaluation of oral-motor control and swallowing
5. Sensory responses around food as well as in general
6. Mealtime pattern including relationships and interactions around eating
7. Family history of eating challenges or food intolerance

An evaluation of feeding involves obtaining a history as well as an observation of eating, including preferred and less preferred foods, and novel foods. Hypotheses are formed about a child's barriers to eating and enjoyment of mealtime. Based on the detailed history and observation, a feeding team is able to select appropriate feeding goals and strategies. Priorities are ensuring (1) that eating is safe, (2) that the child receives adequate calories and nutrition for growth, and (3) that the child is calm and enjoys eating. By placing a high priority on the pleasurable aspects of eating, whether derived from the taste, alleviating hunger, or from the social experience around eating, a child will have a foundation and motivation for advancing other oral-motor or dietary goals.

Unless it is absolutely necessary in order to ensure caloric intake, it is counterproductive to force children to eat, or coerce them to comply with eating through unrelated rewards. Long-term success with eating occurs when a child is motivated to eat because it is intrinsically pleasurable. A developmental approach to eating is based on establishing a social environment with trust and warmth, and advancing through playful interactions to food exploration, building curiosity, and the child's discovery of foods he enjoys, as well as enjoyment of the social interaction around eating.

> *Reed only ate chicken nuggets from one fast-food restaurant. In fact, that was the only meat that he accepted. The family had gotten into a pattern of going there every day at 4:30 to pick up his chicken nuggets for dinner. Over time, this routine became a hardship. If Reed was not offered these particular chicken nuggets, at home, while watching a particular show, he would not eat at all.*
>
> *A feeding assessment revealed that Reed was generally healthy but had many challenges with sensory processing. In addition, he had significant oral-motor challenges. The chicken nuggets that he liked had a soft consistency and bland flavor. During a one-year course of therapy, with once weekly sessions with his mother or father, as well as activities for home, Reed was gradually engaged in food play, and then, as trust was built, was able to engage around eating, without the need of distractions. A number of therapeutic techniques were used to improve his oral-motor skills, while at the same time increasing his participation in selecting foods, experimenting, and discovering a wider range of foods from the families repertoire that they could enjoy together.*
>
> *One of the strategies that was useful for Reed was to help him be more conscious of feelings of hunger and fullness. His attention was also drawn to all of the sensory properties of food. He was encouraged to explore and make choices. At the same time, he was challenged to stretch his interest and bravery within the context of a trusting relationship with the therapist and his parent.*

Some practices are ineffective or even cause regression in feeding development. Using distractions for example can sometimes help a child eat, but distractions do not support advancement of eating skills. To gain initiative and self-control, children must be engaged in the eating process. Tricking a child will destroy trust. Likewise, using food as a reward for unrelated behaviors undermines the development of healthy eating habits, where eating is related to hunger, and occurs at regular biologically based intervals.

Some children with developmental disabilities are able to consume enough for marginally acceptable growth during the school-age years; however, the rapid growth spurt of adolescence greatly increases their caloric needs. Teens may feel hungry and not have the skills to consume the needed amount of food. Their eating may be slow, and they may not be able to eat within the time limits of school lunch, or they may have difficulty eating in the school environment. For some children, a calorie supplement or a gastrostomy tube placement for supplementation may need to be considered at that time. Physicians, dieticians, therapists and parents can help to identify when a child needs additional calories and consider all of the factors, including family lifestyle and preferences to determine the best way to provide the nutrition needed.

Overeating can also have multiple causes, and requires a full assessment. Sensory experiences and emotions are involved with eating, appetite, and food choices. Often, the entire family overeats, which may be related to food selection and lifestyle. Intervention is most effective when there is family participation.

Pica, or placing nonedible items in the mouth, is a serious behavioral problem because it can lead to life-threatening complications. The mouth is highly sensitive, and children may seek sensory input there specifically. It is imperative to provide very close supervision to prevent pica and help children find other activities to meet their sensory needs.

Eating is a basic part of daily routine and essential for good health. A child that has difficulty eating creates great stress for a family. Because eating is complex, with multiple possible factors leading to challenges in feeding behavior, it is important to ensure a complete feeding assessment, and that specialists are able to direct the feeding intervention. A registered dietitian is an essential member of the team to evaluate nutritional intake and help guide dietary goals.

Interoception

Interoception is the perception of sensations from inside the body. This includes feelings of hunger, fullness, the need to urinate or defecate, being hot or cold, burping, hiccups, and so on. Interoception also includes feelings during illness such as stomachache, headache, or sore throat, and feelings caused by a response to emotions, such as a racing heart or a stomach in knots. Some children may have decreased awareness of sensations or altered perceptions of feelings from inside the body.

Some children seem to have a decreased response to pain from inside their body as well as from touch. They may not react or may have minimal reactions to tooth caries or even broken bones. This becomes important when evaluating sickness or injury, as well as self-injurious behavior.

It is difficult to understand why a child would engage in self-injurious behavior. For a child with a combination of altered sensory processing along with challenges in emotional regulation, inducing strong sensory experiences may be soothing, or at least may override a more distressing sensation. One sensory modality can block out another. For example, by humming or making noises, a child can block out sounds that are disturbing. By rocking, a child can gain input that overrides uncomfortable feelings when still. Picking at a scab, biting a hand, or hitting one's head may override another feeling, and is often done when a child seems to be experiencing overwhelming distress.

An approach to self-injury begins with a thorough overall evaluation. Only with this information can a clinician develop a logical hypothesis of cause and a corresponding treatment plan. The goal is to help the child avoid self-injury and to develop regulation, shared attention, and trust in social relationships. These relationships then become a source of pleasurable engagement and comfort during distress. Part of the treatment plan may include the use of soft splints, other barriers, or medication. With ongoing monitoring and assessment, appropriate environments, activities, and relationships can be created to support overall regulation.

Cognition and Executive Functioning

Cognition can be described as the ability to acquire and remember information, and then use that information efficiently for adaptation and problem solving. Children with developmental and behavioral challenges may have average, low, high, or mixed levels of cognitive function. Cognitive abilities, like other areas of individual difference, develop and change over time.

Cognitive abilities often do not correlate with the degree of disability overall. For example, a child may have strong social skills, motor ability, or other specific areas of high ability yet have relatively low levels of cognition, or significant challenges with sensory processing, motor abilities, or social functioning but have a high level of cognitive function. It is always best to assume that children have the capacity for high cognitive function; that is, assume competence and set goals to help them communicate and develop those skills.

Executive functioning is the specific part of cognition related to the ability to focus and maintain attention, shift attention, hold two or more ideas in mind at one time, remember, and plan. It includes the ability to anticipate the future, monitor ongoing events, and flexibly adjust plans in progress. A child with advanced executive functioning might create a complex play scenario with multiple characters and sequences of interaction happening concurrently, and adapt the story by incorporating others' ideas.

As the most advanced level of thinking, executive function links multiple cognitive functions including emotion and memory. Stanley Greenspan provided the insight that information is learned and new ideas generated through their connection with affect (Greenspan and Shanker, 2004). Experiences are noticed and remembered according to their emotional salience. Even concrete ideas of quantity, time, and space are initially learned through affective experience. For example, children learn about quantities of "more" and "less" based on whether something is more than they hoped for or less than they wanted.

Time and space concepts are also related to emotion. Something coming fast and near may be frightening, whereas something approaching slowly or at a distance may feel safe. Waiting for Mom to return can seem like a long time. Being surprised by a sound happens quickly. Feelings around movement inform a sense of distance. Going up high on the swing or down a long slide can be exciting, fun, and perhaps scary. Going just a little way feels easy and relaxed.

Sensory experience is linked with emotion, and sensory-affective information is categorized to create ideas. Some children have difficulty forming useful concepts. For example, many sensory experiences contribute to the concept of a food. Some children may have difficulty differentiating aspects of a food, or other object, from co-occurring sensory-affective information. For example, a child may learn that pancakes taste good, look a certain way, and are eaten in the kitchen, in a certain chair. The kitchen, chair, and pancake are all part of one concept of pancake. Obviously, this overextension of a concept can lead to significant difficulties with rigid behaviors. The child cannot eat a pancake in another location because it is no longer a pancake. With support, these concepts can be gradually reformed to become more adaptive.

The ability to sequence physical movements with motor planning contributes to the ability to sequence ideas in the mind. Developing visual-spatial-temporal thinking allows a child to engage in big-picture thinking and planning. She can then make a plan to get a ball that has gone over a fence, or construct a story that links ideas in a coherent and connected story line.

A child needs a balance of skills between thinking in grand concepts and focusing on details. Some children only look at the big picture and have difficulty considering detail. While they have strengths in visual-spatial skills, they may have weaknesses in noticing and describing detail. They may speak in grand abstractions and generalities. These children need help to discern and isolate feelings within larger experiences.

A child who has weak visual-spatial skills may become lost in detail, with fragmented and disconnected ideas, especially when stressed. Such children may have advanced verbal abilities and memory to describe the detail that interests them; however, they never create a bigger story, or they lose track of their initial idea.

A child focused on detail may experience feelings as isolated from each other and have difficulty seeing how feelings are connected and relate to each other. She may have difficulty connecting ideas about now and later, cause and effect, or multiple influences on an event. She may act impulsively in reaction to things she sees or thinks and seem not to consider options or consequences. An impulsive child often reacts to a detail rather than considering the big picture. She can benefit from help in considering how facts, feelings, and events are related.

> *George is a 5-year-old boy who is always on alert. He notices everything. With every little sound he startles nervously and asks, "What's that?" At school and at home, George is often in trouble for hitting. George is very verbal and can carry on long conversations with adults. He can say what he did, and what his punishment is, but cannot explain why he hits.*
>
> *Further assessment reveals that George has poor motor planning and visual-spatial skills. Intervention focuses on strengthening his sensory-motor processing and helping him to recognize big-picture concepts. His parents are guided to provide firm but gentle broad limits on behavior. By having some choices within those boundaries, George is able to gain better self-control of his behavior.*

Cognitive abilities are vulnerable to stress, and can be particularly fragile for some children. They may have difficulty focusing attention, remembering, or problem solving when they are frightened, angry, or confused. Their thinking may become scattered, or they may only focus on details or perseverate on a particular topic or action.

> *Joshua was fascinated by alien creatures that he had seen in a video. He frequently talked about them by name, and carried the little figurines. He seemed to focus on particular aspects of each character, such as their dress, powers, or weapons, but was unable to connect the facts to a coherent storyline. It was concerning to his teachers and parents that he would dwell on these creatures, which were often involved in violence and destruction.*
>
> *With the advice of a therapist, his parents were able to find a book about the alien characters and the story. Rather than watching the video, they read the book together, slowly, discussing each picture and event. Whereas previously Joshua was overwhelmed with a confusing mixture of strong, fast-paced emotions, he was now able to gain an understanding of the many strong feelings that were aroused by the video. Now, Joshua is able to play out the story and is flexible about introducing new ideas.*

Developmental relationship-based intervention is based on the premise that affect-based interactions support the advancement of development, including cognitive and executive function. Creativity, understanding the perspective of others, and the ability to make judgments and develop personal values all evolve from the linking of information and affect.

Individual Differences Related to Functional Emotional Developmental Milestones

Individual differences in health, sensory processing, motor skills, language, and cognition, and the continual advancement and refinement of these abilities, either support or impede functional development at each milestone. Some factors are particularly related to specific functional developmental milestones.

For Milestone 1, basic regulation and shared attention, good health may be a large contributor to the ability to stay calm and focus beyond bodily sensations. The capacity to modulate sensory input can also allow a child to recover from a strong stimulus and regain basic regulation or shift attention from a compelling sensory experience. When children have difficulty connecting sensory experience with human interaction, they may engage in a repetitive activity such as watching a car roll back and forth or clutching a balloon. With support to entice affective interactions with others, these repetitive behaviors decrease and development can advance.

> Tony, an 18-year-old with severe cognitive limitations, would often hit objects against his teeth. He seemed to find some pleasure in that sensation. After an evaluation to rule out dental or health issues, intervention focused on utilizing his apparent pleasure in strong tactile, proprioceptive, and auditory input to engage him in playing a drum in rhythm with his aide. He also was enticed into playing a game of catch, using a large weighted ball. Over time, he became more engaged in doing activities with others while wearing a headset to listen to music. He enjoyed helping in the garden, pushing a cart and picking up leaves. The more often he was occupied, the less he engaged in hitting his teeth.

Milestone 2, shared attention, intimacy, and trust, is typically supported by enjoyment of shared gaze, the sound of a human voice, and human touch. For a child that does not enjoy these experiences, a parents must find alternate ways to engage children to build a sense of intimacy. Parents can easily feel discouraged and rejected by a child that is overwhelmed by these sensations, but by matching the child's individual profile, parent and child can form a special bond. Similarly, a child that has low responsivity may require exceptionally strong input to reach a good level of arousal and interest.

Milestone 3, two-way communication, is supported by a child's ability to initiate movement to form purposeful gestures. Through careful observation, an adult can help identify and create meanings from subtle movements and sounds. For a child with severe motor impairments, movements of eyes or any voluntary movement can serve to support reciprocity.

Success at Milestone 4 is supported by visual-spatial skills and motor planning. Without these skills, a child is more likely to retreat or avoid problem solving and may become resistant and defiant, or anxious. In either case, a child is prone to develop a sense of incompetence and inadequacy. With strong abilities to sequence actions, and with a clear sense of distance and space, children can work through problems with others and form a connected and coherent sense of themselves that includes challenges and victories, disapproval and acceptance.

Milestone 5, the creative use of ideas, is dependent on advancing cognitive skills and executive function. Children draw upon their memory to create and use increasingly complex symbolic ideas. All sensory systems can now be represented in a symbolic form. Depending on an individual child's profile, different sensory-symbol systems can be used to support behavioral goals.

At Milestone 6, cognitive capacities and language continue to develop. Individual preferences, related to sensory experience, help to form aesthetic value judgments in music, sports, art, or literature, as experiences of beauty, disgust, or inspiration. Children may be able to accurately reflect on their own individual differences with acceptance and pride. This insight can provide the confidence needed for self-disclosure and self-advocacy.

The Pattern of Individual Differences Within Relationships

The individual differences of both parent and child impact the course of their interactions and relationship. A parent's individual profile may be a naturally good match for the child, or the parent's style of interaction may need adjustment to better fit the child's profile. A child with generally low arousal who interacts best with roughhousing play may be more successful with a dad that engages in this type of interaction. Or a child may be easily overwhelmed and interact more successfully with a mother who has a quiet, gentle manner. Once parents understand their child's individual differences, they can learn to interact in ways that meet the child's developmental needs.

Limits are conveyed and enforced most effectively when they are aligned with a child's individual differences. A child that is bright, aware, and very sensitive will respond best to firm, gentle limits that simultaneously soothe and comfort. Children with low arousal who are generally underreactive may need a more dramatic response such as big gestures and a loud voice before they register that a boundary has been crossed. A child that is very active and sensory seeking does best with a parent that can also actively provide physical support for boundaries as needed.

A pattern of manipulative or defiant behavior may occur when a child is frequently confronted with tasks that are difficult and contrary to the strengths of his individual sensory profile. Adults who recognize a child's individual differences can help transform the relationship to have more trust, warmth, and mutual respect.

Harold would regularly sit under the table in his kindergarten class, to the point that his teacher was stymied by his defiant behavior. Among other sensory-motor challenges, Harold had significant delays in fine motor skills and was largely unable to complete the work he was given. After the demands for writing were adjusted and his teacher used a more patient and gentle approach, the confrontations diminished and Harold no longer retreated to sit alone.

Individual profiles and developmental demands are constantly evolving. A parent's or other adult's style may be a better match in some circumstances and at some stages of development than others. If adults are aware of their own individual differences, and can tailor their interactions to match the child's needs, there is success in forming warm, trusting relationships that support behavior and development.

Intervention Related to Individual Differences

Recognition of individual differences provides insight to understand a child's behaviors, as well as to help form a pathway for developmental progress. There are specialists that focus on each of the areas of individual difference. Physicians and other health care providers address health issues. Occupational therapists specialize in sensory processing, the integration of sensory systems, and the motor skills involved in daily activities. Physical therapists focus on gross motor skills, strength, and coordination. Speech and language pathologists support communication; psychologists and educators assess and teach academic and cognitive skills.

Other specialists, including audiologists, optometrists, dietitians, and music therapists, all contribute to the understanding and support of individual differences. Specialists in mental health, including psychologists, marriage and family counselors, and clinical social workers, also consider how individual differences contribute to social and emotional development, relationships, and behavior.

In the developmental approach, all clinicians and educators are challenged to look beyond their traditional fields to consider the impact of all the areas of individual difference on a child's development and behavior. While respecting disciplinary boundaries, a clinician would seek to understand a child's abilities or weaknesses and pursue consultation from other disciplinary specialists as needed.

Specialists that work with children are particularly aware of the importance of experiential learning. Well before children have the capacity to think and reflect on what they are doing, or why, they act and interact based on sensory experience. Many behaviors have a reflexive or automatic quality. Gradually, they develop the capacity to use language to communicate their ideas, and later they are able to think in more advanced ways. Even then, primitive pathways also continue to function and influence behavior. In providing intervention, it is critical to use strategies that are matched to their developmental ability in the moment. Children who are being challenged or stressed may not be able to use their highest levels of reasoning and reflection.

Intervention may be roughly divided into strategies for remediation and those for accommodation. Remediation is directed at improvement of specific weaker abilities. Accommodation strategies provide supports to mitigate or avoid weaker areas, in order to allow a child to concentrate efforts toward other goals. For example, if a child is easily distracted by visual detail, play materials might be offered that have solid colors and little detail to support interaction and shared focus of attention. An accommodation might also include provision of additional supports, such as adding a movement activity to the schedule before a seated activity or modifying the environment by providing a different chair. Remediation would have the direct goal of increasing focus and decreasing visual distraction in environments with gradually more visual information.

The balance of accommodations and remediation can be viewed in the moment, and also in a longer time frame of days, weeks, or years. A continual awareness of sensory, motor, language, and cognitive differences can help in selecting priorities and goals for intervention. Accommodations may be offered in some areas, while focusing on remediating weaknesses in other areas, to find the just-right level of challenge, as well as support.

Steven was an extremely active 7-year-old. He had a short attention span and always seemed distracted. He was receiving many therapeutic services, but almost all involved being in a small therapy room. At school, he had 30 minutes per day of recess, and he had occupational therapy in a big gym 1 hour per week. Steven and his parents lived in a small apartment with his baby sister, with little opportunity to play outside. After a team recognized his need for more physical activity to match his individual sensory-motor profile, a plan was made to incorporate large movement into all of his therapies. His parents also made a plan to go to a neighborhood park every weekend. With these accommodations to meet his sensory needs, Steven had better focus and made good progress academically.

Intervention strategies can be used flexibly depending on the demands of the moment. In particular, a child may require more accommodations during times of stress. Stress may occur in the moment or may accumulate. A child may be stressed by illness, lack of sleep, or the physical, sensory, and emotional demands of daily life. While maintaining limits on behavior, an adult can provide the needed supports and accommodations for a child's success.

Most important, areas of individual strengths usually correspond to interests and preferences. Special interests can cause self-absorption or distraction, or they can be transformed into opportunities to support overall development. If a child enjoys cars, for example, playing with cars may support two-way communication or shared problem solving. Using the developmental framework, a clinician applies strategies that take advantage of a child's natural abilities, skills, and interests to motivate progress toward developmental and behavioral goals.

A preferred activity can motivate performance but should not be used as the primary means to achieve compliance. If a child enjoys cars, they should not be withheld and only given as a reward for accomplishing an unrelated activity. If a preferred object or activity is used as coercion, a child may feel resentful and lose the desire for that activity, and more importantly, he may develop a conflicted sense of engagement with the person withholding the source of enjoyment. In addition, an opportunity for taking advantage of that interest to support engagement and expand and elaborate on the interest may be lost.

On occasion, a special activity could be earned as a reward, with the adult working as a partner or cheerleader for success. Some parents remove a desired object as a punishment. In using this tactic, it is important that children clearly understand how they are responsible for their actions, and how they can regain their privilege and good standing with their parent. Giving or withholding activities that bring pleasure should be occasional at most, and not used frequently due to the tendency to undermine trust and warmth in relationships.

In a developmental approach, each child's unique individual differences are appreciated and respected. Areas of weakness can be strengthened. Areas of natural facility and interest may not only support developmental goals but may lead to lifetime pursuits, pleasure, and pride. Recognizing the contribution of individual differences to challenging behavior allows clinicians to form effective intervention strategies tailored to each child and family.

Chapter 4

Relationships

*Development arises from being a participant in a
dynamic discourse with other people.*

—Alan Fogel

The third component of the DIR model is represented by (R), for relationship. Recognition of the importance of relationships to learning and behavior broadens the focus of assessment and treatment of a child's behavioral challenge from a child's actions alone to the patterns of interaction between a child and others. In each step of assessment, a professional has the opportunity to learn more about the relationships between parents and child. In addition, the assessment process is the critical beginning of creating a relationship of trust and respect between the professional and the parents.

Assessment and Relationships

Assessment of child with a behavioral challenge includes both gathering a history and making observations of the child and parent-child interactions. The developmental approach is particularly concerned with the emotional component of parent-child relationships. A comprehensive assessment supports the creation of an effective treatment plan.

Referral

Parents may seek out professional help of their own accord because they recognize a problem behavior and seek a remedy. They are then part of the assessment from the beginning. Or a child may interface with a professional for another concern, such as delayed language or motor skills, and the professional then identifies a behavior that interferes with progress. In that case, the professional will need to decide to either address the behavioral issues themselves or give the parents a referral to another professional.

In a school setting, a teacher may identify the behavioral challenge and may then need to take the lead in sharing the concern with the parents. Teachers often face barriers to even finding time to meet with parents, and some parents may be resistant to acknowledging the challenging behavior of their child. Yet a complete assessment and effective intervention require knowledge of the key relationships in a child's life and parent-professional collaboration. Fortunately, parents universally care about their children, and professionals can tap into parents' concern to overcome any obstacles to partnership.

The perception of a child's behavior as challenging or acceptable may vary depending on the person, time, or place. What one adult finds problematic and worrisome another adult may applaud as fun and admirable. For example, one parent may happily partake in argumentative negotiations, while another may consider a child's disagreement as a disrespectful affront to authority. Even when behavior is viewed universally as unacceptable, the degree of tolerance will vary depending on an adult's attitude in that moment, and personal histories, hopes, fears, and expectations.

Role of the Parents

Participation of parents is critical to understanding a child's behavior and for the creation of an intervention plan. From the outset of the parent-professional interaction, important messages are conveyed regarding the parents' role in the assessment and for the subsequent intervention. Through the process of gathering the history, a professional can express a genuine interest in the parents' views and in the parents themselves. Through an attitude of respect and sensitivity, the professional begins to build trust. By valuing the parental role in the child's development and behavior, a clinician is beginning the needed partnership for effective intervention, whether with that clinician or another professional.

During the assessment, a clinician will gather information about the child and her place in the family dynamics. A parent typically approaches professionals with respect for their knowledge and authority, and with some degree of anxiety about possibly being judged negatively. Professionals are wise to always be aware of the trust placed in their hands, and the vulnerability of parents who disclose their private lives and personal weaknesses. Clinicians can encourage parents through recognition of their care and efforts on behalf of their child and can instill hope for the future.

An agreement about confidentiality should be explicitly defined at the start. Who will participate in the assessment and who will provide and receive information? Some parents may not want to share information from one professional to another for a variety of reasons. Complex confidentiality issues can arise, for example, if a child is in foster care, or when there are multiple parents through divorce and remarriage, or simply when one parent does not want to be involved. Some therapists may require both parents to consent to assessment before beginning. In a particularly complex situation, a professional can seek guidance in order to comply with both legal and ethical standards.

Gathering the History

An assessment of parent-child interaction has two components: history and observation. Mistakes and misunderstanding can be avoided by diligently obtaining a thorough history, listening openly, and patiently inquiring about actions, interactions, hopes, and concerns. Like other aspects of the developmental model, the format of history taking is not standardized, but develops its own dynamic flow beginning with open-ended questions, such as, "Tell me about Alex." By following a parent's lead, a clinician can gather information that is most relevant to understanding a child's development and the parent-child relationship. While a great deal of information can be derived from spontaneous narrative, a clinician can introduce new topics and specific follow-up questions to gain a more complete understanding of children and their interactions.

A developmentally based history has a broad focus: child, parents, and the interaction between them, as well as interactions in other key relationships in a child's life. Assessment includes information about the course of a child's development (motor, language, cognitive, social), pregnancy and birth, medical events, school experiences, history of specific behaviors, individual sensory-motor profile, interests, and, importantly, the dynamic patterns between parents, other family members, and child. To gain an understanding of a child's experience, it is helpful to review a typical daily schedule, combined with who is involved in providing child care.

Family history includes not only medical history but a social history of family structure and extended family roles. Beliefs and values regarding discipline and child behavior may be expressed by each parent. Parents may or may not have the same values or the values of their larger cultural group. Many factors can contribute to the mood in a family: marital relationship, financial status, deaths, births, and illness. Parents may have experienced some trauma in their own childhood that has left them vulnerable to certain feelings or experiences with their child. And parents and caregivers may have their own developmental, health, or mental health issues.

For each milestone area, the interviewer should help parents to elaborate on their narrative to discover what factors support a child to function with higher-level skills, and what factors may hinder optimal performance. Considerations might include demands of the environment in relation to sensory-motor profile, health, and developmental skills. Rich information is derived from how the stories are told, what is included, and what may be omitted.

Obtaining Historical Information About the Milestones

A developmental history considers a child's abilities within the framework of functional emotional capacities in relating and communicating with others. A history attempts to discern strengths and constrictions within each milestone, and factors that support or impede these capacities. Areas of weakness often correspond directly to challenging behavior. A child's developmental achievements and areas of strengths become the foundation for growth and advancement.

The following is information that would be sought in the course of an assessment interview, organized in the framework of developmental milestones.

Milestone 1: Regulation and Shared Attention

At the first level, consider the ability of a child to organize a stable, alert state and share attention with a parent in a variety of experiences, and the ability of the parent to attune to the child and provide needed supports.

- What does the parent recall about the child as an infant in regard to regulation? How successful were the parents in reading and responding to the child's cues in order to support the child's state organization (sleep, calm attention, excited, distress)? How has that progressed over time to the present?
- How much time are they able to spend with the child, in nonpressured, calm experiences, with shared interest and attention?
- How often is the child exposed to new experiences and how does he or she react?
- Are the parents able to identify their child's sensory responses and reflect on their own sensory responses?
- How frequently is the child overwhelmed with distress? How do the parents respond? How effective is their intervention?
- How often does the child withdraw or become self-absorbed to entertain himself or to calm down?
- In describing the child's behavior and their interactions, how do parents describe their own regulation? Do they lose control themselves?
- Are parents anxious, depressed, angry, or distracted? In other words, do they display a stable sense of regulation themselves?
- Does either parent mention challenges with attention? Are they able to maintain attention during the interview?

Milestone 2: Engagement

For Milestone 2, consider the quality of shared pleasure, warmth, and intimacy each parent has with the child, and the general quality of warmth overall.

- How much time do the parents have together with their child? What activities does each parent enjoy doing with the child? How successful is this play in generating a sense of intimacy, warmth, and joy? As parents become more comfortable with the clinician, they are more likely to share stories of personal moments and games that they enjoy with their child. When parents have difficulty with this question, there is an opportunity to reflect on their efforts and the associated feelings. The assessor may help parents to recall activities that they enjoyed together in the past.
- Do the parents express warmth and nurturance toward their child? In talking about their child, do they convey a sense of warmth, or anger, embarrassment, disappointment, and frustration? What events are associated with these feelings?
- How well do parents feel they can comfort their child? Have them describe examples of how they console their child.
- Does the child's behavior indicate a positive sense of self-esteem?
- Does the child engage in pleasurable activities with others or show warmth toward others—grandparents, caregivers, extended family, friends, peers?
- What activities, careers, hobbies, or interests do parents enjoy? By expressing an interest in each parent, the assessor not only begins to build a relationship, but is also gaining information that may be helpful in identifying activities that will be mutually enjoyable with their child.
- Do the parents evoke a sense of friendliness and warmth toward each other? How do the parents relate to each other, particularly when discussing the child's behavioral challenges? And with the interviewer?

Milestone 3: Two-Way Communication

For Milestone 3, the assessor wishes to ascertain the parents' and child's ability to engage in two-way reciprocal communication, and a child's ability to organize and communicate primary emotions with affective gestures.

- What activities are described that involve purposeful interactions?
- How does the child communicate desires, protests, and choices?
- Does the child initiate interactions?
- Can the parents describe what makes their child happy, sad, afraid, angry, and surprised? How are those feelings expressed and how do they interact at those times?
- Does the child have an in-between range of emotional intensity or are there only extremes?
- Do the parents describe both verbal and nonverbal communication on the part of the child and themselves?
- Do the parents have a dynamic range of affect in their conversation during the interview?

Milestone 4: Coregulation and Shared Problem Solving

History for Milestone 4 seeks to determine if a parent and child are able to sustain long continuous sequences of back-and-forth coregulated communication through a range of different emotions, and work together toward a common goal.

- Do the child and parent enjoy activities of exploration, adventure, and challenge, including outdoor play, construction-type activities or other goal-directed games, hobbies, or crafts?
- How does the parent describe interactions around instances of emotional distress in the child? Does the child seek and/or accept help?
- Does the child recognize and respond to others' expressions of emotion, such as confusion, sadness, fear, anger, or frustration, in a sustained interaction?
- In describing an example of a problem behavior, does the parent relay a sustained dialogue or flow of interaction or are there frequent breaks in shared attention?
- Does the parent describe the child's emotion during a behavioral challenge? Is there a progression of different emotions?

- In the scenarios shared, does the parent tend toward a rigid, rule-based, and directive stance with the child or a more flexible approach?
- Do the parents respond to a behavioral challenge with affectively flat, logical responses or do they describe their feelings and the child's feelings?
- Do the parents tend to cut off or avoid interaction around certain strong emotions?
- Do the parents seem defeated and discouraged, confused or inconsistent?
- How do parents balance limits and rules with accommodations and support?
- Do the parents encourage the child to attempt new challenges or try to keep the child calm and happy?

> Co-regulation occurs whenever individuals' joint actions blend together to achieve a unique and mutually created set of social actions. Co-regulation arises as part of a continuous process of communication, not as the result of an exchange of messages borne by discrete communication signals. Co-regulation is recognized by its spontaneity and creativity and is thus the fundamental source of developmental change.
>
> —Alan Fogel

Milestone 5: Creative Use of Ideas

Inquiry about Milestone 5 is focused on a child's capacity for symbolic thinking and parents' engagement in pretend play and conversation about ideas with their child.

- Have the parents observed the child doing pretend play? Can they describe the content of the play? Do they play with their child?
- Is there evidence of elaboration of ideas, or a repetitive and restricted range of play ideas?
- Does the child have time to explore a wide range of themes in pretend play, or is the time structured and full of directed teaching?
- Do parent and child enjoy conversations about ideas, such as favorite characters or books, planning for a future event, or recalling the past?

- Does the child explore a range of emotional ideas—things that are exciting, scary, sad, or frustrating?
- Can the child use words to describe her feelings without necessarily acting on them? Or does she use other symbols such as drawing a picture, writing a note, or acting in character to show her feelings?

Milestones 6–9: Logical, Multicausal, Comparative, and Reflective Thinking

Assessment of Milestones 6–9 includes a child's ability to connect ideas as reflected in conversation, or other symbolic expressions of ideas.

- In examples of conversations with their child described by the parents, does the child attempt to link ideas? Is there evidence of logical thinking?
- Does the child use words to express her feelings and others' feelings?
- Does the child ask and answer "why" questions, and are the answers logical?
- Is the child able to express opinions about why things should happen?
- Does the child show particular interest in artistic expression of ideas?
- Does the child show an appreciation for consequences of his behavior or others' behavior?
- Do the parents use reasoning in conversation with their child? Does the child seem to understand? Even when upset?
- Do the parents use reasoning exclusively with their child rather than empathic emotional attunement and comforting?
- Does the child try to negotiate with the parents? How successful is it?
- Does the child try to appeal to parents separately to obtain different results?
- Can the child reflect on degrees of feelings?
- Does the child show evidence of an internal standard for behavior?

Obtaining Historical Information About the Behavioral Challenge

To obtain a history of behavior, it is helpful to begin with more open-ended questions, with follow-up inquiries about details. A clinician might ask, "Tell me about times when your child becomes upset." The parents' response might suggest that a child does or does not distinguish emotions. Follow-up questions can examine each emotion: "Does he seem to have any fears?" "Has he had experiences that made him sad?" In this way, a clinician can elicit information about the child's emotional development, as well as parents' responses and interpretations of behavior.

It is also helpful to have parents describe specific examples of behavioral challenges, including the sequence of events, with as much detail about context as possible. It is important to gather information about what all the parties did or said, and how the behavior might vary in different situations.

Further description of the behavioral challenge would include the chronological history of the behavior or previous challenges. In addition, it is important to inquire about parents' ideas about the cause of the behavior and their efforts in the past. Each parent may have a different perspective to share.

While parents are relaying information about the behavior, an interviewer would note their affect and take any opportunity to reflect with them about their response to the challenge. Here, it may be appropriate to learn more about the parents' lives, work, and other life events and how the behavior may impact daily life. Many parents of a child with autism or other disability have underlying grief about their child's diagnosis. It is important for professionals to listen empathetically so that parents are encouraged to disclose their feelings, hopes, and fears, including the possible impact of the child's behavior for his or her own future and for the family.

In closing the interview, it is often helpful to inquire more about a child's interests. In this way, a clinician can help to focus on strengths of the child and the family, as well as provide ideas for the subsequent play-based observation. The interview process is an important first step to forming a trusting relationship with the parents as the foundation for further work together. Following the interview, a clinician has enough information about the child's developmental capacities to set up an individualized play session.

For those clinicians not from a mental health field, inquiry into parent-child interactions may be uncomfortable. Yet, in order to help with behavioral issues, it is helpful for professionals from every discipline to participate, at least to some extent, in assessing the interaction patterns in families that contribute to a child's behavior. Without this, an assessment and treatment plan may completely miss the source of the behavioral problem. A guiding principle is that information about family life is important to the extent that it affects a child and the disciplinary goals. For example, if parents are arguing, or there is an illness or death in the family, a child's awareness and understanding may become relevant. For behavioral challenges, family matters are usually significant.

Observation

An unstructured play-based observation is used to gather more information about a child's functional emotional developmental capacities. Through observation of spontaneous interactions, a clinician can obtain a broad array of meaningful information in a relatively short amount of time. A play observation usually is scheduled for 1 to 1½ hours. If possible, the session is videotaped for review.

Prior to the observation, parents are informed that the play session will take place in a room set up with a variety of toys or play materials, and that the goal is to observe spontaneous play interactions, occurring as naturally as possible. The toys selected can be discussed at the end of the previous interview, so that the parents and clinicians are already working in partnership. A clinician might ask, "What toys do you think would be good to have out?" The goal is to have some toys that are familiar and would likely be successful for both child and parent, and also to have play materials that might challenge a child at the higher milestones.

Play materials are also chosen in consideration of a child's sensory profile and to be appropriate for the child's age. Materials may include opportunities for gross motor, fine motor, sensory, and pretend play. The following are examples of materials that might be made available as arranged by milestone level:

Milestone 1
Climbing structures, seesaw, slide
Tub of beans, bubbles, water toys, vibrating toys
Buckets and shovels
Musical instruments
Blankets and pillows
Pop-up bus or tent
Two-person swing or ride on toy, wagon

Milestone 2
Big cardboard blocks
Scarves for dance and musical instruments
Nursery rhyme books
Books with pop-up or texture elements
Playhouse with windows that open and close
Big tunnel
Feathers or bubbles

Milestone 3
Balls
Train or car, with track, tunnel, or a ramp
Basketball hoop
Cause-effect toys

Milestone 4
Art materials for gluing, taping, cutting
Construction games
Cardboard blocks, chutes, and marbles
Tools and repair kits
Models, train sets
Puzzles
Simple board games

Milestone 5
Dolls and dollhouse
Kitchen and food

Stuffed animal families
Baby dolls, carriages, bathtub, toilet, crib
Cars and trucks, garages
Airplanes, boats
Puppets
Farms
Doctor kits
Tools and repair kits
Magic wands
Pirates, swords, soldiers
Kings and queens
Castles
Villains
Aliens
Dinosaurs
Sharks, alligators, lions
Superheroes
Dress-up dolls, jewelry, doll clothes
Armies
Teams of pirates, gold, and treasure
Open-ended toys: Play-doh, clay

Milestone 6
Pirate ships and little figures
Fighting figures, armies
Dollhouse and families, smaller with more detail
Open-ended art materials, clay, paint
Houses, forts, castles, and figures
Board games with more complex logic
Science kits

It is important that the room is set up to be inviting for both parents and child. Mats or area rugs can provide borders, and pillows or bean bags offer comfortable places for a parent to be on the floor. When a toy is set out with some of the pieces in place, such as a partially completed train track, or a car sitting at the top of a ramp, there is an obvious invitation to engage in play. While several toys should be available, it is equally important that the space is not visually cluttered or spatially challenging. A comfortable, fun, and safe play space is inviting for both parents and child.

Typically, a clinician will not initially interact with the child but will invite the parents to join the child in play, following the child's lead. Minimal further instructions are given. Several strategies can help parents and child to feel at ease and thereby reach the highest levels of interaction. Sometimes parents are anxious that their child begin to engage in some type of structured play, and will try to organize and direct the child. Here, a clinician can reassure a parent, "Children often want to explore what is here first. Feel free to just explore with them."

Some parents may seem particularly uncomfortable with being asked to play in this way. A clinician may need to initially sit nearby to encourage and compliment their efforts. If two parents are present, a plan might be discussed for one parent to begin, and then to trade places with the other. A relaxed atmosphere can decrease apprehension and help to achieve an interaction at the highest level. Sometimes a professional can join the parents in some silly play, thereby giving permission to act in ways that seem a little foolish, to help to establish a comfortable environment for play.

The facilitator must ensure that each parent is allowed to pursue his or her efforts without interference. Sometimes, in their eagerness, parents actually compete for a child's attention or give conflicting directions. A facilitator may need to intervene and ask one to wait, then engage the parent in brief conversation about what he or she is observing, and then find an opportunity for the parents to switch roles.

A clinician may make comments that help a parent playing with the child to feel at ease, without directing the interaction. For example, if the child is not responding to the parent, an observer might comment, "It seems you are really working hard to get her attention. Is it always this difficult?" Thus the observer can also ascertain if the behavior is typical.

A clinician can also encourage parents and guide them to elicit even more skills by a comment such as, "He really likes the way you do that." Generally, a clinician should say as little as possible in order to observe the interaction, but also use comments to help parents feel confident in their play.

If the play engagement is faltering, a clinician might be tempted to coach or join in prematurely. However, it is important to allow the interaction to progress in order to observe how obstacles are addressed. Of course, a clinician would intervene if the interaction was so poor as to risk undermining the trust being formed in this setting with the professional. Then the clinician would offer support just to the level needed for a parent and child to recover and continue.

After first observing the spontaneous interactions between parent and child for approximately 15–20 minutes, a clinician might use coaching to see if the child could reach a higher level of engagement or more complex play. A clinician might initially coach a parent to try an idea, saying, "Let's see what will happen if you . . . " Challenges follow the child's lead and encourage them to increase their skills in thinking, relating and communicating. A challenge might include waiting longer for an expected next step in a simple game, the introduction of a mechanical problem in construction, or the introduction of a slightly more threatening or scary character in pretend play. It is important that a parent not step in too soon to help or direct the child through the challenge, thereby eliminating the opportunity for the child to respond in their own way.

The behavior which was initially of concern may manifest in some way during this observation. It is important for the clinicians to take the opportunity to observe how the parents and child interact at that time, without intervention. Later, they may offer some strategies to try in order to gather additional information about the child's responses.

Next, either at the same visit, or at another visit, a clinician may interact directly either with the child or with parents and child together. Now is the time to observe the child's response to a new person, who may be able to provide a further level of challenge or support. The clinician can observe and join a child either very gradually or more directly depending on the child's level of wariness about interacting with a stranger.

Even while interacting with a child, clinicians can continue a relationship with the parents, either by explicitly talking about the idea they are trying or their observations, or by positioning themselves to face the parents, with frequent eye contact and shared facial expressions. They may look for opportunities to include parents in the play.

Sometimes the clinician is more successful than the parent in eliciting higher level skills from the child. Some parents may be discouraged by their own lack of skills, while others are encouraged by their child's potential, or a combination of both. It is helpful for a clinician to solicit the parent's reflections toward the end of the session or at a subsequent visit.

Throughout the observation, the clinician takes a stance of interest and curiosity, while holding a relationship of warmth and acceptance. An empathetic disposition toward both parent and child is necessary. While clinical impressions are formed, parents are in a vulnerable position. They are worried about their child and aware of being judged. They are often insecure and even feel guilty or ashamed for being unable to manage their child's behavior. The initial assessment and the beginning of treatment is a critical time for establishing rapport and setting a compassionate tone for a successful therapeutic relationship

Additional Observation, History and Review of Records

The clinician should inquire of parents if the play observation was typical of the child's behavior. It may be helpful to expand observations to a second visit and to other settings. Observation at home, in school, or at child care can provide valuable information. Some parents are able to videotape specific types of challenging behavior, which can also provide invaluable information to augment an assessment. Similarly, historical information from multiple sources can provide significant insights to a child's abilities.

In addition to history and observation, review of records may provide additional information. The goal is to gather as much information as necessary in order to form a working hypothesis about a child's abilities and formulate a treatment plan. Sometimes consultation from another discipline is indicated to probe a child's skills in specific areas. Assessment is an ongoing process that continues throughout the course of treatment.

Recognizing Challenging Patterns of Interaction

While gathering historical information, observing interactions, and playing with the child, a clinician begins to formulate a profile of the child's strengths and constrictions, individual differences and relationships. The clinician is also forming impressions about the parents and their interactions with their child. Particular situations and types of parent-child interactions contribute to challenges corresponding to the developmental milestones.

Milestone 1: Regulation and Shared Attention

Some parents may have difficulty being available to their child to support basic regulation and shared attention because they have concrete and tangible barriers to basic security, such as lack of housing, food, or the basic necessities of life. In some instances, parents have limited time to spend with their child, perhaps due to their own busy work schedules or perhaps because they are consciously or unconsciously avoiding difficult interactions. Parents may be unavailable because of medical problems, addiction or mental illness. Professionals may be able to help a parent connect with health and mental health services and are bound to contact authorities if a child is truly neglected.

In other families, parents have experienced so many traumas concerning the child that they are coping consciously or unconsciously by avoiding interaction with the child. Some parents bury themselves in work, or schedule their child every waking minute so that they actually have almost no direct interaction with their child. By helping parents recognize their value to their child, a therapist can help parents build their confidence and ability to relax and enjoy being with their child in less structured activities.

Another pattern of parent-child interaction that can disrupt basic regulation occurs when parents relinquish authority to their children. Children rely on their parents to protect them through boundaries and limits and are comforted by the belief that their parents are powerful and knowledgeable. In some relationships, the balance between the perceived omnipotent role of the parent and the apparent power of a child can become confused. If a parent fails to create limits, confides in the child, or frequently apologizes, a child may have difficulty forming a sense of security.

Milestone 2: Engagement and Intimacy

Strength at Milestone 2 is based on the deepening of a close, intimate bond between parents and child. When the relationship is filled with joy and closeness, trust in the relationship actually allows a child to go into the world with a sense of security, and advance development to higher capacities. Many parents are discouraged because they do not feel warmly connected with their child despite their best efforts.

Many circumstances might impinge on a warm engagement. A sense of loss and grief may sap some parents' energy. Caring for a child with special needs may severely impact a parent's career goals, finances, and simply time for their own needs. A child may be physically violent toward them, or restrict their abilities to leave their home. Parents may feel embarrassed by their child's behavior. In addition, they may be dealing with loss of friends or marital issues.

If a mother was ambivalent about her pregnancy, or if issues of abandonment occurred in her childhood, if there is marital strife, or if other family members have intense needs, parents may have difficulty in developing genuine feelings of love and connection toward their child. They may even admit that they do not want to be parents, and harbor guilt about their wishes, or blame themselves for their child's condition. Negative feelings about being a parent may occur with any child and can be intensified if developmental or behavioral challenges exist. If a caregiver is aloof or angry and abusive, a child may develop unhealthy patterns of being detached or engaging indiscriminately.

Some parent-child combinations simply have a mismatch of temperaments. Some children need strong affective cues, and the parent may be naturally quiet or less expressive. Other children respond slowly while the parent talks and moves quickly. A professional may be able to guide parents to use a more effective style to connect with their child.

A more challenging pattern of interaction occurs when parents are unable to provide a soothing affect to counter balance their child's extreme emotions. If a child becomes overly excited, a parent can be a stabilizing and calming influence. Or, if a child is becoming discouraged, a parent can offer hope and enthusiasm. Unfortunately, some parents tend to respond in kind to their child's moods. If the child is anxious and rigid, the parent becomes even more anxious and rigid themselves. The result is that both parent and child fluctuate between extremes of affect and are unable to modulate their behavior to correspond with the realities of their situation. There can be an increasing spiral of more anxiety for both parent and child. A clinician can provide the guidance needed to transform this unproductive pattern of interaction.

It is important to recognize parents' challenges in connecting affectionately with their child. The foundation of a healthy parent-child relationship is the sense of joy in sharing moments of pleasure and the intimacy of these experiences. If there are challenges in engagement, a priority for intervention is to build this capacity as the basis of further progress.

Milestone 3: Reciprocity and Two-Way Communication

A goal of Milestone 3 is for the child to engage in a balanced, reciprocal flow of communication using a range of affective gestures. Circles of communication are accomplished when a parent follows a child's lead, the child responds, and then the parent responds contingently. In this way, the child is encouraged to use initiative and expand autonomy.

Sometimes, parents who are worried that their child may be delayed in some aspect of development try to compensate by teaching their child a variety of skills. They may teach rote skills such as naming animal pictures, letters of the alphabet, or actions such as putting a puzzle together properly. Parents may be very proud that their child has learned to perform these skills, and the child may enjoy them as well.

In their desire to have their child learn specific skills, parental communications can sometimes become predominantly giving directions. The flow of communication becomes one way, rather than a reciprocal back-and-forth exchange. A child may receive a plethora of commands: "Put it in here." "Give me that one." "Sit up." "Roll the car to me." While all parents teach their child, in this case, there is a lack of balance in the interaction, and the child does not initiate or enter into a more even flow of communication.

Unfortunately, parents may be encouraged to teach their children in a directive fashion, either explicitly or by example from other professionals. The developmental approach can help parents regain natural shared enjoyment in two-way reciprocal interactions with their child. By recognizing, encouraging, and celebrating a child's intent, parent and child can enter into a natural flow of spontaneous interaction.

Another frequent pattern of interaction that inhibits progress at Milestone 3 is when parent are anxious that their child not become upset. They may strive to accommodate their child's wishes to keep the child happy. It is easy to imagine how a pattern of walking on eggshells can develop. A parent learns that if a certain threshold of emotional intensity is crossed, the child's behaviors become extreme. The child may be very difficult to console, and even after some recovery may continue to be irritable for a prolonged period. Any parent would seek to avoid such events. Over time, the pattern of daily living can be dictated by avoiding those upsets.

> *Teresa had great difficulty starting social skills group. She had never been separated from her mom. Because Teresa was frightened by change and new environments, her mother tended to stay at home. There was just the two of them in the home, and they did everything together. At social skills, Mom wanted to come in, and then sneak away when Teresa was not looking. Of course, when Teresa discovered her absence she was quite upset.*
>
> *A plan was developed to help Teresa and her mom to feel comfortable with being apart. The plan included routines for saying goodbye and for greetings upon return, and opportunities to practice many times each day. The initial separations were just minutes, and Mom enlisted a neighbor to stay so that she could make a quick trip outside. The length of the separations increased very gradually. Throughout the process, Teresa's feelings were acknowledged and she was offered the comfort of another person. Although it was not easy, Teresa came to look forward to her sessions with her peers and was proud of her independence.*

Depending on developmental capacities and individual differences, other specific strategies can support the process of separation. If a child has challenges with visual-spatial awareness, it may help to see where Mom goes, and even go there with her at first. For children with an awareness of time, it may be possible to give them a specific time so that they can anticipate a parent's return or link it to some known event, such as when the movie ends. And intervention strategies would also be geared to the parent's concerns that may be contributing to difficulty supporting the child's independence.

Another pattern of interaction that is a barrier to progress is when a parent who is upset by the child's actions simply disengages. Although they may be able to engage in reciprocal interactions during positive experiences, the parent cannot tolerate the feelings of anger or disappointment evoked by the child's behavior. If the interaction is abandoned, there is no opportunity for a child to learn and practice more modulated expressions.

An intervention plan can provide a pathway for parents and child to expand their capacity for reciprocal, balanced interactions. Through these interactions, a child learns to organize different emotions and express intent with a graded intensity of feeling.

Milestone 4: Coregulation and Shared Problem Solving

Milestone 4 is achieved when a parent and child are able to sustain shared problem solving through a range of emotions. A pattern that can constrict a child's development of coregulated interactions may occur when parents are uncomfortable with conflict and negative emotions. A parent might then have difficulty sharing a moment of distress with a child long enough to work through problem solving.

Parents naturally want to soothe their child's distress and help with maneuvering through life's challenges. A parent might distract the child from distress or attempt to fix every problem. When a child shows anxiety and rigidity, or becomes frustrated, a parent may quickly intervene by offering solutions. "How about if we . . . ?" "Why don't we just . . . ?" "Can I . . . ?" "Do you want to . . . ?"

A parent may distract the child by laughing, making jokes, or teasing. A parent may use humor or sarcasm to cover feelings of embarrassment or tension. Unknowingly, the parent is not respecting or honoring the child's feelings and is not allowing the child to join in reciprocal problem solving, with the opportunity to practice functioning across a range of emotion.

If a child expresses anger, especially toward the parent, the parent might seek to immediately disengage from the interaction and leave. As parents attempt to avoid their own feelings, they may be constricted in the range of emotional cues that they provide to the child. In a subtle and continuous fashion they create distance from genuine expressions of emotion and opportunities for coregulated interactions.

When a parent is uncomfortable with conflict they may fail to set and maintain limits or, in the opposite fashion, they may become overly rigid in imposing rules and consequences.

Penny felt very comfortable in the clinic. She blithely opened the door and headed down the hall. She ran around the corner, and darted in and out of rooms. Mom waited on the couch. At home, Mom often deferred to Penny's wishes. Further assessment revealed that mother had long-standing discomfort with conflict, which was now increased by criticism of her parenting.

Parents that are uncomfortable with negative emotions may seek to control their child and set up a pattern of unequal competition for power. In play, a parent may be domineering and use more advanced skills to win at games, use subterfuge to undermine a child's intent, or simply interrupt and counter his ideas. In play, a parent may attack before the child is ready, or may dominate the child physically.

A parent may also use threats and physical strength to control a child. Outbursts of angry commands may be directed at the child (or therapist) or expressed diffusely. Or a parent may anxiously maintain strict schedules and routines.

Jesus was an active little boy. When it was time to go, he ran behind the playhouse and then around the yard. Although Jesus had not gone very far, Dad became enraged. This momentary loss of control triggered a disproportionate emotional response from Dad.

A plan for intervention begins by recognizing both the history and ongoing patterns of interaction. A plan can then be created to challenge a child in small increments, and likewise help parents to tolerate negative emotions and exchange feelings in sustained coregulated interactions. Unproductive patterns of interaction do not change quickly, but with the support of a sensitive clinician, relationships can be transformed. A parent and child can achieve more effective ways of relating with sustained, coregulated shared problem solving.

Milestone 5: Exploration of Creative Ideas

Success at Milestone 5 develops as children are able to use words and pretend play to explore a wide range of emotional ideas. They need opportunities to use their imagination and engage in spontaneous play, conversations about fantasy, or unstructured artistic expression, and to be encouraged to delve into strong feelings and elaborate their ideas. An impediment to advancement at this level is simply the lack of opportunity and time in their daily schedule for play. Other children need appropriate play materials and adult facilitation to become more creative.

Similar to the examples at earlier milestones, parents who are uncomfortable with their child's expressions of aggression, sadness, or fear may limit this expression, even in pretend play or conversation. A parent may create rules to limit aggression in play or rush to the rescue when the child enacts a distressing scene. They may avoid conversations about sad or traumatic events or ideas from books or movies.

> *Tobias seemed to live in a fantasy world. He frequently spoke in the voice of a character, and referenced his 'friends' and plans according to this other world experience.*
>
> *Although it might be considered that Tobias had a serious disorder, he was able to relate coherently at times. An assessment revealed that Tobias had intense feelings about many events in his life. His parents were uncomfortable talking with him about them, and preferred that his play was polite and focused on safe themes. Tobias felt safer in his fantasy world and powerless to grapple with events in his real life. A plan was created for his parents to increase their comfort and ability to support him with his strong feelings, and, moreover, encourage him to expand his range of symbolic ideas.*

Milestone 6: Logical Emotional Thinking

Helping a child move into logical bridging of ideas requires patience and understanding of a child's true abilities. Children will often begin to say "because" before they are consistently making logical connections. As the sense of time, space, and quantity are emerging, these concepts are only partially available for reasoning. Children may not fully understand the motivations and consequences of their behavior or others'. A child who is distressed may have even more confusion or misperceptions around reasoning.

Difficulty often arises when a parent or other adult tries to use logical reasoning with a child before the capacity to utilize this level of thinking is fully developed. The parents become frustrated by their child's failure to respond to reason, and the child may become frustrated as well.

Similarly, if parents believe that their child has higher-level abilities to reason than the child actually does, they may expose their child to ideas that are beyond the child's ability to truly understand. The child can then become fearful and distressed. For example, a child may be told about a catastrophic storm at a great distance, but not have the capacity to understand time and space. Then he might fear that the storm is imminent. Or a single parent might confide adult concerns and situations to a seemingly precocious child. Parents generally protect their children from adult levels of concern; however, a child's true ability to understand and use logical reasoning may be misperceived.

A troubling pattern of interaction can occur if a parent frequently deceives a child. While children enjoy pretending, they can become confused if fantasy and reality are continually mixed. Sometimes parents resort to fantasy tales because the truth makes them uncomfortable and they are trying to protect their child from having these feelings as well.

As parents become more aware of the child's abilities to use logical reasoning, particularly during times of distress, and the importance of separating truth from fantasy, they can adjust the information provided and their expectations for response. An adult can also more accurately consider how understanding or misunderstanding of events might contribute to a child's behavior.

Informing Interview

The informing interview is the occasion for a professional to share their impressions with the parents. Depending on the discipline and the context of the assessment, this may or may not include a formal diagnosis. In regards to specific behavioral challenges, this is an opportunity to reflect on patterns of behavior and interaction, and the contribution of a child's individual differences.

After impressions are shared with the parents, the professional and parents begin to work together to set priorities and goals. Strategies may be discussed in regards to responding in the moment of a challenging behavior, as well as the formation of a long-term plan to build the underlying capacities that may be contributing to the unwanted behavior. The parents' perspective, values, and culture continue to inform a collaborative process.

PART II

RESPONDING TO CHALLENGING BEHAVIOR IN THE MOMENT

Chapter 5

The Initial Response

With adult support, children, including those with developmental challenges, learn to act within acceptable limits of behavior and gradually acquire self-control. Usually the most troublesome behavior occurs when emotion overwhelms the child's higher-level capacities for thought and reason, and he begins to function at lower developmental levels. In the moment of a difficult behavior, the goal is twofold: to get the unwanted behavior to stop, and to help the child learn a different and better way to act in that circumstance in the future. The developmental approach helps children both change their behavior and learn new skills by systematically helping them to move back up the developmental ladder.

In the developmental approach, intervention is directly aligned with an understanding of a child's functional emotional capacities, individual differences related to sensory, motor, language, and cognition, and patterns of interaction in specific relationships. During a behavioral challenge, intervention is guided by the level of functioning at that moment, all of the unique factors for both child and adult, and by an understanding of the universal hierarchy of developmental functioning.

The developmental approach uses three basic steps in the moment: (1) attunement and organization of the affective experience, (2) helping the child move up the developmental ladder, and (3) coming to a genuine resolution of the event. Although a myriad of factors may possibly impact behavior, these three steps help to organize the response.

The primary feature of intervention is the adult's ability to use affective attunement in a compassionate way to move the child up the developmental ladder as they work together through the challenge. Through respectful interaction, a child advances to higher levels of development and also experiences sensitivity and compassion as relationships are strengthened.

Ben has had a good time, but now it is time to leave. Ben is told, "We are all done. It's time to go." Before a second has passed, Ben has bolted out the door. The adults are thinking, "Wait! He should help clean up. I wish he would say goodbye." They run after him and do their best to slow him down, and help him to move safely out the door and into the car. It happens so quickly.

Jeremy's teachers have learned to give him several warnings before it is time to stop playing. Still, when the final word is given, "Okay, Jeremy, now it's time to stop playing. It's time to clean up for snack," Jeremy continues playing, then suddenly knocks the toys over and begins to kick his classmates.

Aaron typically responds to the news that he must leave by arguing back: "You said I could play until the red car got all the way, and it's only halfway. It still has to cross the barrier and you have to stop the green one!"

What is the right thing to do in the moment? How can we help Ben, Jeremy, and Aaron learn to transition from one activity to the next without such difficulties? There are innumerable varieties of children and behavioral challenges, and each situation is unique. However, the developmental approach provides a universal framework for intervention that guides the child to higher levels of developmental capacities.

In the following chapters, the three steps to use in the moment are described in detail. Later, there is time to reflect on a behavioral pattern that is reoccurring and create a long-term plan. This chapter provides an overview of the overall approach in the moment.

Three Steps in the Moment

The three steps for immediate action are (1) attune and organize, (2) help, and (3) resolve. The first step is for an adult to closely observe the child and empathetically consider what he is experiencing and how he might be feeling. An adult attempts to assess where the child is functioning along a developmental continuum at that moment. Recognizing that emotional development begins with basic state control and moves gradually toward greater emotional differentiation and organization, the adult can support the child at the earliest levels to calm down enough to gain shared attention and begin to help organize affective experience.

The second step is for an adult to help the child move up the developmental ladder with the goal of functioning at the highest level of emotional organization, awareness, and insight possible in coping with the challenge at hand. The adult is not necessarily helping the child get what she wants, but rather providing the needed support to manage feelings in an adaptive and socially acceptable way. The developmental framework provides a hierarchy of levels of support to guide the intervention. Help is provided in a form that encourages the child to be in charge of creating solutions, within a supportive relationship.

The third step is for an adult to help the child recover, repair, review, and possibly rehearse for a future event. The goal is to help the child bring closure to the incident in a way that becomes an opportunity for learning and increases pride and self-esteem.

Applying the Developmental Model in the Moment

The goal of developmental intervention is for children to organize their emotions and emotional thinking so that they can bring their highest skills to bear on the problem at hand. By providing the just right level of support needed for successful behavior, children, as well as adults, build a true sense of shared accomplishment. Children have the opportunity to progress in their ability to organize and manage feelings, to function socially, resolve conflict, negotiate, and solve problems with others. Through experiencing compassion and forgiveness they learn to be considerate and kind toward others.

Consider Ben, the boy who suddenly bolted out the door. Using the three steps, the adult would:

1. Attune and organize: Trying to attune to his experience, an adult would want to consider everything known about Ben, including his relationships with the people there, individual sensory-motor and language profiles, and his developmental capacities. With that information, an adult might deduce that Ben is feeling a mixture of excitement and anxiety in regard to a change of activities, and that he naturally seeks movement for self-regulation. An adult would start by regaining shared attention by physically joining him (Milestone 1). By using high affect in facial expressions, gestures, and vocal tones, an adult would help Ben organize his excitement and at the same time provide information to organize the experience and decrease his anxiety. Together they create a warm, safe shared experience (Milestone 2).
2. Help: Now an adult would continue to help Ben to organize a pleasurable experience together of leaving, such as marching down the hall, perhaps incorporating a goodbye, and moving up to simple reciprocal interactions (Milestones 2 and 3).
3. Resolve: An adult could use familiar social gestures to acknowledge the transition of leaving (Milestones 1, 2, and perhaps 3).

There will be time later to create a plan to help Ben learn more about how to function while experiencing the emotions involved with leaving.

For Jeremy, who suddenly becomes aggressive when told to clean up, an adult could use the three steps in this way:

1. Attune and organize: To begin, an adult might perceive that Jeremy is reacting with a primitive fight response. She would consider what is known about Jeremy and perhaps conclude that Jeremy has difficulty understanding auditory cues, such as the announcement of cleanup time, and has difficulty with visual-spatial orientation. He is often anxious when other children are moving near him in unexpected ways. He may also be frustrated that he had to stop his current play and unsure about what to

do next. While immediately stopping the aggression, she would remain empathetic to the strong feelings that are overwhelming to Jeremy. Through a reassuring tone of voice and gentle holding, she would help Jeremy calm down. She might help him organize the experience by providing information about what is happening (Milestones 1 and 2). Other adults would simultaneously help the other children.

2. Help: Using the safety and security of a trusting relationship, the adult would then utilize strategies to help Jeremy use some gestural or verbal interactions to express his feelings, moving up to his highest level of functional skills. He may simply want to restore a sense of trust by clinging to the adult (Milestone 2) or may gesture or use words to indicate what he is thinking (Milestone 3). Through a reciprocal communication, acknowledging his feelings and desires, and counterbalancing with the limits of the situation, the adult helps Jeremy to put away his things and move to the snack area. He might be able to sustain a shared problem-solving interaction (Milestone 4).

3. Resolve: An adult would then help Jeremy to regain his baseline composure. Actions might include picking up the toys, making amends to the other children, and resuming the typical routine of snack time (Milestones 1–4).

While Jeremy is provided with support for a successful transition, this does not mean aggressive behavior will be condoned in the future. A long-term plan will recognize that Jeremy will initially need more adult support, as he learns the skills needed to independently end play and transition to the next activity.

For Aaron, who argues about why he cannot stop playing, an adult may use the three steps in this way:

1. Attune and organize: An adult recognizes that Aaron is not utilizing logical reasoning. His pseudo-logic belies an underlying rigidity and anxiety about change. An adult must gently and sensitively respond to the feelings underneath the brash behavior. Aaron's need to be in constant control might indicate poor

self-esteem and some sadness and loneliness. An adult might simply say, "I know it is really disappointing that we have to stop." This statement helps Aaron to calm and listen, and immediately forms a more trusting connection with the adult (Milestones 1 and 2).

2. Help: While Aaron might continue to assert various reasons for his actions, an adult will help Aaron move from reciprocal interactions (Milestone 3) up to sustained, coregulated problem solving (Milestone 4). With time, Aaron might even be able to use higher-level symbolic thinking, such as "This makes me so mad" (Milestone 5), and logical reasoning such as, "If I put all this away, then I can start at the same place next time" or "That would only be fair if everyone follows the same rule" (Milestone 6).

3. Resolve: An adult would want to help Aaron find closure with some comments that help him reflect on the process and conclusion. "It took us 5 minutes to stop playing today. But we finally did it. I'm glad you figured out how to mark your spot for next time." The goal would be for Aaron to participate in the discourse with either verbal or gestural signs to indicate closure and the release of tension. Through reviewing what happened, including a successful resolution, Aaron has gained a sequence of interactions that may build toward an anticipated pattern of success (Milestones 1–6).

The long-term plan for Aaron might include creating opportunities to practice problem-solving negotiations at the just right level of challenge, with a focus on reviewing and rehearsing situations that are frequently difficult. The plan might also include extra supports to decrease anxiety and celebrating successes to build self-esteem.

Moving up the Developmental Ladder

In these examples, each child has different levels of organization and intent in his behaviors and has different capacities to move up the milestones in the moment.

Ben is running out the door, not necessarily trying to escape, but rather overwhelmed by excitement. In this case excitement is disorganized and leads to primitive flight with elements of surprise, anxiety, and confusion. There is little sense of plan or purpose. Such behavior can sometimes be dangerous as children have little awareness of the consequences of their actions. With help, Ben can gain regulation, shared attention, and engagement and advance to perhaps beginning Milestone 3 with purposeful interactions.

Jeremy, who becomes aggressive and bites, is equally disorganized. He falls into primitive behaviors at a low level of emotional functioning. He may be overwhelmed by the commotion and his limited ability to understand the strong and mixed signals coming into his sensory system. Primitive survival reactions overtake his body but, with help, he can advance to shared problem solving (Milestone 4). To be helpful, an adult must recognize Jeremy's low level of functional capacity at that moment and support his organization so that he can ascend the developmental continuum.

For Aaron, who typically argues, the adult must see past the surface behavior to recognize that the controlling behavior is a sign of a child that is anxious and insecure. An attempt to address only his negative behavior will not be successful in helping Aaron to become confident and self-controlled. With help, Aaron can reach beginning capacities at Milestone 6—logical bridging of ideas.

The developmental approach uses a continuous appraisal of a child's functioning to guide the interaction. Through having opportunities to advance to higher levels, the child is not only achieving the desired behavior but is learning the skills needed to expand developmental capacities and initiate creative problem solving in the future.

Understanding Intent or Purpose of Behavior

A developmental approach interprets intent depending on developmental level. At Milestone 1, a child is often responding and reacting to primitive emotions with resulting survival behaviors. Any child (or adult) is sometimes overwhelmed and reduced to such primitive feelings and responses. At Milestone 2, the child's behaviors reflect the pleasure of engagement and trust, or the lack of security in relationships.

At Milestones 3 and 4, behaviors have more apparent purpose, as thoughts and feelings are tied directly to actions. However, for a child with developmental challenges, emotions may be disorganized with incongruent expressions, making interpretation of emotion more complex. At Milestones 5 and 6, behaviors may or may not be aligned with the child's thoughts about feelings. She may act in a certain way, but have dramatically different actual feelings about her actions.

In a developmental approach, the function of behavior is interpreted in light of a child's functional developmental capacities and affect in the moment. The constant priority on empathetic attunement provides a child with reaffirming experiences of trust and care. Through these experiences, a child grows to become an adult who in turn is able to empathetically care for others.

Consequences and Rewards

The developmental approach to behavioral challenges is mostly concerned with the process of helping a child through a challenging experience, rather than through feedback for obeying 'correct' behavior as dictated by an adult. Nevertheless, behaviors do have consequences, and part of an experience is learning the impact of behaviors. Therefore, children need to learn the natural outcomes of their behavior. If a toy is broken, then there is sadness about its loss, and it is not immediately replaced. If a privilege is abused, then that privilege may be revoked. Likewise, children may be encouraged by earning praise and rewards. Such behavioral principles are common in everyday life and can be incorporated into the developmental approach; however, consequences and rewards should not replace the primary process of reciprocal interaction and supporting relationships.

The Three Steps Are the Same for Adult Interactions

The basic steps of attune and organize, help, and resolve are the skills needed for adult success as well. The goal is for children to experience and learn these steps so they will be able to utilize them throughout life. Consider these adult experiences:

Joanne is struggling with her college statistics class. She is on the verge of giving up, but she needs the credits. Joanne calls up her best friend and describes the problem. She tells her friend she is angry that she has to take this class because it seems unrelated to her ultimate career goals. She is tired from staying up late to do the work, and disappointed in her poor grades. Her friend listens patiently and makes some empathetic comments as Joanne reflects on her predicament (Step 1, attune and organize). Together they each think of some alternatives. Joanne decides to call a resource number for a graduate student tutor (Step 2, help). Even before the tutoring begins, Joanne is hopeful that with help she can learn the material (Step 3, recover).

Adults often talk to a friend, receive help, and resolve a problem through this process. Even when a friend is not available, they may play through a dialogue in their mind, using memories of past supportive interactions to work out a solution. In terms of developmental milestones, adults continue to expand the breadth of capacities at all levels: regulation, intimacy, initiative and reciprocity, coregulation, and symbolic, logical, reflective, and abstract thinking. With experience, the three-step process for coping with emotional challenges becomes internalized as an effective approach to a wide range of distressing experiences.

Simon has lost an important paper.

Step 1: Attune and organize. He tells himself, "Don't panic. I know I can figure this out," and takes a deep breath.

Step 2: Help. Simon then goes through his memory to think where he last saw the papers and where he might have gone with them. He conducts a step-by-step search.

Step 3: Recover. Once he finds the papers, he is so relieved that he celebrates with a little shout. He then makes a resolution to always place important papers in a folder on his desk.

The following are examples of using the three steps to manage problems in the workplace.

Susan is very upset at a perceived injustice at work. She slams her notebook shut and walks out of the room. The supervisor utilizes the three steps.

Step 1: Attune and organize. The supervisor approaches Susan and sees that she is on the verge of tears. The supervisor first suggests that they go to a quiet place, and maybe get some water or take a walk. Then the supervisor expresses concern for her and asks Susan to describe the problem.

Step 2: Help. The supervisor helps Susan to think logically, consider multiple perspectives, problem solve using reflective and abstract thinking.

Step 3: Recover. Then the supervisor helps Susan to find closure, regain composure, and consider ways to repair and/or rehearse for the future.

Richard is simply in a bad mood and is rude and insulting to his coworkers. Richard's supervisor approaches him to confront the situation.

Step 1: Attune and organize. The supervisor creates a time to talk in a calm and considerate way with Richard, helping him to become more aware of his mood and behavior, and helping him consider the impact of his behavior on others.

Step 2: Help. They consider options such as taking time off or changing work assignments.

Step 3: Recover. Together they make an agreement about how Richard will act in the future, including supports available, and consequences for future behavior.

In each case, adults are using the same general framework. It is common for adults to share their difficulties with close friends, to ask for and receive help, and to achieve resolution. With success, the capacity to manage success, tragedy, and major life dramas expands to create the wisdom of old age. By using this pattern in our response to children, we are helping them through challenging experiences, and helping them to learn this effective approach to dealing with life's challenges.

Problems When a Step Is Missed

Step 1: Attune and Organize

Each of the three steps is essential for a child to learn to successfully manage emotions. The first step, attunement and organization of feelings, can be missed if a child is distracted and the emotion is thereby discounted or avoided. When a child's attention is moved quickly to something else, an unwanted behavior may stop, but the child has not learned to manage the feeling.

This pattern is actually typical and acceptable at times. When the goal is to continue an activity of some type, a parent or teacher might want to quickly redirect the child and fix the problem.

Mom is trying to get Melinda into the car seat and she is fussy. Mom hands her a favorite doll to engage her while she quickly fastens the seat belt.

Sam is working hard to draw within the lines. His crayon breaks, and teacher quickly hands him a new one.

In these examples, the goal for the activity was achieved, and helping the child learn about dealing with emotions was not the goal.

If this pattern is repeated so that almost all negative experiences are avoided or immediately fixed, the child will not have the opportunity to learn how to handle emotions and will likely have breakthroughs of overwhelming emotion. Distraction or redirection may essentially bypass the work necessary to organize and communicate a feeling state.

Likewise, if a child is distracted or overwhelmed by a secondary emotion, such as a fear of a negative consequence, or a feeling of ridicule and shame he may not learn to attune and organize his original feelings. Over time, true emotions may become unrecognized or denied.

Adults may misread or inaccurately deduce what the child is feeling. A child may hit another child, and the adult may think he was angry, when in fact it may have been a flirtatious gesture to get the attention of a favorite classmate. Mistakes in communication are common in everyday life. By taking the time to interact in a reciprocal way, it is possible to adjust and repair these misperceptions. When interpretations are accurate, the child will respond in a way that reinforces the interpretation; however, if it is not, the child's actions will lead to a reconsideration of the meaning of the behavior. The child is also learning the important process of communicative repair.

The process of an adult attuning to children's experience and helping them to organize their feelings is a powerful connection that provides the opening for further growth in a trusting relationship. Without this connection, opportunities for further development are lost. Part of attunement and organizing affective experience is an empathetic shared attention that helps a child to feel secure and build trust. If the child is not helped to calm down, behaviors tend to continue to escalate, or other difficult behaviors emerge.

Step 2: Help

The second step of helping allows children to bring their highest abilities to a problem. If a child is left with only attunement, as an adult repeats, "I know you are sad. Oh! That's so sad." and does not provide any help, she can be left with prolonged distress. A child may eventually become despondent or find other dysfunctional patterns of coping with their feelings on their own.

Children who are not encouraged to problem solve with their highest abilities may become dependent on being rescued and directed. This type of rote learning deprives them of the opportunity to learn fluid, creative, and dynamic problem-solving skills. An opportunity for learning to use higher-level skills, building self-confidence and self-reliance, may be missed.

Step 3: Recover

A child who does not fully recover from a behavioral challenge may stop the specific behavior, but continue to be irritable, sad, or anxious. By moving on quickly, rather than taking time to review the events and repair relationships, the child is likely to repeat the unwanted behavior and is more likely to develop a negative sense of self.

Each of the steps has important goals. It takes an investment of time to help a child move through each of the steps and extract as much learning as possible from each occasion. While the practicalities of a situation may dictate bypassing steps for expediency in the moment, the more often time can be devoted to helping a child move through each step, the more quickly she will expand regulatory and behavioral capacities.

Steps 1, 2, and 3 Not Necessarily in Order

While the three steps form the basic components and order of developmental intervention in the moment, they do not necessarily happen in a neat sequence. Often a child begins to calm down and organize her experience, and may even move up the developmental ladder to creative problem solving, but then regresses and slides back into disorganized distress. Even when working on recovery and review, a child may become distressed. A caregiver must then go back to the first step and help the child calm down and organize herself again.

There is also overlap in the steps. Step 1 often has simultaneous elements of helping. Sometimes a parent or clinician must move in immediately to help because of danger to the child or others, while simultaneously trying to use attunement and organization. Elements of recovery and repair may be intermixed with helping discussions.

The important aspect of this process is that it is a continuous learning interaction. A parent or developmental interventionist would actually take advantage of this work to draw out the process to glean as much as possible from every stage of this effort. The process of coregulation is the medium for learning. In subsequent emotional challenges, the child will benefit from the practice from all of the previous work together. A parent, teacher, or clinician can be guided in actions and language by an awareness of the child's developmental levels and an appreciation of the process of emotional coregulation taking place.

Is Interaction Always One to One?

Following a developmental framework, emotional and behavioral regulation initially begins with one-to-one interaction, typically with a parent in infancy. At the earlier milestones, children are only able to use their highest skills in interaction with one person at a time. Imagine a typically developing 2-year-old who wants a truck that is stuck behind the couch. He will try to get Dad's attention, and may sustain an interaction to work through the problem with multiple steps, and even play with Dad, have the truck become stuck again, and continue the interaction. In this Milestone 4 type of interaction, the child is successfully moving through multiple emotions in a sustained way with one adult.

If Mom and Dad both give verbal and nonverbal cues, the toddler might easily become confused or have a more fragmented interaction. If a sibling enters the mix, it is unlikely that the toddler will be able to sustain a problem-solving interaction at the same level as with Dad alone. If a babysitter is caring for the child, where there is less of a sense of knowing each other, the process is also less likely to be as smooth or complex. By 3 years of age, a child may be better equipped to negotiate a problem with strangers, multiple adults, and even peers.

In the midst of a behavioral challenge, children often function at the lower milestones, and need individual support to become calm and organized. Intensive one-on-one support in a classroom setting is not always possible. Within the constraints of staffing, a developmental behavioral plan can include adequate support so that the child will have the benefit of individual attention from trained staff as needed in moments of distress. In addition to time dedicated for individual support after a behavior occurs, additional support to facilitate interactions at other times may help a child to advance more quickly and perhaps avoid some of the unwanted behaviors.

As children develop higher level skills, a variety of symbolic strategies can be used to communicate with a child in a group or even independently. The intensity of support can be individualized according the child's developmental capacities as well as utilizing the sensory systems that are most effective for that child.

Who Provides Help?

To support a child in the moment of a behavioral challenge, the first decision is who will be intervening with the child. That, of course, depends on the context; however, the best person is the one who has the closest relationship with the child. The strength of that relationship provides the foundation for moving up the developmental ladder.

In the clinical setting, the best person to intervene would be the parent or caregiver. Here, the therapist and parent work together as a team, with the clinician coaching the parent as needed. Working with the parent is important because the bonds of care and trust in that relationship will support the child to do the difficult work of organizing, problem solving, and recovering from distress. Although a less familiar adult may be able to get a quicker or in some cases more skillful resolution, an opportunity for learning for both parent and child will be missed.

In a school setting, or when no parent or caregiver is present, the teacher, classroom aide, or adult who knows the child best will be most successful. In this case, it is best to assign one teacher or aide to be the primary person to work with the child. This person will be able to build the trusting relationship needed to support the child in moments of distress. They will also be better able to read the child's cues, understand behavior, and perhaps intervene before it becomes problematic.

Even when parents are not present for the problematic behavior, it is imperative to devise some way for the clinician or teacher to communicate with them. Recognizing the primary role of parents in a child's life, the professional would want a partnership with them to better understand the child's history and daily experience, as well as to create a shared vision and plan for helping the child. In a long-term plan, the child's goals may be to manage emotional challenges with the support of specific people, moving from primary caregivers to those that are less familiar, to support from community members, such as police, clerks in a store or school, or supervisors at a workplace, as well as in interactions with peers.

Drawing Upon Humanistic Qualities for Support

The developmental model is not linear or reductionist, but rather embraces the complexity of human interaction. It may be difficult to fully understand the emotional experience of a child with developmental and behavioral challenges and to know how to help. Parents and other adults also contribute their own individual differences and feelings to their perceptions and interactions. Professionals can only approach children and families with humility, recognizing that they can never know their sensory or emotional experience with certainty. Yet, by drawing upon the humanistic qualities that enable attunement and communication, adult and child can find comfort in a shared experience of care and compassion and move towards higher levels of shared purpose and cooperation.

Chapter 6

Step 1:
Attune and
Organize

In the moment of a challenging behavior, the first and most important step is for an adult to attune to a child's experience and help to organize the feelings that are at the root of the behavior. Through an interactive process utilizing strategies corresponding to a child's developmental capacities in that moment, a child is supported to connect feelings, thoughts, and actions, and advance in functional developmental level.

In the developmental approach, an adult draws upon the human capacity for shared emotion and the innate ability to recognize and empathically feel what another person is feeling. Beginning with an almost instantaneous assessment of a child's experience, an adult's attunement continues through an ongoing consideration of a child's perspective and available developmental capacities.

A child communicates through movement, posture, facial expression, vocal intonation, language, and the dynamic flow of all of these factors together through time. It may be more difficult to interpret these signs when a child has a developmental disability, yet with practice an adult can learn to be sensitively attuned to each child's unique ways of showing thoughts and feelings.

Emotional development begins in infancy with general states of sleep, alert interest, and distress. As development advances, children form orga-nized emotional states such as happiness, anger, sadness, and fear, and then later express even more subtle and complex emotions. A child with developmental challenges may continue to express only general states of excitement or distress or have emotional expressions that are limited, or mixed and conflicting. A child may have incongruent expressions and actions, such as smiling while angry, or running away when happy.

Emotions may fluctuate rapidly or may be experienced within a pro-longed mood. A child may shift erratically between emotions such as laughing and then crying just moments later. One emotion can lead to another, such as becoming frightened when anger is aroused. Rigid pat-terns of behavior may be a coping strategy as a child tries to avoid these angry and anxious feelings.

Affect may also be associated with physiological state, such as being hungry, tired, cold, or in pain. A perceptive adult will try to discern these various experiences and, by using specific strategies, help a child gradually organize and connect all of the different feelings and the asso-ciated thoughts and actions.

Using Relationship to Organize Experience

Adults provide an important force to help children learn to regulate their behavior and organize their emotions by embodying authority and power, not through dictating actions, but through a relationship that helps them feel safe during moments of distress. Through an adult's physical presence, calm, regulated state, and attunement with the child's emotional experience, the adult provides a secure context for learning. By recognizing a child's level of functioning, an adult can provide the type of support needed for the child to engage in the two-way interactive process needed to achieve mastery of feelings and actions.

The acceptance of a child's genuine experience creates a trusting bond between an adult and a child that is at the same time reassuring and respectful. Especially when connecting around a negative experience such as fear or anger, a sense of comfort and security is gained from being understood, and through the power of an adult to help hold and manage the disturbing feelings. Adults can help children embrace their feelings and tolerate a deeper intensity and range of experience while keeping arousal in a functional zone.

Children benefit when an adult does not bypass or obfuscate their emotions but rather provides an honest appraisal of their experience. If a child tends to dismiss a feeling, an adult may actually help the child perceive that emotion by focusing attention and amplifying the affect. The safety and support embodied in a trusting relationship make it possible to regulate emotions and incorporate those feelings into adaptive functioning.

It is sometimes difficult for an adult to maintain an accepting attitude toward a child's emotions, especially when the behavior is unacceptable. An adult may interpret a child's behavior to represent any of a variety of negative attributes, including being cowardly, mean, jealous, bossy, stubborn, spoiled, or lazy. Parents might easily react with anger or fear that their child was developing such traits. A developmental perspective can assist an adult to consider a child's developmental weaknesses that underlie the behaviors and avoid negative judgments. Rather than assuming that a child knows better, an adult would then be oriented to help the child gain the ability to function successfully even when in distress.

The interaction during the process of supporting a child through problematic behavior reflects caring and a desire to build and maintain a warm and trusting relationship. While it is not possible to ever completely and precisely know another's experience, there is great value in the continuing process of interaction that leads to closer and closer approximations of true mutual understanding. In the process of attunement, children have the opportunity to refine their communication and repair or correct miscommunication. While supporting emotional organization, the interaction becomes a cocreated experience, building not only the child's capacities but also trust, intimacy, and shared knowledge in the relationship.

Milestone 1: Regulation and Shared Attention

Before children can learn to manage behavioral challenges, they need help to achieve a basic level of regulation so that they can access higher level skills of thinking and communicating. As a child experiences distress, their level of functioning slips down to lower levels. At a base level, actions fall into general patterns corresponding to primitive survival instincts of fight, flight, or shutdown. At this level, emotions are not differentiated; there is only safety and distress. Here is where children may engage in spitting, thrashing about, running, screaming, or hitting themselves. Or they may cover their ears, bury their head, or freeze.

In distress, children may become so overwhelmed that they are truly unable to attend to others, hear, see, or feel at a full capacity. The ability to process sound, understand or produce language, or process any sensory information may be greatly impaired. Sensations may simply not register, or the sensation may be altered.

The ability to move easily may also be lost under stress. A child may become immobile and have difficulty initiating any volitional movement or using coordinated sequenced steps. Cognitive skills including memory and visual-spatial processing may be impacted as well.

By incorporating shared attention with another person in the process of achieving regulation, they form the basis for advancing skills. The important factor is that the adult is caring, present, and part of the soothing and regulatory process. If children are comforted and their emotions are assuaged in a solitary way, such as being given a toy or music to use by themselves, an opportunity is lost for beginning a relationship that can advance development.

Using the Sensory Profile to Support Regulation and Shared Attention

While some children are extremely vulnerable to particular sensory experiences, conversely, almost all of them respond to comforting sensory experience. An adult can provide calming sensory experiences to dampen strong reactions, matched to the child's profile and paired with the adult's body, in a way that facilitates soothing and shared attention.

A toddler falls and is crying after hurting their knee. A parent says, "Oh, honey, did that hurt? Let me give it a kiss." Here, the parent recognizes the child's distress, and simultaneously conveys concern and comfort. In addition, the parent may help the child recognize where the pain is from, and diffuse a general sense of panic, through this caring, intimate moment.

Through countless daily encounters, a child learns to gradually tolerate and manage increasingly stronger and more differentiated emotional experiences, with the help of a trusted and caring adult. For a child with autism or other challenges in emotional regulation and communication, these types of interactions may not occur as readily.

It may take close observation to discern which sensory experiences are soothing, and how an adult can be part of that sensory input. Movement and strong proprioceptive input are often calming. However, sometimes in seeking out comfort and proprioceptive input simultaneously, children may bite, pinch, hit, kick, or squeeze the person with whom they feel the strongest connection, ironically, as a sign of their positive connection with that person.

Violent Behavior

An adult can attune, soothe, and help the child achieve regulation and shared attention even when behaviors are more challenging. Sometimes, a behavior such as spitting or yelling does not need to be addressed directly. By attuning to the underlying feelings, a child may spontaneously shift to using more appropriate ways to regulate and communicate.

Consider how this might happen for a typically developing tired toddler at the end of the day:

> Max is upset because he wants more cookies, and is now throwing anything within reach. Because she recognizes that he is tired and has limited capacities at that moment, Mom reacts with patience and compassion: She helps by both physically stopping the throwing, picking him up, and soothing him. Mom says with a sympathetic tone, "I know, Max, you wanted more cookies, but, no more cookies tonight." Max shifts from throwing to clingy behavior and soft crying. Mom says, "Let's go read a book." The tone of voice and gentle holding help Max to organize and cope with his feelings of frustration and anger. His emotion shifts to sadness and a desire for affection.

On a different day, the parent might choose to restate rules, such as, "No throwing." However, if the parent recognizes that the child is functioning at Milestone 1, the priority is on soothing the child.

A similar level of support may be needed for an older child with developmental challenges that is attending a new social skills group:

Charlie, a large 9-year-old boy with cognitive deficits, is becoming disruptive at the start of a social skills group. He is making sudden, unpredictable movements around the room, flicking the lights off, picking up and throwing whatever is within reach, knocking the phone off the hook, and pushing other children. His face is fairly unexpressive, but he occasionally says "go" as he lunges for the door.

Many feelings can be provoked by a violent, out-of-control child, in both parents and professionals. To soothe a child effectively, the adult cannot contribute to the child's distress by displaying fear or letting him think that the adult is intimidated. Similarly, overt anger will not help an extremely dysregulated child function.

It is important for the adult to act with confidence, so that the child can utilize a sense of safety and security from both the calmness and limits presented in that relationship. An adult can not only help the child to calm, but can also redefine the experience, and communicate a different perception of the experience. A child might be afraid of fireworks, and a parent might hold the child close and say, "Look it's pretty!" Or, a child might be afraid of a costumed character, and a parent could reassure them with a smile that it is safe.

The therapist approaches Charlie in a way that physically blocks him from other children and objects. With a warm smile and calm, slow movements, she reassures him, stating repeatedly, "We are going to play." Even when he tries to throw something, he is met with a physical barrier, or a gentle hold, along with a reassuring smile and tone of voice. The therapist carefully notes and responds to each movement or vocalization with an attitude of care and support so that Charlie is drawn into a close relationship. Even as limits are set, by saying, "No throwing"; "It's okay"; "We're going to play," the therapist conveys a feeling of warmth and helpfulness.

The therapist then brought out a preferred activity, bubbles, and helped Charlie engage with a sense of rhythm: "One, two, three, blow!" He enjoyed the bubbles, and as the therapist was able to slow the pace, the other children joined in as well. Gradually, variations in the game were added, and Charlie was able to participate in simple, reciprocal, happy exchanges with his peers.

Safety for the child and others is always a priority, and safe holding techniques may be needed in accordance with the policies and roles of the professionals involved. Even while containing a child's behavior, an adult can continue to soothe him, letting him know that his emotions are being appreciated and recognized, and that the adult will help him calm down.

> *Dad was holding Robert, who was thrashing, trying to bite, and occasionally spitting. He held him in his strong arms while sitting on the floor against a wall. Dad used a calm voice while making comments such as, "I know this is hard. I know you wanted the red one. I'm just going to hold you until you can calm down. I'm going to help you. We are going to wait until you are ready. I know you don't want to act this way. I'm not going to let you bite."*
>
> *Dad's holding and comforting tone continued for over 10 minutes. Gradually Robert relaxed and engaged in some dialogue. After some more time had passed (and they worked up the milestones), Dad said, "Are you okay now? Shall we go get a drink of water?" All of this was said with a calm, warm tone of voice, conveying Dad's understanding that Robert was overwhelmed with distress, and that he could provide the help needed in a loving way. Robert eventually regained his composure and then gave his dad a hug.*

Adults' ability to protect themselves is essential so that they can be confident in their own safety. Parents may need to learn safe holding and self-defense techniques and should be aware of emergency resources such as what in the environment might be used to help manage the child and who can be summoned for help. For a child that responds negatively to touch, it may be particularly difficult to hold or contain aggressive behaviors. Alternatives include touching or holding with deep pressure rather than light touch, combining touch with rhythmic or auditory cues, or using pillows or bolsters between adult and child. A careful plan can help an adult act in a manner that not only quells the behavior but supports the child's self-regulation and developmental progress.

Milestone 2: Building Trusting Relationships

A trusting relationship is established through respectful, consistent, and supportive interactions. In a trusting relationship, children can expect to be understood, as well as anticipate that through the interaction they will gain a deeper understanding of their own experience. The process of achieving organization and regulation is satisfying, and as their feelings and ideas are appreciated, they experience pleasure and increasing positive self-regard. Trust and enjoyment in relationships becomes a resource in facing future challenges.

An adult creates patterns of interaction that are consistently soothing and respectful by empathetic attunement. For example, an adult can help a child to cope with disappointment about stopping play by saying in a voice reflecting an understanding of the disappointment, "We have to clean up now." By using the word "we" and simultaneously helping the child start the process of cleaning up, the adult is providing a supportive relationship. Accumulated experiences of support create a relationship in which the child anticipates that this special adult can provide soothing and comfort. The child may not only seek out that adult when upset but can also be soothed more readily.

Ironically, a foundation of close, trusting interactions enables children to move toward independence as their skills advance. Relationships become imbedded in the child's sense of self. The capacity to withstand negative feelings and persist despite them, is grounded in a secure sense of self. The warmth, trust, and acceptance created in a relationship provide the secure sense of self that children require to independently seek out new experiences and manage a full range of feelings with confidence.

A child that is just beginning to build trusting relationships will typically not yet display differentiated emotions. They may express a global distress or pleasure, such as screeching, jumping, bouncing, or flapping their arms when excited and may have different sounds or movements when happy or upset. More importantly, a child that has weaknesses at this level may be difficult to comfort and will not seek out a particular person when distressed.

Over time, children with deficits at Milestone 2 may tend toward depression, self-absorption, or irritability. While they may give the impression of not wanting or enjoying human interaction, they may yearn desperately for friendship and warmth. The intimacy of being known and knowing others provides acceptance, and its absence may be experienced as a profound rejection.

A goal in the developmental approach to behavioral intervention is to strengthen the bonds of trust within key relationships. In moments of distress, an identified key person can utilize familiar actions to comfort and soothe the child. These actions can draw from activities that are done together at other times that are pleasurable, and often involve repetition, rhythm, and anticipation, such as a particular song or a particular type of shoulder squeeze.

Is This Indulgent?

One might be concerned that a focus on sensitive attunement is unnecessary or, worse, may be creating a child that is too dependent on nurturance and unable to function within limits. Ironically, a gentle and attentive response builds a child's capacity to be resilient and better able to cope with strong feelings. Being attuned does not mean allowing the child to get what she wants. Rather, attunement leads to a compassionate attitude toward the child's struggles with behavioral control. Children who are treated with kindness will learn not only to value themselves but to treat others the same way, as they engage in the dynamics of social interaction.

The challenge for parents, clinicians, and teachers is to teach limits on behavior, while also respecting that the child is learning and will benefit from their understanding and support. This is the basic tension in child rearing, which becomes magnified for a child with developmental challenges.

Self-control develops gradually and adults' expectations should align with ability. For a child with a developmental disability this process may be hard to appreciate since it may occur much later than in children with neurotypical development, and skills may be uneven and fluctuate greatly at times. Consider this progression of self-control in typical development:

Sidney, an 11-month-old, was in the high chair and was finished eating. She was becoming a bit disorganized as she waved her arms over the tray, flipping food onto the floor. Before she started to cry, Mom picked her up and said, "All done."

Jay, 18 months old, has just rejected his peas by throwing the spoon. Mom says sternly, "No throwing." Jay looks at Mom, touches a pea on his plate, and looks back at her. She says, "Mm-mm," shaking her head, and Jay puts the pea back on his plate.

Dylan, a 2½-year-old, runs in the store. Mom says, "Dylan, what is the rule?" Dylan says, "No running" and then immediately starts to run again. Mom smiles knowingly as she helps Dylan to slow down and take her hand.

Margaret, a 3½-year-old, has been carefully building a tower, and it collapses. She is so upset she stomps her feet, acting out her rage. Dad says, "Aww, honey, what happened?" After being comforted, she is able to talk about what happened.

Matteo, at 5 years of age, runs to tell Mom, "Joey took the red car and that's not fair. He had the red one yesterday!" She encourages the boys to talk to each other and solve the problem. She helps them talk about what they are thinking and feeling.

These examples represent stages in a child's ability to learn self-control. When a child has just hit or spit or broken something, the first instinct of a parent or clinician may not be to soothe a child's distress. It is natural to show displeasure and enforce a limit. However, a child who is overwhelmed also needs adult support to help manage distress, which can only come from an empathetic adult. The adult is not condoning the errant behavior, but recognizes that the child may lack the skills needed to deal with the situation more appropriately. In time, the child can be helped to work back up the developmental ladder, perhaps becoming able to consider the perspective of others, problem solve, and use reflective thinking.

Milestone 3: Two-Way Interaction

When children function at the level of purposeful gestures, their intent is usually apparent. They will connect feelings with actions such as saying "apple" when they want an apple, pushing a hand away when they don't want someone to touch their toy, kick or hit when angry, select a choice between two objects to show preference, or give a drink to a doll in play. Feelings and actions are directly connected. A child at this level lives in the moment, and interactions concern the people and objects in the immediate environment.

It is at Milestone 3 that a child begins to organize and express differentiated emotions such as anger, sadness, and fear, and acts purposefully while experiencing these emotions. In fact, emotions help to organize their actions. Affective expressions become congruent: facial expression, actions, and vocalizations all align with the emotion being experienced and communicated.

For a child with autism or other developmental challenges, the process of developing a range of simple, affectively differentiated gestures is often delayed or incomplete and the child's feelings, as well as the meaning of the behavior, are not clear. A child may have incongruent or undifferentiated expressions. Expressions may express global feelings of happiness or distress, or may only organize around one specific emotion such as fear and anxiety, but not anger or sadness. Emotional expressions as well as the underlying experience can be confused. For example, someone may take a toy, and the child responds by clenching her hands while smiling. Another child may grab a toy with a flat expression. Or a child that likes another child may go to his desk and push his chair while attempting to express a desire for closeness.

An adult who recognizes that a child is having difficulty with emotional differentiation and congruent organized expressions can use strategies to support this level of skill. With success a child will learn to engage more successfully in communicating and acting across a range of organized emotional experiences. The goal is for the child to use simple back-and-forth interactions with purposeful gestures to respond as well as initiate reciprocal interactions while experiencing a range of differentiated feelings.

Using Affect

A basic developmental intervention strategy is for adults to use their own affective expressions to help the child organize his experience. If adults use slightly exaggerated facial expressions, movements, vocal intonations, and words to express the feeling they perceive a child to be experiencing, they can help that child identify and focus on their feelings, while at the same time receiving comfort from the shared understanding with an adult.

José was pestering his mother. "Can I go?" Mom responded, "No." Again José asked, "Can I?" Again, she said, "No." After the third request, she answered with irritation, "I already said no." José then started pulling boxes off the shelf.

How might have this been handled differently? Using a more attuned and empathetic response, Mom might have said, "I know that really looks like fun, but we can't today." José could whine, "But I really want to." She then could reiterate slowly, with a lot of expression in her face and voice, "I know, but we can't." Although no one wants to encourage whining, in this case, it is better than acting out anger physically. With a simple recognition and attunement with José's desire, Mom can help him manage his disappointment.

> *Gus keeps trying to balance his little zoo animals on the shelf, but as soon as he balances one, another topples over. Dad says, "Oh no! It fell over again!" using a vocal tone, look, and gesture that help to communicate a feeling of exasperation and frustration.*

Such an interaction helps a child experience and learn to communicate around varying degrees of anger and frustration. It is important for the adult to maintain a genuine level of empathy and attunement to a child. When the adult says, "Oh, that keeps falling!" there is a tone of voice and facial expression that communicates frustration and, importantly, also demonstrates tolerance or acceptance of the frustration. The gradations in emotion must be nuanced, depending on the child. The expression can be mixed with a touch of humor if needed to increase the tolerance. "That silly thing doesn't want to stand up." There is a risk of being overly dramatic, to the point that the communication is no longer genuine and becomes distracting and silly. Even with humor, the adult must maintain a quality of authentic shared experience.

Adults may also use their affect to simultaneously modify and organize a child's experience. If the child tends to have intense emotions and dramatic behaviors, the adult can provide a muted reflection of the child's expression help to modulate experience.

> *Pam was loud and boisterous. She was playing in the kitchen area at preschool. She was heard to yell in an angry tone, "No! I'm making cake!" The teacher went over to check and calmly asked, "Pam, what's going on?" Pam said, "I am making cake for the dolls." Martha frowned and said, "But I'm making cake." The teacher waited. "Um . . ." Then Pam and Martha decided to both make cakes.*

Later, it was time to clean up. The teacher gave a one-minute warning. Pam dramatically stomped her feet. The teacher calmly said, "Pam, you can leave your cake in the oven until later." Pam closed the oven door tightly.

By providing a calming influence, the teacher helped to diminish Pam's heighted affect. At the same time, she conveyed both respect for Pam's distress and help to contain its intensity. Through these types of interactions, Pam will feel supported and accepted. A response that focuses on the behavior and increases the tension, such as a stern "No yelling in class" would not provide the support Pam needs to calm her intense feelings. With patience and support, a child with strong emotions can achieve greater self-control and regulation.

Attunement and empathetic responses may be difficult to achieve. An adult may not be attending to a child's actions or words, or the child's emotional communication may be subtle or confusing. There is a risk of not reading a child's experience accurately; however, if the adult is incorrect, the child will likely provide further clues to his or her true feelings.

A child's feelings may make an adult uncomfortable. The adult may correct or contradict a child's feeling, such as saying, "That's not scary!" An adult might use mixed verbal and nonverbal expressions such as, "Oh, that piece went the wrong way!" but with a smile and a cheerful voice. The adult may also be anxious about avoiding potential distress and may quickly fix the problem.

There may also be a tendency for an adult to act too quickly when using bold affect, as energy and arousal are heightened. Ideally, the adult would use clearly defined affective gestures, but slowly enough that the child has the opportunity to fully appreciate all aspects of the expression and organize around it. This combination may require practice.

Narration

A technique that is helpful in supporting emotional organization is narration, which is saying for children what they would say if they could say it. It is based on the idea that children may have difficulty using language when under stress. An adult can supply the language that is then borrowed or used by a child.

Olivia does not want to leave her speech therapy session. She seems to be ignoring all requests to end play and put the toys away. The therapist says dolefully, "I don't want to leave." Olivia, copying these words, turns to Mom and says, "I don't want leave, Mom." Almost magically, we now have shared attention and a congruent and organized affective communication. Mom then says, "I know it's hard to stop, but we have to go home now." The interaction moves forward with cleaning up and saying goodbye.

Narrative expressions help to organize experience, so that children are then able to move forward in the security of being understood. The emotional attunement can help a child calm down and halt an escalating emotional reaction.

Some children that do not yet have expressive language will also benefit from narration, because they are able to understand language. They appreciate that an adult recognizes what they are feeling. The following is an example of using narration in play and in a more problematic behavior:

Chris constantly says no, either verbally or nonverbally, such as pushing away people or things. As he is pretending to cook, Mom offers him a cup. He pushes it away. Mom uses narration and says, "Not that one." She offers a different one, and he also pushes it away. "Not that one either!" she says. This continues with Mom using a lot of expression. "That one's not right." Chris notices and begins to look in anticipation of what she will offer next. Mom uses bigger affect—"Eww, no!"—and tosses it aside. Now Chris is amused. Mom offers a shoe instead. Now Chris smiles as he rejects it. The game continues, as she offers objects in a variety of ways. A fun game has been created by building on Chris's desire to assert himself and say no.

While Chris is being dressed, he rejects his shoes by kicking them away. Dad says, "No shoes." Chris does not yet have language, but he listens and stops kicking. Dad says again, "Chris says no shoes." Now Chris is looking intently at him. Dad says, "I know you don't want shoes, but we have to put shoes on now." Dad patiently empathizes. "I know it's hard." With this shared understanding, Chris fusses but allows Dad to help put his shoes on.

When children recognize that their "no" is heard, it can decrease the level of overall global distress and help them to organize around a particular feeling. Often a general primitive fight-or-flight response will be transformed into a more specific angry ("I don't want to!") or sad (crying) response and communication. This creates possibilities for more advanced interactions.

The strategy of narration continues to be useful as a child moves into higher levels of interaction, including coregulated interactions, considering others' perspective, and the level of ideas, separating ideas from immediate actions.

Sophia has poor visual-spatial awareness. She is playing in a busy preschool yard, building with blocks. Another child approaches, and she pushes him when he comes close. She doesn't use any language and is not clearly expressing her concern. An adult attunes to Sophia and steps in to help her organize her feelings and connect them with her actions. "Sophia, you seem worried that James may touch your blocks. I think he was just coming to look at them. You could tell him, 'Don't touch my blocks.'" Sophia looks and listens, and says, "Don't touch my blocks, James!"

After facilitating the subsequent interaction between Sophia and James, the adult will remember to cue Sophia the next time James approaches by saying, "James is coming to see your blocks!" An adult could remind her to say, "Don't touch my blocks" if needed. By helping Sophia to feel safe, the adult could eventually help Sophia and James enjoy playing together. The important factor is that Sophia is learning to connect her feelings with ideas and words; she is beginning to appreciate the motivations of others and to separate her feelings from immediate actions. Through a trusting relationship, she is able to negotiate her anxiety, knowing that her feelings are respected and that support will be available when needed.

Is the Child's Problematic Behavior Malicious?

Sometimes an adult has the impression that a child is purposefully confrontational or deceitful and willfully disobedient, manipulative, or testing the limits. The adult may be inclined to respond with anger and punishment.

Deliah looked straight at her mom and said, "You can't tell me what to do!" Mom was indignant. She could feel her face flush with anger. She thought, "I will not allow my child to speak to me that way." But, instead, she took a deep breath and considered her response. Then, she said, "I know you want to be in charge, but this is a decision for Mom. I say, you are going to put the toys away now. I will help you."

It is always worthwhile to consider a child's developmental level before reacting. It is particularly important to recognize behaviors derived from reflexive survival reactions. A child who is acting on primitive survival responses may bite, spit, or fight without the possibility of using words and ideas to mediate these actions. Without experience with mutual regulation and attunement, these behaviors can become habitual. Negative consequences will not help a child learn to quell panicky feelings.

A common misperception is that a child's behavior is designed to get attention. It is viewed as a fault that children demand constant and immediate satisfaction of their desires. The response may be to try to teach them to work independently. Ironically, they will learn to manage independently when they are initially provided with more attention and supportive interactions. When they know how to use interaction with an adult for support and are able to build trusting relationships, they increase their capacity to tolerate disturbing feelings and learn to be patient and persistent, as well as how to coregulate their behavior with others.

An adult may suspect that children pretend to be helpless when they could do the desired action. Here it may be helpful to wonder what emotion may be undermining their ability and at which level. To attune to the child compassionately, an adult may say, "I know, this is tough. But I know you can figure it out," offering both empathy and encouragement. Or an adult may find an appropriate level of support or advice to offer.

Another misperception is to assume a child is being manipulative, such as thinking, "He is doing that so I will give in and give it to him." The child may indeed be learning to coregulate and may be testing limits. This is a natural stage in development that is best countered with calm and consistent limits, and help in reading adults' emotional cues.

Sometimes, a parent may interpret behavior as manipulative, such as, "He does it to make me angry" or "He likes to hurt me." Such conclusions can cause deep hurt and resentment for a parent. Happily, this is rarely an accurate view. It is particularly important to assess the child's developmental capacities to determine if he is capable of planning at this level, especially when in the midst of strong emotions. At earlier stages, children are likely acting out of their own desperate feelings and need for help.

Sometimes a child will use provocative statements such as, "I like to kick," or provocative actions, like purposefully knocking over a vase. Such disturbing acts and sentiments require careful examination of all levels of developmental capacity and patterns in relationships. Frequent provocative behavior may be evidence of a significant deficit in the early milestones of regulation, trust, and warm engagement.

If adults feel their authority is threatened, the response may be harsh. A mismatch in a child's true level of functioning and an adult's interpretation can lead to spiraling patterns of increasingly problematic behavior. At the first step of attunement, it is critical to consider behavior in the context of the developmental hierarchy of abilities and to avoid overestimating a child's capacity for planned, malicious, or manipulative behavior.

Why Is He Laughing?

Laughter is basically a release of tension, a quick slide down from emotional tension and suspense to relaxation and resolution. The same basic flow occurs with many forms of pleasure. Consider a story line with buildup of the plot to a climax, and then resolution, or the flow of a piece of music with dissonance and then resolution of the chords. A comedian will create tension or suspense, and then resolve it an unexpected and fast punch line. Comedy occurs when tragedy is averted: Consider the laughter when we slip and harmlessly fall. The quicker the descent from tension, the more likely is a laugh.

Parents often recognize the raucous laughter that signals overarousal and warns of imminent disorganization and behavioral problems when a child is full of excitement. Laughter can signal that a child is becoming overwhelmed, even with a fun and exciting experience.

Children with developmental delays may have a limited capacity to organize and maintain a feeling of stress and arousal. As their tension dissipates, they may laugh. Therapists are familiar with the nervous laugh of a child on a therapy swing or touching a wet slimy substance. Children may be excited and anxious, and becoming overwhelmed. They laugh as their ability to organize their feelings is lost, and their primitive reaction is to giggle or laugh. Therapists know that such a child probably needs to end that activity before she loses more functional capacities. Some behaviors can be mixed with seemingly incongruent laughter.

> *Marissa is in a therapy room that is new to her. Mom is talking to the therapist and neither is paying attention to Marissa. Marissa has tried to get Mom's attention to help with her sense of uneasiness in this new place, but isn't noticed. She then comes over and pinches Mom! She turns away with a giggle. Mom is angry and bewildered. Why is my child laughing when she hurt me?*
>
> *Marissa's giggle is associated with releasing tension through her preferred route of strong proprioceptive input, in this case a pinch. Here it is also connected to her mom, her source of comfort. Whether by pinching or biting, Marissa's stress dissipates in conjunction with a little giggle.*
>
> *Marissa repeats this pattern of pinching and laughing whenever she is feeling distressed. Through recognizing the meaning of this pattern, her mother is able to anticipate Marissa's behavior. Now, when she sees Marissa approach, she reaches out and says, "Oh, do you need Mommy?" and at the same time provides her with a little squeeze and pressure. Now the pattern of interaction is converted to a comforting and pleasant experience for them both.*

It is important to attune to laughing, to ascertain the shift between arousal and the release of tension. It is then possible to interpret laughing as a sign of organization or disorganization in state control, and help to interpret the overall meaning of the associated behaviors.

Milestone 4: Shared Problem Solving and Coregulated Interactions

Interaction at level 4 can be recognized by the use of many verbal and nonverbal gestures in a sequence, across a range of emotions, and by the child's ability to respond contingently to another's affect during a sustained interaction. At this level, a child's words and actions are still closely tied to immediate experience and actions in the environment.

> *Two children are sitting at a table drawing, sharing one set of colored markers. Mina looks at Bethany with an expression of irritation, then put her fists on her hips and says, "I need that one!" Bethany responds with an expression*

of confusion, saying, "Which one?" Mina responds while pointing, "That one over there!" Bethany says, "Wait, I need to finish this part first." Mina is annoyed, but is able to wait. The interaction continues with a sustained animated dialogue, with each girl sharing delight in her drawings, sometimes becoming aggravated when they get in each other's way, and then resolving it and continuing an excited and happy dialogue.

Through such interactions, children learn to solve problems in social interactions. They are learning to deal with success and failure, and develop persistence and patience.

Children who are having difficulty at this level may be able to sustain interaction when happy, but cannot continue when they are angry, frustrated, or disappointed. They may have difficulty clearly organizing and conveying their own feelings as well as have difficulty reading another's expressions.

Ronald and John had been playing together well, building a road and track set. Now they are engaged in a verbal volley about where a truck should go, along with a physical push-and-pull struggle. John looks briefly at his mom, whose face is disapproving, and the fighting abates momentarily; soon the discord begins again as John slyly takes the truck when Ronald isn't looking. Quickly, he pushes the truck down a ramp and knocks Ronald's car off the road. When Ronald protests, John points to the road and says, "Your car was in the way."

Here, an adult would recognize that Ronald and John are building skills at Milestone 4. They are engaged in a sustained interaction, closely tied to the physical environment. John is able to coregulate at some level by considering Mom's look of disapproval. However, the boys are having difficulty considering each other's feelings and resolving their conflicts. An observing adult might be concerned that the situation is on the verge of deteriorating and wonder if support is needed.

It is important for adults to be sensitive to children's struggles to learn coregulated interactions and to support their ideas without providing a solution too quickly. The just-right level of support includes bolstering a sense of safety including the availability and understanding of a trusted adult.

Mom moved closer but did not need to do more. The boys looked up at her and then returned to more peaceful negotiations about where the cars could go.

Patterns of interaction, particularly with parents, establish children's sense of self. If their ideas and efforts are treated with respect, they learn to feel confident. If their ideas are discounted, they may learn to feel ineffective and incapable. If adult responses to behavior are harsh or shaming, children may develop a negative sense of themselves as being worthless and impotent or, worse, actually evil. Sometimes a child will even act out in accordance with this negative sense of self.

Using Affect

At Milestone 4, an adult can focus the use of affect to help a child identify a broader range of differentiated feelings and levels of intensity of emotions. At this level, children begin to reference adult expressions to modulate their own feelings and actions. An adult can use expressions, both verbal and nonverbal, to support children in organizing their own feelings as well as understanding others'. In this manner, the shared affective experience becomes organized and understood by both.

It was time to leave, and Ivan did not want to go. After the usual countdown warnings, Mom said, "Ivan, now it's time. We need to leave." Ivan looked at her, ran to the far side of the room, and then looked back. Mom looked at him again, shook her head, and said, "No, I'm not playing. We really have to go." Ivan sat down, picked up a toy, and held it. Mom walked over to him and said, "I know you want to stay, but we have to leave the toys here. It's time to go."

This is a common confrontation for parents. Will Ivan relent? Will his behavior escalate? How will Mom let Ivan know that she has authority? Through many interactions, children learn to read a parent's expressions and adjust their behavior based on the level of intensity in the other's communication. This skill often begins with a parent's expressions of limit setting, from "No! Stop!" for a child about to do something dangerous, to a firm, "No, not now," to "No, I don't think so" (but might be persuaded). A child can learn to read an expression of disapproval from across a room.

The same variation in expressions as in limit setting apply to communicating the full array of feelings and intensities in sadness, worry, and confusion, as well as the infinite mixtures of feelings such as surprised and happy, or the happy fear of a rollercoaster ride. Expressions are also not static or solitary, but are communicated through multiple looks, sounds, and movements in a row. For a child with developmental challenges, an adult's attunement at this level includes a conscious use of complex affective signals to support a sense of shared understanding and emotional organization.

Facilitation of Peer Interaction

Using attunement with a group of children follows similar principles as with a child alone; however, the adult role is now to help each child both read and respond to another child.

> *Pablo and Jason were playing ball. Pablo kicked the ball and it accidently hit Jason in the head. Jason started to cry and looked angrily at Pablo. Jason said, "You hit me! I'm going to kill you!" Pablo watched with a worried look, and took a few steps backward.*

An adult who observed this scenario would probably want to intervene to help both children. The process of helping each child to use his higher skills begins with respectful attunement to how they are feeling in the moment. Both Pablo and Jason may have a flood of different feelings. On the surface, Jason is in some degree of pain, and is surprised and angry. The pain may lead to worry, and with further reflection he may also be sad that his friend would do this. Pablo might be feeling surprised and worried, and also, with more reflection might be sad. The emotions come with different intensities and evolve through the interaction.

In these situations, the goal might be to help each child organize and then communicate his feelings, listen to the other child, and negotiate a solution together. If an adult simply resolved the problem, an opportunity for learning would be lost. After gaining shared attention with each child through affective attunement, an adult might facilitate the interaction with phrases such as, "Ask him," "Tell him," "Did you hear what he said?" "Look at Pablo's face. How does he look?" "How do think he is feeling?" An adult may need to clarify, "I think he looks worried."

Sometimes, an adult can repeat what a child says, in a way that helps communication. "It sounds like you are trying to tell Jason that it was an accident." Through this social facilitation, the adult is emphasizing not only the sequence of actions but also the feelings of each child. Through attunement to their emotions, an adult can provide the safe holding space for each child to learn to negotiate through strong emotions.

Sometimes an adult can help to redefine an experience by lowering the emotional valence, and put the problem in perspective.

Jerry and Reese were painting a fence together. While they had enjoyed this activity for some time, now they started to argue about whether a bird they saw was an eagle or not. Mom came over to see what the problem was. When she heard, she offered a look of puzzlement, saying, "Is it really that important, guys?"

Mom could encourage them to question what was important- or not, and by her attitude and presence convey that it probably wasn't. She might use humor as well to discharge some of the tension, "Maybe it was an ostrich!" If they needed more support, she could help them describe all the work they had done, and get them to talk about what was coming next.

Stop! Freeze the Action!

A powerful technique for halting an escalating situation is for an adult to step in with a big affect and gesture to stop—holding out the hands with eyes wide open. Often no words are needed. If words are used, it can simply be an expression like, "Whoa!" Most children will stop, even if momentarily, to see what the adult is doing. That is the moment needed to give the next affective gesture, which could be a look of confusion and questioning, or disapproval, or concern. Sometimes the adult stepping into the midst of a problem gives children the opportunity to stop, organize and correct themselves, or reach out for help.

It is important to provide time and focus on calming before moving on to higher-level problem solving or discussions. It is easy to assume that a child is capable of logical thinking and reasoning, and to be tempted to engage initially at this level, even though the child is showing evidence of being overwhelmed with distress. The adult may need to slow the interaction to allow the child to consolidate regulation before moving up to problem solving and negotiating.

Providing Information

An adult can help children organize their experience by providing information to clarify events, explain motivations and consequences of behaviors, and provide a sequence of events in time. In addition, the adult can help interpret sensory experiences, sounds, or sights that may be confusing, frightening, or irritating. Information can be valuable at all functional developmental levels.

- "You're okay. That was just a big truck going by. It was loud!"
- "We can sit here and both go down the slide together."
- "That screw just won't fit."
- "Daryl looks like he is sad. His cracker is broken."
- "Mark was just coming to look."
- "The teacher had to take the list to the office. She will be back in 5 minutes."
- "Mary was hoping that her picture would win."

Providing information helps children organize and understand their experience through interaction with another person. Facts are relevant to the extent that they help to connect thoughts, actions, and feelings in a way that is meaningful at a child's developmental level. While a child may be reminded about rules and potential rewards or punishments, the value of information sharing is that it offers an opportunity for an attuned connection to the child's experience, and helps build the foundations for developmental growth.

Asking Questions

Another strategy to support attunement is for an adult to ask questions. Here an adult can ask directly or wonder aloud about what a child is thinking and feeling. This strategy is obviously useful when an adult is unsure about a child's perspective, but is also a useful way to help children reflect on their own feelings.

Asking for clarification shows interest and respect for a child. With a gesture such as upturned hands and a puzzled expression, an adult might simply state, "I don't understand." Implied is a genuine desire to understand. An adult can further cue a child by suggesting, "Show me," or even offering some options: "Did you mean . . . ?" "Were you trying to . . . ?" Patient, expectant waiting and responding to nonverbal as well as verbal responses will support a child to organize ideas.

In questioning a distressed child, it is generally more successful to start with easier questions first. Inquiries may start with "what," and then "where," "when," and "who." An adult may be inclined to start with, "Why did you do that?" However, "why" questions are often the most difficult. An adult can help children organize their thinking so that they can answer questions about their motivations, or otherwise link thoughts and actions with causality and logical thinking.

The adult may look concerned while giving comfort and support. "Oh no! What happened?" Gradually the adult might offer information: "It looked like you were trying to get that to balance, but it kept falling." "I know, Sally came over and took your car." The adult might specifically ask about emotions: "Was that scary?" or "I wonder how that made you feel."

Both giving information and using questions can help children connect their feelings and actions. It is important to balance questioning with other types of interaction. If a child is unclear about his own feelings, finding answers can be difficult. Eventually, the child may simply stop responding. If questions are alternated with other strategies, such as providing information, the child will be more likely to sustain a shared problem-solving interaction.

Milestone 5: Using Emotional Ideas

When children are able to use words or symbols to express their feelings, wishes, and ideas, they are functioning at the level of symbolic thinking.

An adult can interpret the underlying meaning of a child's use of symbols and encourage a child to elaborate their ideas.

Cindy said, "I want to go swimming!" Mom replied, "But it is too cold out today. Look, it's cloudy and windy outside." Cindy argued back, saying, "I have my swim suit on! I want to go swimming now!" She even brought Mom her car keys. Mom said, "I know you are disappointed, but we just can't go today. Maybe we can go tomorrow." Cindy acted as if she were going to kick over a lamp, but didn't actually do it.

Cindy is functioning in the world of symbolic ideas, but logical reasoning has little influence on her. She can talk about her wish and imagine the swimming pool. She is even using a symbolic gesture to express her anger. For now, Mom will need to support her by acknowledging her feelings, yet know that logical reasoning is unlikely to be helpful.

A child with higher-level abilities may at times be overwhelmed by emotion and then only use symbolic expressions of feelings in a repetitive or ritualistic way.

Whenever Stacey was feeling nervous, she recited lines from a favorite story. She had memorized many parts of the script. Her favorite line was, "And then he told Vox, 'Bejon is on the way. Death to the Zombies!'"

These words were alarming to many around her that did not know her well. Stacey's insightful aide recognized that she was functioning at the level of symbolic ideas and suspected that this line had emotional significance. After some inquiry she learned that Stacey tended to use that line when there was a change in routine or a new or unexpected event that caused her to feel anxious. The line corresponded to a character, Bejon, who came to the rescue. This idea made Stacey feel more secure and even brave.

With this knowledge, an adult can appreciate the feelings behind Stacey's scripted lines. Knowing that she is able to use symbolic thinking, Stacey might be encouraged to use other words and ideas to elaborate on the feeling of being afraid, or use drawings to help her connect the feelings with the script she has chosen. In the moment, an adult can begin by listening and respectfully considering the meaning in her use of this particular symbol.

Sometimes words betray an underlying feeling that is the opposite of the words. Megan often stated, "I am the best in the whole world at playing Ninja." This boasting was usually not well received by her peers. In reality, Megan often felt insecure. Fortunately, adults have the capacity to suspect and hypothesize the true feelings that may be behind behavior, and can attune to them both in the moment, and in the long term.

Milestone 6: Logical Thinking

Milestone 6 or higher can be recognized by the ability to connect ideas with logical thinking around causality, time, space, and quantity. Children will be able to link their ideas with another's and connect one emotion with another. At this level, a child can plan and predict, and can discern reality from fantasy. An adult can help by using logical reasoning, not only about facts, but to connect emotional experiences. As development advances, a child is able to use multicausal, comparative, and reflective thinking.

> *Nicholas was hiding in the corner. In talking with the interventionist, he disclosed that he had lost his jacket. Nicholas said, "I'm afraid to tell my dad." The clinician was tempted to reassure Nicholas ("It's okay. I'm sure your dad will understand"), but instead she helped Nicholas to reflect on what he was saying: "Mm, you sound worried. What do you think your dad might say?" "What do you think your Dad will feel?" As the dialogue continued, she listened and encouraged him to reflect on his feelings: "How worried are you?" "How does it feel to be that scared?" Eventually, she was able to help him think logically about what his father might feel, think or say, and then what he might say.*

Ultimately children will be able to engage in negotiation, including planning and consideration of how alternatives may affect others. It is beneficial to engage them in these discussions and negotiations. While not everything is negotiable and parents need to maintain their authority, providing children with practice in defining their arguments, particularly when they are passionate about something, can lead to creation of strong personal moral and ethical values. Without this experience, they may become passively compliant or deviously avoid external rules.

> *Juan argued with his brother, saying, "You told me yesterday that I could be first today. You are always first. That's not fair!"*

Juan is displaying an understanding of quantity and time concepts as well as fairness. He may be capable of connecting reasons and feelings, such as why his brother wants to be first, and may be able to negotiate a solution to the problem.

Dawn was playing a marble game with her friends. It was very difficult to get the marbles to hit the target. After a while, her friends agreed to bend the rules and move their marbles closer. Dawn was distraught. She cried, "No you can't do that!"

Dawn was having difficulty being flexible around an unexpected and seemingly random change of the rules. It made her feel completely disoriented, confused, and worried. An adult needed to step in quickly.

A teacher helped her to feel safe by his presence and he listened as she told him about her concerns. He asked her what she wished would happen. Eventually, she was able to describe why she thought cheating was wrong, and how it made her feel. The teacher facilitated a conversation between Dawn and one of the other girls. Together they worked out a plan to finish the game that Dawn could accept.

At times, an adult may respond as if a child had higher-level capacities, when in fact, she is not yet functioning at the level of logical thinking.

Maria wanted to get a pretty doll in the store. Dad said with a serious tone, "No, it costs $12 and we already spent $20 on groceries."

Maria may understand and accept "no" but probably would not understand the concepts implied in the family budget. Sometimes, anxiety is created when a child hears about their parents' emotional struggles but cannot fully understand them.

If a child has language abilities to use sentences and vocabulary, but does not yet have logical thinking, his utterances can be baffling.

Rodney often said, "I will die if I lose," and sometimes said, "If I'm second, I'm a girl."

An adult might be alarmed by these statements and be tempted to respond with logical reasoning; however, attuning to Rodney's feelings can help him to better organize his experience. Rodney was overwhelmed by the feelings aroused by the loss of control in not winning or not being first. He was disappointed, angry, and confused about what to do, all leading to anxiety. Through empathetic attunement with an adult, he was able to gradually gain more confidence in his ability to withstand these feelings, and learn ways to successfully interact while feeling some disappointment and sadness.

Moving Up and Down the Ladder

It is not uncommon for children with higher-level capacities when calm, to collapse to lower functioning under stress. An astute and sensitive adult will be continuously aware of a child's level of functioning and provide commensurate supports.

Collin said, "Marty took my ball and I'm gonna kill him!" Collin raised his fist and started to move toward Marty.

Although Collin can use words to express an idea, if he is beginning to act on this aggression, he is not at the fully symbolic level. He needs help to calm down before he can converse about his feelings and ideas. In the midst of this conversation, he may bolt and try to hit again. He will be back to Milestone 1, and needs further calming and soothing. With practice, both adult and child become adept at working through difficult challenges with greater ease, and at higher levels.

The structure of the developmental framework helps to clarify which responses are appropriate for the circumstance. If children with severe disabilities are distressed, pacing, shouting, and thrashing about, it is appropriate to simply soothe and comfort them, while trying to determine the source of their distress. If another child with higher capacities is upset because he was told no, and is hitting and biting, he would also need a soothing interaction, but could then move up the developmental ladder to conversation and shared problem solving. By always beginning with regulation and trust at the earliest functional levels, an adult will be more successful in helping a child move to higher-level capacities.

An adult response that is not matched to a child's abilities is unlikely to help a child through a behavioral challenge. Patterns of ineffective interactions may be formed by a frequent lack of this alignment.

Devon grabbed Susie's toy and she began to cry. Dad said, "Look, you made Susie sad." Devon looked confused. Dad then took the toy and gave it back to Susie. Now Devon began to cry.

Devon was just learning to act with intention, and was not yet able to understand how his actions connected to another's feelings. Dad moved Devon so that he could no longer reach Susie's toy and then soothed him by talking to him and giving him something else. With more experience, Devon was able to learn how his actions affected others.

Although the process of moving up and down the functional emotional milestones can take more time than other responses, it is exactly through this process that a child learns. The time spent is rewarded in increasing skills. Each time a clinician or parent helps a child to work through these feelings contributes to progress evident in less time spent in such interactions and growing capacities at higher milestones.

Acting with Calm Confidence

Parents, teachers, and clinicians may all have their own strong emotional responses to some children's behaviors. If a child spits, screams, throws, kicks, bites, and so on, it is natural to have a flood of nervous energy, or even a shutdown, flight, or fight response. Whether parent or professional, an adult's emotions of courage, confidence, and responsibility must override the negative emotional responses in order to be helpful. An adult must not only assess the situation for danger, but also remain calm, or at least act calmly, to be the emotional anchor needed by a child.

While authoritarian and harsh responses may stop a behavior, the child may only learn to stop that particular behavior. In addition, harsh responses can undermine a trusting relationship and a child's feeling of self-worth. More importantly, a child may actually learn to restrict or avoid initiative, discovery, and creativity.

Some adults become so nervous about a child's possible behaviors that they impart this anxiety to the child. This can quickly spiral into a shared sense of anxiety. Patterns of interaction can become geared around avoiding emotional upset by avoiding challenging situations, quickly fixing problems, or ignoring signs of distress. It is essential that the adults in a child's life are able to convey a confident and calm strength that can withstand a child's negative feelings.

Self-calming is a skill that can be learned and practiced. Specific actions can be used to calm, such as slow deep breathing, moving slowly and with determination, speaking slowly, and using a lower pitch. Saying certain phrases aloud can be helpful for all, such as, "I am going to help you" or "You're okay." Even adults who are feeling anxious can learn to act calmly.

Helping a Parent First

Ideally, a clinician would coach a parent to interact with a child in the moment of distress. However, the clinician will first need to attend to the parent's emotional state. Misbehavior evokes emotional reactions in a parent, which may include anxiety, embarrassment, anger, and discouragement. During a challenging behavior, a clinician may begin by calming and supporting the parent before attending to the child. Or the professional may need to support both parent and child simultaneously.

Nathan was told he could not play with a particular fragile object. He sat on the floor and screamed in distress. His mother initially tried to talk with him, but he continued to wail loudly. Eventually she resigned herself to simply sitting on the couch, watching and feeling hopeless. Nathan's screaming was loud and alarming, yet he was sitting and not causing any harm.

In this scenario, Nathan could be 2 years old or 12. The goal is the same: for Nathan to learn to tolerate disappointment and bring his highest developmental capacities to bear on the problem. He does not yet know how to independently calm himself. If the clinician can help the mother to fulfill this role, she will be learning how to help her son, and they will be building their relationship.

The clinician sat on the couch next to Mom and said, "This is really hard. I think you can help Nathan calm down. You are really the most important person to him, and he needs your help." The clinician continued, "What usually helps Nathan?" Mom says, "I just let him cry and eventually he stops." "Is there anything you do together that he likes?" "Sometimes I give him my phone." "Is there anything else that you do together?" "Sometimes he lets me rub his back." "Okay, let's try that."

Mom then sat by Nathan, and the clinician sat nearby. The clinician encouraged her, saying, "Nathan, Mom is here to help." The clinician also supported the interaction by humming a little tune in rhythm with her strokes. Nathan's sounds gradually abated, and he then leaned into Mom and looked at her.

The clinician's calm presence, voice, and affect helped both parent and child to be soothed. Through this experience, Nathan and his mother learned that they could stay connected. Mom was able to help Nathan to move from unregulated distress to becoming calm and gaining shared attention and warmth. With practice, Nathan will learn to anticipate this help from his mom, and will be able to seek it out and avoid episodes where he feels detached and alone, with overwhelming distress.

In other moments, a clinician may coach a parent while simultaneously helping to calm and contain a child.

Jack had a difficult day at school. He arrived in the therapy room, and when a preferred toy was not where he expected, he started to grab anything within reach and fling it across the room. Dad reached his arms around Jack and held him gently yet firmly.

Sometimes, an adult must act immediately. Fortunately, the father felt empowered to act and did not wait for the clinician. If he had hesitated, the clinician could have quickly asked him to please step in and help Jack stop. By her position in the room, tone of voice, and coaching, the clinician then helped the father to act calmly even while physically holding his child.

Dad said in a calm and measured tone, "I know you're upset, but you can't throw things. I'm going to hold you until you calm down." Jack was writhing, trying to get free. He kicked his legs, and Dad repositioned to prevent him from kicking. Then Jack tried to bite, but still Dad was able to maneuver his body to prevent it. Dad continued, "Jack, you need to calm down." He repeated, "That's my boy," in a slow, rhythmic way. The struggle continued for over 10 minutes, with a gradual increase in dialogue and interaction. Jack was sweating, and Dad was hot and tired as well. But his patience was rewarded as Jack gradually relented.

Throughout the episode, the clinician was sitting across the room, directly facing Dad, providing verbal and nonverbal messages of approval and encouragement. Ready to provide backup if needed, the clinician nodded, and told the father, "You are doing just the right thing. You are helping Jack to calm down. Keep using that low, slow voice." If the father had started to use a threat or distraction, the clinician might have coached him: "Let's just keep holding him, and letting him know that you will wait until he is ready. We know he can do it."

A clinician should always consider his or her physical position in a room. If a parent needs to physically hold the child, then the clinician may need to help hold or position the parent and child. Often, a clinician simply needs to be next to the parent to offer coaching or calm reassurance. Perhaps a touch on the arm will help reinforce this support. Sometimes a connection of support can be established from across the room, if clinician and parent are directly facing each other, and at eye level.

Additionally, the clinician must consider where the child is in the room. The clinician would not want to block or interfere with nonverbal communication by placing herself directly between parent and child, unless that level of support is required for safety. A clinician might support parent-child interaction by moving toys or furniture to help decrease distractions or obstacles. By encouraging and supporting the parent to aid the child, a clinician is opening the opportunity for growth in their relationship. Through an alliance with a clinician, parents gain trust and hope, especially as they experience growth and success.

"Go to Your Room!" and Other Time-Outs

Time-outs are generally known as a consequence for bad behavior and are often used as a threat. In the developmental approach, time-out is used as a placeholder, to give each party breathing room to calm down and organize before beginning an interactive process around a behavioral problem. In the heat of the moment, it may sometimes be helpful for parents and child to separate, or for a child to separate from the source of conflict. If parents are at the point of becoming dysregulated themselves, then sending a child to his room or another quiet place can provide a needed break for everyone to become calm. Ideally, children see their room as a safe haven where they can calm down as well.

Parents who are attuned to their own emotional state can recognize when they need a break or when their child will benefit from a few minutes alone. Such a time-out should be followed in a short time by a reunion of parent and child where the process of working through the incident can begin together. During a time-out a child may apply reasoning skills to connect actions and consequences, learning that a certain action leads to a certain consequence. However, the value of time-out is diminished if there is no subsequent interaction around the incident, where parent and child are able to reflect together.

If a child is withdrawn from an activity, such as playing with peers, then an adult may be able to sit with the child and help her process what occurred. Initially, the adult may simply sit with the child, to let her know the adult are available when the child is ready to talk. The message imparted is that the adult accepts the child, even though the behaviors are not condoned. Children are always treated with respect, and time-out is never used to embarrass or shame them for their behavior.

This chapter has focused on the importance of attuning to a child's experience, recognizing their developmental capacity at the moment, and using strategies to help the child soothe, calm, form a warm, shared, and trusting relationship, and organize at the level of their ability in the moment. This first step provides the foundation for an interaction in which the adult will now help the child to move up to higher levels and continue to learn from their experience.

Chapter 7

Step 2: Help

> *Assumptions by clinicians and researchers suggest*
> *that they have forgotten that reciprocity needs to be*
> *mutual and symmetrical—that reciprocity is a*
> *two-way street.*
> —M. Gernsbacher (2006)

Marco is angry because his baby sister has broken a prized toy. He is trying to push her away. Mom rushes to separate them. She looks at Marco and says with a look of understanding, "I know. Macy broke your toy." Marco is so upset that he can barely speak.

Now what? How do parents shift from attunement, comfort, and organizing to helping a child learn acceptable behavior? How do adults help children use their highest skills to problem solve and recover, and eventually do this all on their own?

This chapter presents a systematic framework for the process in which adults help children advance from their level of functioning at the moment of distress, to climb up the developmental ladder to the highest level possible. The process is a shared experience between adult and child.

Helping begins after an adult first attunes to a child's distress and recognizes his level of functioning. This directs the starting place. If

Marco was punching and wild, his mom might need to provide support at lower levels such as holding and soothing, and gradually move up to the point that Marco could return calmly to play. On the other hand, if Marco was loudly complaining and reporting what happened and how he was feeling, Mom might be able to help him move to an acceptable solution through negotiation and reflection. Recognizing the starting point and knowing how to provide the needed incremental levels of help allows children to gradually gain ownership of their own regulation.

Anyone can fall back to lower levels under stress. Even an adult in a moment of panic may lose the ability to speak or act purposefully, or in sustained periods of intense stress may lose the ability to recall information or think logically. The first step is to recognize where the child is functioning in the moment. This level does not necessarily indicate how high or how quickly a child may be able to advance in overall functioning.

The second step for handling a behavior in the moment is called "help" because the focus is on how an adult helps the child learn to manage experiences of distress. The medium for learning is the relationship between adult and child, which creates a place of safety and security, builds a child's positive self-concept, and forms a desire to please others. Through these interactions and an ability to communicate about feelings with a trusted adult, a child builds an understanding of the social world.

Helping children does not mean simply helping them regain their composure or stop a particular behavior; it means helping them advance toward the highest level of their ability to think, communicate, and problem solve in stressful situations. With these skills, a child is able to adapt flexibly to new challenges, and can seek and utilize help from others as needed.

For a child with autism or other developmental disability, it may be difficult to know the amount of support that is needed or the child's capacities for recovery. Utilizing the milestone framework provides guidance in how to support children, regardless of their chronological age or developmental challenge, through the process of dealing with distress. The hierarchy of levels can be reliably used so that a child is moving toward greater mastery of self-control during stressful events.

Help Moving up the Milestones in Sequence

Carl was building a train track with his dad. They were happily talking, deciding which direction the tracks should go, and connecting the pieces. Then Carl tried to connect a bridge piece and was struggling to get it to fit. He worked on his own, and tried and tried. The conversation stopped. Finally, he stood up and kicked the whole train track apart. Dad was startled and angry, but also compassionately attuned to his son's extreme level of distress.

Using the developmental framework, Dad began to attune, calm, and organize. He moved near Carl, blocking his way from further kicking, and gently soothed him. "It's okay, Carl." No more words were needed. Carl melted into his arms, with tears in his eyes. Now, Carl was ready for Dad's help to move up the developmental ladder.

Milestone 1: Attain calm, shared attention. Dad has been able to help Carl to calm a little, organize his movements and feelings, and he is now listening to Dad.

Milestone 2: Attain sense of warm engagement and trust. Dad is using gentle holding and a soft, soothing voice to let Carl know that he is safe, and that Dad is there to help.

Milestone 3: Two-way communication. Now Dad would like to help Carl begin to communicate, either with words or gestures, about what happened and how he is feeling. Dad says, "What happened?" Carl initially doesn't respond. Dad says, "Were you working on the bridge?" To this, Carl kicks his leg at a nearby piece of track. Dad says, "I wonder if you were having trouble with that tricky bridge." Carl gives a big sigh, and utters "uh" along with another little kick. Dad says, "So frustrating, huh?" He waits. Then Carl picks up another piece of track and throws it. Dad says, "It's okay. I can help," while still holding him gently. Dad waits. Then Carl starts to sit up and look at the track pieces. Dad notices that he is looking at the bridge piece. Dad picks it up and brings it over. "Was this the one you were trying to fit?" Carl stares at it with anger. Dad offers, "Would you like some help with it?" Carl nods. Dad says, "Okay, where is the other half?" Carl picks it up and hands it to Dad.

Milestone 4: Shared problem solving. Dad and Carl are now working together. Dad solicits Carl's help to hold one side as they try to fit it. Dad purposefully adds a number of small steps and mistakes, and follows Carl's lead so that they practice with trial and error, now working through successes and failures, until they finally get it the way they want. In the process, Carl begins to relax and is talking more as they work to reconstruct the rest of the track.

Milestone 5: Use of symbolic ideas. Dad and Carl's conversation now expands into a discussion of the train city they are building. They are now using words to describe which pieces are the most frustrating or easiest to put together.

Milestone 6: Logical bridging of ideas. Dad and Carl might even begin to elaborate on how designers should modify their designs so that they are not so frustrating.

Using a developmental approach in the moment of distress takes time. It may be more expedient to soothe a child, stop a behavior, or gain compliance through simply giving in, using distraction or deception, or threat or reward. However, the goal in a developmental approach is to build developmental capacities and thereby help a child gain the ability to function at higher levels. In the example above, Carl will learn that Dad is available and able to help him to work through strong feelings of frustration, so that in the future, he will seek out this help before dropping to lower levels of functioning.

Help Advancing All the Milestones at Once

Often children need continued support at lower milestones, even as they advance. Sometimes, they may advance and slip back several times within a dynamic of helpful interaction. Still, the framework of developmental milestones provides an adult with appropriate strategies to match the child's capacities from moment to moment.

Mabel, an 11-year-old with an intellectual disability, is bored and frustrated because she has to wait in line for a turn at a game that she loves. She starts to whine and complain loudly, "This game is stupid. Mark shouldn't go first. Me next!"

Mabel's aide, Ms. Nancy, knows that Mabel can use higher-level thinking when she is calm, but that she is also prone to acting impulsively and might easily dart away or push another child at any moment.

Ms. Nancy attunes to Mabel's feelings. She calms and organizes, saying sympathetically, "Mabel, I know you have been waiting for a long time in line. It's really hard to wait." Mabel answers, "I hate waiting. I want to play now!" Ms. Nancy has her attention. Mabel does not act out but looks to the aide with anticipation that she will help.

How can Ms. Nancy help Mabel learn to cope with the frustration of waiting? Mabel is able to communicate what she wants and how she is feeling, but is having difficulty at all levels, from regulation to logical thinking.

Milestone 1: Regulation and shared attention. Through her caring response, Ms. Nancy has conveyed that she is present, listening, and available to help. For now, Mabel is able to regulate her actions (she is not pushing or running away).

Milestone 2: Engagement, warmth and trust. Fortunately, Ms. Nancy has a good relationship with Mabel, and Mabel is telling her what is bothering her, providing an opportunity to help. However, for Mabel, this engagement is fragile, as Mabel is threatening to leave.

Milestone 3: Two-way communication. Mabel has initiated sharing her ideas and is responding in conversation. The goal is to build on this capacity, and keep the conversation going, in order to help Mabel continue to calm down and advance to higher levels.

Ms. Nancy decides to build on Mabel's idea about waiting. She knows that Mabel understands time and might be interested in looking at her watch. She says, "Would you like to see my watch?" Mabel's curiosity is aroused. "Let's see what time it is." Mabel comments on the watch and a dialogue has begun. Ms. Nancy asks, "What time did you get in line?" Mabel is still talking loudly but talks about the time, and gradually softens her tone a little. Ms. Nancy's calm demeanor is continuing to help soothe and calm her distress, while gradually helping her focus on the concept and feelings around waiting.

Milestone 4: Coregulated, shared social problem solving. Now Ms. Nancy helps Mabel think about the goal—having a turn in the game. Their con-

versation is more animated, with a range of expressions, as they focus on the fun in the game, anticipating the next move as they watch, and noting how they are advancing in line. Ms. Nancy includes the other children in the conversation. She is helping Mabel to wait through a coregulated dynamic interaction. Once, Mabel begins whining and turns as if to leave, and Ms. Nancy responds with calming and organizing again.

Milestone 5: Symbolic thinking about emotional ideas. In their conversation, Ms. Nancy is also talking about Mabel's feelings as her turn is getting closer. She notes that Mabel is smiling as she watches a big hit. She asks, "Are you excited?" Mabel says, "I want to hit the ball over the top! That would be fun!"

Milestone 6: Logical thinking. After her turn, Ms. Nancy finds time to sit and review with Mabel. "It was hard to wait. Was it worth it? If only two kids were in line, would it be better?" Now that Mabel is calm, she can reflect, "It's okay to wait if there are three kids, maybe five, but never 10."

In the developmental approach, there are no specific correct words to use. Each child is unique, and each situation is different. Adults utilize what they know about the child's individual differences, and build on the trust in their relationship. By thinking of the developmental milestones, an adult is cognizant of the goals from moment to moment, as they provide the degree of support needed for a child to move up to their highest capacities.

Help With an Attitude of Caring, Kindness, and Confidence

In this step, an attitude of caring, respect, and kindness is constant. Often, a challenging behavior arises from the inability to use social supports to regulate feelings and behavior during times of distress. An adult encourages a child to trust and use others for support in acceptable ways.

Through a confident attitude that success is possible, children are empowered to exert their best efforts. When they are treated with a belief in their competence, even in moments of distress and difficult behavior, they learn to respect themselves and treat others likewise.

A wise father commented, "No one enjoys being out of control." His son, Sean, was thrashing about as Dad tried to restrain him. Sean was trying to bite and kick and sometimes would even spit. He was intermittently saying something to the effect, "I hate you." With incredible patience, Dad told him, "I know you don't like feeling this way." His recognition of the tremendous turmoil inside his son allowed him to calmly offer his help as his son was able to gradually regain his composure.

An attitude of helping may be completely contrary to an adult's natural instincts in the moment of a child's difficult or belligerent behavior, especially when the child has hurt the adult or someone else or has caused damage. An adult may interpret behavior as being purposefully mean, hurtful, and selfish or believe that a child knows better. Sometimes a child knows a rule and still does not follow it.

In a developmental approach, it is possible to recognize that a child's functional level in the moment may be reduced. The response is graded to the moment. With a view that a child needs support, adults may be more willing to take an attitude of helping, and respond with patience and empathy, even counter to their initial instincts.

Shame, in particular, is not a productive strategy. Shame is a strong and painful feeling of exclusion or separation from the warm, shared sense of connection between adult and child. Experiences of shame erode a positive sense of self and undermine a trusting relationship. Children do feel ashamed at times, as they recognize that their behavior is unacceptable. However, adults can help them know that behavior, no matter how egregious, will not cause parents to break their bonds of care and affection.

Through repeated patterns of interaction, children learn to anticipate that they will be embarrassed, blamed, corrected or dismissed. Or they will be heard, respected, helped, and supported in times of need.

Learning About Authority and Limits

For parents, a basic question of discipline is: How can I tell my children they have done something wrong and that I am not pleased, but that I still love and accept them? The message of disapproval must be communicated in accordance with developmental level, and also framed in a broader message that the parent is there to help children learn from their experience. Each unacceptable behavior is an opportunity for building developmental capacities and strengthening relationships.

It is essential that children learn about limits from an early age. It is instructive to think about how infants typically learn the meaning of "No!" They hear it when they are about to, or have already, crossed some limit. Maybe they throw food, put paper in their mouth, reach for the stove, or pull Mom's hair. The word is accompanied by Mom or Dad's hand gently stopping the errant behavior. Gradually, children learn that this word, with a particular tone of voice and facial expression, means to stop what they are doing. At some point they no longer need a parent's action to provide the meaning.

In a similar way, children learn about many limits, first with maximal levels of support, and then expanding to more contexts and less support. Toddlers might only need part of the message—a disapproving look and shake of the head. Later, they might even anticipate a response, and turn to a parent expecting that look to reinforce their proper behavior. A graduated response allows children to steadily develop more responsibility for their actions. Their success engenders a sense of accomplishment, empowerment, and pride, both for the child and the parents.

Although it can be helpful, it is not always necessary to state the limit as a rule. In fact, it is impossible to make a rule for every occasion. In the example of Carl above, it was not necessary or relevant for Dad to tell Carl not to kick the train tracks. The words would not have provided the level of support needed for Carl to calm down, organize, and regulate his behavior. Dad helped him stop by physically blocking him. Through Dad's help, Carl is learning that his strong feelings can be managed with help, and thus he will learn to avoid out-of-control actions.

Later, when calmer, Carl might try to grab his sister's cookies off her plate. Dad might quickly appraise the situation, including Carl's level of functioning. Dad might simply give Carl a look of disapproval and say, "Hey, don't take her cookies!" Because Carl is acting in a purposeful and more organized way, he would be able to listen and obey without difficulty. The level of support needed to obtain the desired behavior is determined by the child's functional level in the moment.

Gradually, a child learns the boundaries of acceptable behavior, with unspoken as well as explicit rules of expected conduct. At the earlier levels, a rule can be accompanied by a physical action: "No touching Mommy's glasses" as a hand is moved away. Then, a physical cue may be used: "Stay in the sand area at the park." Later, a rule may represent a concept: "Play nice."

Behavioral strategies can be used to reinforce compliance with rules. A child with capacities at Milestone 6, logical thinking, may be taught, "Do not play on the computer until after your homework is done." She would understand both the actions requested and could anticipate how Dad would feel and act if she failed to comply. She may know that she would likely receive a punishment for noncompliance. Such cause-effect consequences are part of daily life; however, if used in isolation, they bypass important opportunities for learning. At times, an adult could discuss a rule with the child and engage in shared problem solving about how to achieve the necessary outcome.

Children need help to manage their feelings, and parents provide safety and boundaries as children gradually learn to think and function while broadening their experiences. As children mature, this unequal relationship evolves. Children learn that they are capable of managing more on their own, and are able to get help from a wider array of sources. While children with autism or other neurodevelopmental challenges may need more time and assistance to learn, the process is the same.

Ethan, a large boy, is standing in the hallway of his house and having trouble leaving to go to school. He looks distraught as he talks with his mom. "I want bike!" he says loudly. Mom tries to soothe him, saying, "We can ride bikes after school." Ethan says, "School, no school!" Mom says patiently, "Yes, today is school. We need to go now." Ethan, with a desperate whining voice and concerned expression, repeats, "No school! Bikes! Home!" This exchange continues for over 10 minutes, without progress. In fact, Ethan is becoming more upset and uses fewer words and more pushing. He continues to stand in the same spot. Mom tries to help. "What do you want? We can ride bikes later."

Mom is patiently trying to attune to Ethan's feelings and keep him from becoming more upset, but she must take him to school and get to her own job. She is worried about how she is going to get him out the door, and what might happen if he becomes more upset. Her worry is evident in her pleading tone of voice. In order to help him move forward, Mom must act with authority. It can be difficult with a large child that cannot be physically controlled, but with practice, Mom can build confidence, and Ethan will gain the ability to tolerate his anxiety through her strength and conviction.

With coaching from a professional, Mom learns to respond to Ethan's "No school!" with a strong voice: "Yes Ethan, time for school. Take your backpack." Ethan has difficulty initiating movements when he is distressed, so Mom places his backpack close to his hand and he grasps it. Mom continues, "I am opening the door. We are going to the car now." She says rhythmically, "Let's go. Let's go" to help him walk with her. He makes some sounds of protest, and she responds in rhythm, "It's okay. School today." Ethan makes it to the car and relaxes as he settles back into a familiar routine.

Through her actions, Mom has supported Ethan to strengthen his capacities in the foundational developmental milestones.

Milestone 1: Ethan was sharing attention, but his regulation was tenuous and actually getting worse over time, as his level of distress seemed to be increasing. After coaching, Mom's use of authority and structure provided a level of security for him. The difference included her confident tone of voice, the definite actions expected, the subtle supports for movement, and her own sense of secure regulation.

Milestone 2: Ethan was seeking help by telling Mom what he wanted. She was able to strengthen this bond by helping him move through an anxiety-provoking transition. Using sound and movement created a shared experience that built trust and success in their relationship.

Milestone 3: At the beginning, Ethan was engaged in some level of communicative exchange; however, Mom's responses were not successful in helping with his strong feelings. With more support, Ethan was able to return to a calmer state where he could engage in reciprocal interactions, which initially involved the nonverbal steps grasping his backpack, walking together, and getting into the car.

Limits are paradoxical. On one hand, children resist limits as they arouse feelings of anger and rebellion, but on the other hand, limits and boundaries provide security. A child who is presented with too many limits and too much structure may become defiant, angry, and oppositional or may become passive, self-absorbed, and apathetic. Children benefit from a sensitive balance of consistent limits and flexible respect and accommodation to their wishes and ideas.

A child who becomes overly reliant on routines may become confused and anxious if the situation changes. Alternatively, if a parent routinely capitulates and fails to enforce limits, the child may become unruly, and be both bossy and anxious.

A foundation of trust and security in an adult-child relationship includes the flexible imposition of some structure and limits, with the concomitant support of helping children manage the feelings associated with those limits. A child's ability to negotiate and compromise around limits is also an important skill.

A Dangerous Situation in the Moment

Ethan, who is nonverbal, has had a challenging week. School is on break and his mother has been away for a few days. There are guests in the house and it is noisy. He becomes more agitated and is now pacing and pounding on the walls. Fortunately, Dad is home.

When children are a danger to themselves or others, or may cause harm of any type, an adult may need to move in immediately to help, so that steps 1 and 2 are happening simultaneously. Safety for parent, clinician, and child is always paramount. In the moment of this behavior, the goal is to maintain safety for all, while helping to soothe a child's distress.

The first question is who can best intervene. The person that the child knows and trusts the most will generally have the greatest success in helping. That person is also likely to know the child's individual differences, likes, and dislikes, and will have a repertoire of shared experiences to reference.

Knowing that Ethan is sensitive to sound, Dad asked the guests to turn off the TV and go into another room. Dad approached Ethan, keeping a safe distance. "Hey Ethan, are you okay? Was the TV too loud?" Ethan watched Dad from the corner of his eye. Dad approached a little closer. "Do you want to listen to your favorite music with me? Let's go in the den." Ethan made calmer vocalizations, and was no longer pounding the walls. Dad invited, "We can listen together." Ethan responded by moving a bit closer. Dad waited, and when Ethan looked up, he said, "Come on, let's go. I'll help you." Dad walked by Ethan to the den and got out his favorite music. They sat together in their usual spot on the couch.

Although Ethan is nonverbal, he listened to Dad's voice and heard a comforting and calm presence. He understood Dad's invitation and recalled the times they sat and listened together, and the pleasant experience of the music and being together. Because Dad sensitively waited for Ethan's cues, Ethan was able to use his help to relax.

Help at Milestones 1 and 2

The following strategies support a child to gain basic regulation and shared attention, and support a relationship of warmth and trust between adult and child during moments of distress:

Environmental Considerations

When a child is overwhelmed, consider adjusting the sensory environment, utilizing his or her individual sensory-motor profile. Whenever possible, combine the sensory experience with a personal social experience, such as walking together or singing a song together. Consider where the adult is spatially in relationship to the child: acting as an anchor in the room, in direct line of sight, or at a comfortable distance.

Structure and Routines

Charlotte is sitting in her preschool class. It is story time, and the children are gathered on the rug. It is also a beautiful day and the door is open. Charlotte suddenly runs from the room. Stacey, the classroom aide, runs after her. She stops Charlotte and says, "I know it's fun outside, but it is story time now. It's time to listen to Ms. Marsha." Charlotte likes Stacey and is happy to see her, but gives no indication of understanding. Stacey continues, "Come with me. We can listen to books together" as she guides her back to the class.

Routines are important in everyday life. Numerous sequences of action are accomplished without conscious thought or planning because they are routine. Daily schedules help a child to anticipate changes and tolerate less pleasant experiences with the knowledge that they will end and preferred activities will follow. For children who have challenges with movement, sensory processing, and cognitive understanding, routines are particularly helpful.

Routines naturally evolve around sleep, meals, dressing, and hygiene. Communication about routines can be supported by the use of calendars, picture schedules, and lists, as well as more or less sophisticated depictions of events through time and space. Consistent routines can help with regulation, facilitate compliance, and generally decrease anxiety.

Charlotte is learning the classroom routine. Over time, she will learn to anticipate that story time is followed by outdoor play and will be able to tolerate the feelings aroused by both excitement and waiting. While she will learn to reference a classroom picture schedule, interactions with Stacey and Ms. Marsha will provide the security and pleasure in the classroom experience that help Charlotte follow the expected routine.

While routines are powerful and ubiquitous, it is equally important that children can tolerate and adapt to changes in expected events, and that they exercise choice and initiative. When children are extremely upset by a change in routine, an adult may need to simply soothe and comfort them in the moment in order to proceed. However, when they have a pattern of rigidity around routines, it is important to create a long-term plan to help them move toward greater flexibility.

An Attitude of Calmness and Assurance

An adult's tone of voice, expressions, and movements can all contribute to a soothing interaction. Adults who have been pinched, bitten, or struck by a child are likely feeling strong emotions themselves, making it more challenging to maintain their composure. However, even during holding, they can consciously use deep vocal tones, and breathe and speak slowly.

An attitude of authority and confidence that they can set limits is reassuring to a child. If adults act as if they are intimidated by a child's actions, this may create more anxiety in the child. Communicating an attitude of steadiness and calmness is more effective than specific words used in an interaction.

> *Josue is upset that he can't get the top off a box. He tries various ways to capture Mom's attention, but Mom is preoccupied and misses his cues. Josue then comes over to Mom and bites her arm.*

Biting is a very primitive response to stress and danger. If a child is clamped onto a shirt or even a body, the only option is to help him calm down and relax. An adult must convince him that he is safe, so that he can literally relax his grip. A calm voice and still body, along with gentle words, can ease the tension. A child will often bite or pinch the person that they are going to for help, although this can be easily mis-interpreted. In retrospect, there are often indications that the child was becoming overwhelmed. A careful review of the event may provide clues to contribute to a long-term plan.

> *Joel is playing a game with his brothers. Suddenly, he runs to his room and slams the door. Mom wonders what happened. She waits a moment, and then goes to Joel's room. She opens the door slightly, peeks in, and says gently, "Joel, what's the matter? Can I help?"*

Her calm attitude will help Joel to begin a process of shared problem solving.

Use of a Defining Statement of Help

An effective strategy when an adult must act immediately is to use a statement that defines what the adult is doing to help the child. This statement sets a definitive and authoritarian tone that provides security for the child, emboldens the adult to act with confidence, and sets the tone of the relationship as one of calm helping. The word "help" is a cue and reminder to assume an attitude of helping children manage their feelings and behavior, and to advance to their highest skills.

- "I am going to hold you and help you stop."
- "I am going to hold your arms and help you stop hitting."
- "I am going to help you get down; it is not safe up there."
- "I am going to help you calm down."
- "I am going to hold you until you are ready."

Even children with higher capacities may need reassurance from an adult during times of stress.

After an unusual intense wind storm, Olin was frightened. He had heard about death and destruction on the radio, and now his house was without electricity. He began to pace and moan. His father was able to talk with him, and focused on how he would keep the family safe. "I am going to stay home with you today. We can use our flashlights if we need to." He told Olin about the emergency personnel that repair the electric circuits, and the police that patrol the streets. He also tried to limit Olin's time of listening to the news reports. Dad knew that it was important to stay near Olin and provide a sense of calm and security.

Using "We" and Partnering

A highly effective strategy for building trust and helping children calm down is to join in their experience by using the word "we" or "us" or being a partner in their efforts. By having a calm and secure partner, children gain comfort and reassurance that they can be successful when faced with a difficult situation. An adult might use phrases such as, "What should we do?" "Let's do it together." "I'll help you clean up." Partnering is a more intense level of support, which can be used strategically, and gradually diminished as expectations increase for a child to manage a challenge independently.

Distraction

In some situations distraction is a viable strategy. It is particularly appropriate when a behavior is needed immediately (fasten the seat belt), or when the child may not understand a situation (a workman has to come into the home for repairs) and there is no time to help process the situation. If possible, distractions can include a shared social activity that builds warmth in the relationship. While slipping the seat belt on, a parent might say, "Let's sing a song about going for a ride."

Distractions can also help a child recover from distress.

Carol's balloon had slipped out of her hand and was floating away. She was distraught. Mom and Dad tried to comfort her, but she continued to cry as she watched the balloon float away. After a few minutes, Mom decided to redirect her attention to the swings and slides. Carol was able to stop crying and move on with play.

While distraction can be effective, if it is a primary means of soothing a child, it decreases opportunities for learning to manage feelings together with an adult. Children may even distract themselves, as they suddenly shift attention away from a difficult feeling, or give up on an effort. An adult might want to help them persist by drawing their attention back to the original goal.

Safe Holding Strategies

Sometimes children need support to get their body under control. Flailing movements and aggressive behaviors both indicate that a child needs help. In addition to strategies to organize and calm an upset child, an adult can provide specific feedback about where a child's body is ("Your leg is kicking me," said while gently but firmly moving the leg). Or an adult can move a child to a different location or activity to help organize her movements ("Let's go walk to the table," or "I am going to pick you up and take you to the car"). Or an adult can provide physical limits like pillow bolsters or hold a child if needed.

The most important factor in providing physical restraint is that the adult convey both compassion and firm, calm, and reassuring control. Adults need to act calmly, even while feeling some degree of distress themselves.

Erick was insecure and unsure what to do in the new room. He was lying on the ground and randomly kicking his legs. At times his legs hit Ms. Rita, who was sitting nearby. She surmised that he was sitting close because he wanted to be engaged, but that he was probably fairly unaware of what he was doing with his legs and definitely had no perception that he might be hurting someone.

She gently but firmly grasped his legs at the ankles and playfully tapped his feet on the ground. She cued him: "Your feet go on the ground. Feet go on the ground." She physically prevented him from kicking her and remained close. He looked at her but seemed to make no intentional gestures. After a few moments he stopped his random kicking. She provided physical support to help Erick stand up, and then he joined in a tossing game.

Every parent and clinician that interacts with a child with aggressive behavior must know how to physically protect themselves and the child from harm. As much as possible, the goal is for the child to learn to control his own body. If adults can use a pillow or barrier to protect themselves, and allow the child to direct his own movements, it provides a greater opportunity for learning self-control.

Adults may also need to learn safe-holding techniques and emergency procedures. For a larger child, an adult may need to learn self-defense maneuvers. This may be as simple as standing tall and firm to dissipate intimidation, or may involve fending off blows. It is important to have a plan in place when a child has violent or dangerous behavior.

It takes great patience and self-control on the part of an adult to tolerate extreme and persistent distress in a child, especially for parents. It is physically demanding to hold a fighting child, and arouses many emotions in both adult and child.

Even while holding a child, an adult can engage in dialogue and advance as far as the child is able, including shared problem solving and higher-level thinking. It is important to continue holding until the adult determines that the child is able to maintain a basic level of regulation without physical support. If a child cannot understand "if . . . then" reasoning, a statement such as, "If you say you are sorry, then you can go" may not be meaningful. A statement such as, "When you calm down, we can finish reading the book" provides a simpler plan for moving forward.

Oscar was bucking and fighting while Mom held him firmly in his arms. Mom was seated on the floor and Oscar was in her lap, facing forward.

Oscar intermittently tried to bite or spit. Mom took a deep breath and moved to prop her back against the wall. She made sure Oscar could not reach her arm to bite, and that if he jerked his head back it would not hit her face. Mom had to readjust her legs to cover Oscar's leg, in a gentle squeeze.

Oscar yelled, "You're hurting me!" Mom said, "It's okay, Oscar. I'm going to help you calm down." Oscar wiggled, and Mom held firm.

Eventually Oscar said, "Let me go!" Mom said calmly, "I will let you go when you are ready." The next time, Oscar added, "I'm ready!" Mom continued to hold him, but said, "Okay, when you are ready, what do you want to do? Do you want to play blocks or put them away?" Oscar said, "Let go!" The conversation continued in this haphazard way, but gradually moved to a more coherent flow. Oscar eventually said, "Put them away." Mom said, "Okay, then what? Do you want to get a drink or read a book?" Oscar responded, "Get a drink." Mom continued until they had a three-step plan. She repeated the plan a few times, so that Oscar would have more time to relax. Mom said, "Okay, when you are ready, we're going to put the blocks away, get a drink of water, and then play ball. Right?" Oscar, surprisingly, added, "I want apple juice." Mom said, "But I thought you didn't like apple juice." They continued talking about where they might find apple juice, what kind of ball game they might play, and so on. After some planning, Mom could see that Oscar was relaxed, and gradually eased her hold.

They followed through with the plan. Mom helped put the blocks away, and they worked together to get juice, and then play ball. Later that night they talked a little about what had happened including how hard it was, how upset Oscar was, and how Mom helped.

The whole episode lasted over 30 minutes. Through this stressful time, Oscar experienced his mother as someone that could help him control his body and was calm and safe. Mom helped him to engage in two-way communication, and even the beginning of shared problem solving. Oscar's episodes of behavior requiring this level of support quickly diminished, and became shorter and less intense.

Respectful, Active Waiting and Encouragement

Some children respond to stress by shutting down or withdrawing from interaction, rather than escalating into fight-or-flight behaviors. An adult can help by persistent and respectful attunement to a child's gestures, and patient waiting for tensions to ease through active and warm engagement and encouraging statements.

> *Alex was lying still on the sofa, intermittently closing his eyes, although he was awake. He did not want to go out. Mom sat by him. She spoke softly, saying, "Where's my big boy Alex? I want him to come with me to the store." Alex shut his eyes tighter. Mom said, "Your eyes are closing so tightly. I think you are saying you don't want to go." Alex turned away. Mom said, "Now you are turning away. You really want to stay home." Alex didn't move. Mom described the plan. "We are going to go for a ride in the car, stop at the market to get bread and milk, and then drive through the bank, and then back home again." Alex didn't move.*
>
> *She waited, and then she said, "I can help. Alex, will you give me your hand?" Alex put his hand in his pocket. Mom said playfully, "Where did that hand go? It's gone! Where is the other hand?" Alex put the other hand in a pocket. Mom said, "Okay, can I have a foot?" Alex smiled and tried to cover his foot. She said, "Oh! I still see a foot!" He now opened his eyes, sat up, and covered his feet with his hands. Mom said, "No feet! How can we go to the store with no feet?" Alex stuck out a foot. "Oh, there it is!" They continued a game of hiding and finding his feet for a few minutes. Then she said, "Okay, Alex. It's time to go. Can you help me carry the bags? You're my big helper—thank you!"*

Alex had been tense and shut down because of his level of stress. He needed time and support to help him calm down, open his eyes, look, and listen. Mom noticed his actions and gave them a shared meaning. She confidently provided a plan and offered her help. Mom was then able to entice Alex to act purposefully and engaged him in a reciprocal interaction, while giving him time to relax and regain his functional skills. If Alex had begun a conversation to describe what he wanted to do first, or where he wanted to go on the drive, Mom could have considered making a deal with some negotiation and compromise. Her patience and active waiting helped Alex participate in an interaction that supported his recovery and strengthened their relationship.

Time-Outs

Time-outs can be helpful by removing the child from a situation which is overwhelming and escalating, Time-out can also be helpful if the parent is feeling overwhelmed and needs time to regulate their own emotions or tend to another child. An adult may say, "You need to go to your room and come out when you have calmed down." Or, "Let's take a time-out and sit on the bench for a minute and talk about it." In these examples, the child is learning self-control, with a graded level of support. There is no shame or humiliation, and the child is learning boundaries on behavior.

A parent or clinician must be cautious that a pattern does not develop in which children are removed from every challenging situation, or are left alone before they have the ability to calm down on their own. Time-outs, when used judiciously, can help children learn self-control, especially when they have an opportunity to talk about the event, either during or after the time-out.

Help at Milestone 3

When a child is distressed but has attained basic regulation and engagement, an adult can proceed with a focus on two-way interaction. The goal is to achieve purposeful gestures in a reciprocal flow as the child works through strong feelings. Through the interaction, an adult is also helping a child to discern and clarify different emotions. Through this process, the child learns functional developmental skills while achieving acceptable behavior.

Keep the Conversation Going

An adult can help a child to stay calm and remain engaged by initially entering into an exchange about any topic, and then gradually focusing on the more difficult emotions. This strategy is used to encourage them to participate in a dialogue as they recover their composure enough to focus on their uncomfortable feelings. An adult may initially ask inconsequential questions or offer tangential information, and gradually pose questions or provide comments that help to organize a child's feelings.

Lila is sitting outside the classroom. She has just stopped crying after an altercation with Bobby. She is hot and shaking. The teacher asks her, "Lila, are you okay?" Lila looks at her wet shirt. "Oh, your shirt is a little wet." Lila touches her shirt, breathing deeply. "It's a pretty shirt—is that Violet?" (A favorite character.) Lila nods. "And is that Charmaine?" Lila is breathing a little easier. "Okay, Lila, right now the other kids are drawing pictures." Lila recalls, "Bobby took my picture!"

Now the teacher proceeds with sorting through what happened and makes a plan with Lila. Once Lila appears to be on the verge of acting out again, and the teacher keeps the conversation at a tolerable level by asking, "What was on your drawing?" "A horse." "What color was it? You made a horse yesterday too." By keeping the conversation a bit tangential to the problem, Lila is able to stay engaged.

Offer Choices

By offering options, an adult is inviting a child to actively participate in a plan of action. Similarly, if the child suggests a plan of action, the adult can respond to either accept or reject it, or offer an alternative. By not directing the child's actions, an adult can encourage initiative in acting purposefully and beginning problem solving. Sometimes it is helpful to use a closed-ended choice, where both options are contained within the same action, for example, "Do you want to hold my hand or Dad's hand (as we cross the street)?"

Use of Gestures

During an interaction, an adult can encourage a child to communicate intent by interpreting behaviors as having meaning. As a child pushes a hand away, the adult interprets, "Not that one!" or "You don't want me to touch your shoes." Giving meaning to gestures encourages a child to use more definitive gestures. An adult can suggest a specific gesture to signify a choice, such as, "Show me where you want it to go," or model use of affect gestures, such as shrugging shoulders and hands palms up for "I don't understand" or "Which one?" It is natural for an adult to use words; however, for some children gestures and nonverbal communication are more effective, particularly under stress. The amount and complexity of adult language should be tailored to each child in the moment.

Heightened Affect

An adult can help a child to distinguish and organize emotional experiences by the use of clear and slightly exaggerated affect gestures, including facial expressions, tone of voice, words, and body language. An adult's use of clear affect gestures helps a child to organize experience, join in reciprocal interactions, and regulate behavior.

> *Noah is upset because his choice did not win in the voting. He stands up and protests, moving to tear the paper off the wall. The teacher stands to block his way and says with heightened affect, "It's so hard when you don't win." Noah pounds his fist once on the desk and sits down. Later, when his peers compete in a game of chance, the teacher uses facial expressions and body language to communicate the suspense. Noah looks directly at her and says, "Cross your fingers!" Their animated dialogue continues through victory and defeat.*

Continue Past "No"

Sometimes a child can have very negativistic or defiant behavior. "No" can be a frequent response. In order to help a child learn to modulate this behavior, an adult can respond in a way that respects the child's feelings and also challenges them to consider other choices.

> *Bobby has just angrily knocked the wood box onto the ground. Ms. Sheila says, "Bobby, please pick that up." Bobby says, "No." Ms. Sheila is familiar with Bobby's negativism and knows that raising her voice will not help. She gets down close and patiently says, "Let's see what happened." She continues to comment on what she saw and how the box is now on the floor. She uses rich affect to express her concern. She watches for Bobby's gestures of response. He brushes his arm on the table as if knocking it off again. She responds, "I can see you are angry." Now, he is looking and listening. "Well, we need to pick it up. Do you want to put it on the table or the shelf?" Suddenly, he picks it up and puts in back on the table. Because of her patience, he is able to modulate his initial intense response.*

Help at Milestone 4

At Milestone 4, an adult is helping a child to sustain a continuous flow of interaction, using multiple gestures in a row, through a broad range of different feelings such as joy, worry, disappointment, frustration, and so on. The goal of milestone 4 is not to reach a quick solution to a problem, but rather to engage in shared problem solving involving reasoning about options and consideration of the perspectives of others. The rich affective exchange, with adult and child reading and responding to each other's cues, is called coregulation.

Build on an Exchange of Emotional Expressions

Using an active interest in the feelings behind actions, adults can help children communicate the meaning of their actions, and promote sustained problem solving. Adults may express confusion so that children will more clearly express their thoughts and feelings, through words or actions.

> *Lisa is experimenting with watercolor painting for the first time. She is learning to dip her brush in water and then paint. Lisa and her mom are exchanging comments and pleasure as Lisa discovers the pretty colors she can make. At times, Lisa also expresses frustration with the process. Sometimes, Lisa vocalizes in irritation, but Mom is unclear why. Mom uses a gesture of confusion, gets close and asks, "What's the matter?" Lisa points to her paper. She is apparently unhappy with the way the colors have mixed. Now, they have the opportunity to try different paints or brushes, or start again with another paper. Lisa and Mom now have a dynamic interaction, exchanging combinations of looks, gestures, and words.*

Using a Cue to Designate a Limit

Adult and child can create a cue that signifies a limit, and embodies the shared attention, respect, and calming influence of an adult helping to regulate emotion and behavior.

> *Jessie was waiting for club to start. He asked repeatedly about the schedule for an upcoming vacation, even though he knew it thoroughly. Mom knew*

that Jessie fell into a pattern of repetition when he was feeling uneasy. She said simply, "We are not talking about that right now." Jessie took a deep breath and stopped asking questions. He was familiar with this cue. Mom's calm demeanor, as she firmly reminded him of a limit, helped Jessie to toler-ate his anxious feelings. He listened intently as they moved on to another subject and as he looked to her for further emotional cues and support.

A child can learn to respond to a familiar phrase or action to gain self-control. An adult can prevent a child from descending into self-absorp-tion and repetitive behavior by gentle interference, or can de-escalate a situation by slowing a child's actions or direction. By shifting attention to a compassionate adult, the child experiences both calming regulation and the comfort of a personal connection. Eventually, the child may anticipate this cue, and then be able signal herself by recalling the cue.

Coregulation

In helping children consider the perspective of others, an adult first helps them to deepen their insight and understanding of their own per-spective. The adult can use an organizing statement such as, "Don't let it fall down!" Or "You are trying hard to keep the scary shark behind the wall." Or pose a question, such as, "Did you want to keep the big green one?" A child who is able to organize their own intention first may then be ready to consider the perspective of others.

An adult challenges a child to notice and respond to another perspec-tive by adding their own different affect, such as a look of disapproval, concern, sadness, frustration, surprise, or confusion. With coregulation, children read and respond to another's expressions with a change in their feelings and behavior. It is important that an adult participates in the interaction with genuine emotions, so that the child's experience is organized and meaningful. An adult might say sadly, "You pulled hard on my beads and now they're broken."

An adult can also help a child to use coregulation with peers. An adult might provide additional information to help a child recognize the intent and feelings of others, using a statement such as, "I think Mark wanted it to go all the way to the end." "She might be afraid that it is going to fall." "Yolanda wanted to see too." "Victor looks sad." Or the adult might pose a question, such as, "Look at Mary. Did you see what she is doing?" "Did you hear what she said? Maybe you can ask her." All such statements need to be conveyed with words, clear and appropriate affect, body language, and gestures, to support continuous communication of affect.

Shared Problem Solving

In shared problem solving, an adult does not offer a solution to a child's dilemma, but rather engages the child in a shared process of trial, error, and discovery. This might include making a plan together and considering possible outcomes. It is important to allow the child to try her idea even if it is unlikely to be successful. This provides opportunities to work through various emotions such as frustration, sadness, confusion, surprise, relief, and joy. Offering a solution prematurely eliminates the opportunity for a rewarding shared endeavor. Ideally, adults will hold children at the just-right level of challenge, where they feel supported and ultimately proud of their success in managing their feelings and solving a problem.

Wesley was playing a board game with his older brother, Tim. He was anxious about playing but was excited to be with his brother. Unfortunately he rolled a number that meant his marker had to go all the way back to the beginning. He thought he would now lose. Wesley stood up and ran into another room, yelling,. "I hate this game. I am never playing again!"

Wesley felt devastated with feelings of despair and humiliation. Tim was able to talk to Wesley, and together they considered how they could invent new rules. It took 15 minutes of cajoling, debate, and bartering, but they finally settled on a rule that a player could only go backward one step at most. Wesley bravely joined this new game, which provided the needed bridge to help him continue to engage and gradually learn greater tolerance of winning and losing.

Open-Ended Offers of Help

An adult can encourage a child to join in shared problem solving by using open-ended options for obtaining help: "How can I help?" "What do you want me to do?" or, more subtly, "I wonder if you need help." "I think there is someone here who might know the answer to that." "You can ask for help if you want to" or "Let me know if you want help."

Emily is upset because her doll broke. She is glum and fairly unrespon-
sive. Mom says, "Oh Emily, the doll broke! Did the leg fall off?" Emily
nods. Mom asks, "Where is it?" Emily gestures weakly. Mom looks at
it and repeats, "It is really broken." Suddenly Emily screams, "I hate
this stupid doll. It is always breaking!" Mom knows she loves the doll.
Mom shares a look of understanding of the sadness that is behind Emily's
words. Mom says, "It is really frustrating that it keeps breaking!" Emily
takes a deep breath and cuddles near Mom. Mom says, "I wonder what
we can do." Emily picks up the doll and says, "I can just put pants on
her. No, let's tape it back on." Mom and Emily then work together, trying
to fix the broken leg.

Narration

Narration can help a child to organize their emotions, and can also help
them to move forward to engage in higher levels of shared problem solving. It is important to attend to a verbal child's language ability in the
moment, since language skills may be at a lower level than usual when
they are stressed. One strategy is for an adult to offer a word or phrase
that a child may borrow and utilize.

As Oliver became more anxious, he stopped talking. He wanted the ball
but was only reaching for it and bumping the other children. The teacher
observed him, and said, "Tell Shane, 'I want a turn!'" Oliver immediately
said, "I want a turn, Shane!" Although this phrase would be automatic
in other situations, Oliver needed his teacher's cue to produce it at that
moment. Shane responded, "After I hit it one more time." Now, Oliver was
ready to continue the dialogue about whose turn it should be.

Help at Milestone 5

As children move up the developmental ladder in their work to resolve
a disturbing feeling and control behavior, they may be able to utilize
a capacity for symbolic and creative thinking. At this level they can
communicate about how they feel using words or symbols to express
their emotional experiences, as well as to tell about what they wanted or
expected to happen, and what they wish could happen or not happen.

Dialogue About Emotional Ideas

Building on strategies that support regulation and shared attention, an adult can help children use language and symbols to organize and express what they want to happen, and how they feel. Because their ability to utilize symbols may be tenuous, it is helpful to focus on using words and actions to symbolize meanings rather than the correct use of language or logical reasoning.

> *Lucas has a red face and is holding up a little alien monster figure and growling at Sammy. The teacher quickly comes to stand by the boys. "Lucas, what's wrong?" By her presence, the teacher keeps them both safe and encourages them to talk. Lucas says, "He took the grindle!" Then, turning to Sammy, Lucas says, "I am going to send you a poison curse!"*
>
> *The teacher says, "You really didn't like that Sammy moved the grindle. What do you want him to do?" Lucas answers, "Put it back!" With gestures, the teacher encourages the two boys to speak to each other. Sammy says, "I put it in the space ship." The teacher asks, "Lucas, what do you think about that?" "No, not there! It has to go on the ground. Lucas is about to grab it, but the teacher says, "Wait! Sammy, where is it now?" Sammy says, "It's on a launcher." The teacher repeats the idea. "Oh! Sammy has the idea that the grindle is on a launcher. How do you feel about that?" Happily, Lucas thinks that is fine, and they resume playing together.*

Although it was clumsy, Lucas was able to move through strong feelings without acting them out physically. The teacher did not impose rules, ask for logical reasoning, or expect labeling of emotions. The children simply used words to mediate their symbolic ideas, and an adult encouraged their use of language.

Use of Symbols: Drawing, Writing, Acting, and Music

Children may be encouraged to use symbols with drawing, acting, writing, or music as a way to communicate about their ideas and feelings. Marsha wants Mom's attention and shows this by pretending to be a baby. Mom can help Marsha further elaborate her feelings by joining in the idea symbolically. Or Dad can help George to identify his angry mood by referencing a familiar pretend story: "Are you as mad as the bear in the *Big Bad Bear* story?"

Nick is so angry at a peer that he was sitting in the hallway, fuming and refusing talk. The clinician offers, "Shall we write a letter?" Nick nods, and together they create a long, somewhat rambling note that reflects all the thoughts and feelings Nick experienced. When the note is delivered, Nick is more composed and ready to continue a problem-solving interaction with his peer.

Isaac is rocking back in his chair and hitting the wall. He appears to be in distress. His aide approaches. Isaac gets up and walks toward another wall. His aide follows, gestures that he is puzzled, and hands Isaac his communication device. Isaac types in, "Labby gone." Isaac looks distressed. His aide asks, "Who is Labby?" Isaac uses the icons to mean, "My dog." The aide guesses, "Is Labby lost?" Isaac spells out, "Lost." Isaac's expression changes to sadness and worry and his aide is able to mirror those sentiments. They find the icon for worry. They continue the conversation about what happened, efforts to find the dog, and feelings of concern for everyone in the family.

Help at Milestone 6

In the midst of addressing a behavioral challenge, some children are able to reach the level of connecting symbolic ideas using logic and higher-level cognitive skills. Their conversation may include phrases such as, "He did that because he doesn't like me." "You are making me mad!" "She never plays fair." "If he comes over, Jessie will be jealous and then Simon will hate me." "That's against my beliefs!"

An adult can use strategies to support logical bridging of ideas, as well as reflective and abstract thinking, so that children learn to apply these skills at moments of heightened emotion and distress. Gradually, an adult can help children question or correct their perceptions, and think about alternative viewpoints. When they are able to think and communicate logically about their feelings, they can engage in discussion and debate, and create their own personal standards for behavior rather than acting on peer pressure or concrete and rigid thinking.

Dialogue to Help a Child Connect Ideas

Use questions and comments to help children connect their actions and feelings in the moment, within a sequence of events. Questions that use who, when, where, how, and what lead to considerations of causality or why. An adult can balance questions with summary or reflective statements, such as, "It seems like Manny was angry, and he grabbed the door. Then the door hit your foot. What happened next? How did you feel?" It is important for the adult to be receptive to hearing about any of a child's feelings, and helping the child to connect ideas before attempting to correct or teach proper behavior.

Provide Information About Rules and Natural Consequences

Consequences for behavior—both positive and negative—are ubiquitous realities in life. Within a developmental approach, such contingencies are included as one element within a broader framework that emphasizes an interactive social process of emotional and developmental attunement. Information about possible consequences for different actions may be included if it is helpful to organize the overall experience. Consequences such as praise, reward, or punishment are considered differently depending on the developmental level of the child, and generally become more significant at the third step of resolution. At Milestone 6, a child is able to incorporate thinking about consequences to form logical decisions about actions.

Question Assumptions About Time, Quantity, and Space

An adult can help children think logically by questioning their perceptions about time, quantity, and space. When distressed, some children develop a sense of urgency that something must happen immediately. An adult can help them consider alternatives by saying, "Why now?" or similarly, "Why that many?" or "Why that far?" "What if it were less? Later?" An adult can also help them clarify what was past, what is present, and what might be in the future.

Clarify Reality

Sometimes a child acts out of an idea that is not completely based in reality, but is an extension of fantasy. A typically developing young child might be a 4-year-old that engages in dangerous behavior because he is playing Superman, or a child who eats the wild berries that she is feeding her doll. Youngsters may also think that a person in a costume is real and may hit or kick them, or run away in fright. Sometimes, an adult can simply provide information that helps to separate facts from fantasy, but in other cases, a child who is not yet able to make this distinction may need close supervision to be safe.

> Kim is a 12-year-old girl with cognitive disability. She reported that Lorin grabbed her and kissed her during lunch. The staff confronted Lorin. He reported that in fact Kim had kissed him! After asking other witnesses, it turns out Lorin was correct. Why did Kim lie? Potentially many feelings are involved. Was she actually confused about what happened? The staff helped her to sort out the facts and made a plan for both continued counseling and closer supervision.

For an older child with developmental delay, behaviors based upon a blurring of fantasy and reality can become even more confusing and dangerous. A child may act out a fantasy from a TV show as if it is real, or worse, find a weapon and use it as a magical form of power. Unfortunately, many children with disabilities are inevitably exposed to violent or sexually themed shows, games, or music, or even develop fantasies based on actual news events. A child can become overly focused on these ideas as they struggle to understand and master the emotions that are aroused. Discussion or professional counseling can help a child discern the true values—good and bad—inherent in the characters, actions or lyrics of these genres. In the moment of a behavior where there is some blurring of fantasy and reality, an adult can attempt to clarify the difference, although some children will hold steadfastly to their beliefs. Recognizing the confusion can guide the adult in the moment to at least protect the child from harm as a long-term plan is devised.

Consider Motivations and Perspective of Others

At Milestone 6 a child develops the ability to recognize how feelings motivate behavior and how actions affect feelings for themselves and others. An adult can help children consider these perspectives by asking questions or presenting ideas such as, "I wonder why you hit Sally." "I think you were acting that way because you were worried that someone might take your model." "Why do you think he said that?" "Why do you think he did that?" "What do you think he is feeling right now?" "I wonder if he understood." "I wonder if he didn't see it." "Do you think he was jealous?" As with earlier milestones, it is important to help children to organize their own feelings, before expecting them to be successful in considering another's ideas.

Reflect on Patterns of Behavior

Children who are able to discuss their behavior can be encouraged to reflect on patterns of interaction. Reflection may begin with actions: "What do you usually do when someone takes your socks in gym?" Second, reflection may address feelings: "How do you usually feel when you are the last one picked for the team?" Open-ended questions such as, "What do you usually think about?" can lead to comparison to other experiences with similar or different feelings, and comparison of actions.

Encourage Discernment of Intensity and Complexity of Emotions

As development advances, children can begin to consider multiple possible emotions that may motivate behavior. They can compare emotional experiences, describe levels of emotional intensity, use a more subtle range of descriptors for emotional experience, and describe mixtures of emotions. Now they can appreciate sentiments such as, "I was so embarrassed" or "I'm hoping she will go, but I'll only be a little disappointed if she can't." An adult can support this developmental capacity by exploring the full scope of feelings associated with a challenging behavior.

Hypothesize and Evaluate Possible Solutions and Consequences

Children can be encouraged to consider a range of possible actions and responses. "What else could you do?" "What should the rule be? Why?" Help the child to reflect: "What do you think he would do if you said that?" "How do you think he will feel if you do that?" "Will you be relieved after we are done tomorrow?"

Negotiate, Compromise

Whenever possible, it is good practice to engage children in a process of negotiation and compromise. Encourage them to elaborate on their reasoning. Make a plan together.

Reference Values

As children advance in their ability to connect emotional ideas, they begin to form their own value system, which is less dependent upon immediate feedback from others. Adults can encourage them to consider ethical values related to the current behavior. An adult might ask, "Do you think that is fair?" "Why or why not?" "What would be fair?" "Do you think it is a good thing to hide it from her?"

Moral values separating right from wrong are complex. Behavioral challenges are opportunities for children at this level to progress in the growth of their personal belief system.

Jacob talked about dating incessantly. He was preoccupied with Internet dating sites and wrote letters to his favorite movie idol. His parents were concerned that his behavior could lead to trouble. Fortunately, Jacob belonged to a young adult group where they had frequent discussions about making friends, sexual relations, and dating. He was encouraged to ask questions, explore his ideas, and develop his own ideas about privacy and personal boundaries that helped him to approach dating in a more gradual and acceptable way.

Interaction With Peers

The same strategies used for an individual child can also support peers through a behavioral challenge.

Paul grabs his sister Tina's toy and runs off to another room, and is hiding behind the couch. Tina cries and says, "Mommy, Paul took my toy. I want it back." Mom reassures Tina: "I'll help." She goes to Paul and leans down near him, saying calmly, "Paul, what's going on?" He answers, "I want it." Mom says, "I see you really want it, but Tina wants it too." She moves closer and says, "Let's figure this out." And she offers her hand.

He is reassured by her offer to help and is willing to take her hand and go into the room with Tina. Mom sits between them. "We have a problem. Tina wants her toy, and now Paul wants the same toy." She waits. Tina says, "It's mine." Paul answers, "It's mine." Mother says, "I think it is Tina's," and repeats, "It's Tina's but Paul wants it." Tina offers, "You can have this one," offering another toy. And Paul accepts the offer.

Mother has helped them to share joint attention, helping through her presence to keep them safe and calm. She has encouraged them to speak to each other and clarified facts and feelings. She has allowed them to find a solution. Mom would have been willing to accept any solution that they found mutually agreeable, and stayed to help celebrate by joining in some fun play together for a few minutes.

Adam tries to join his peers in play but he doesn't know how to play the game. The others get mad and quit, saying, "Adam ruined the game!" A staff member steps in to help. "Uh-oh. What happened?" William said, "He doesn't know the rules." The staffer reflects, "Adam looks kind of sad. I wonder what we can do." The staff facilitates a discussion where several children suggest ideas. The staff asks the others, "What do you think? Is that a good idea?" until they formulate a mutually agreeable plan, which includes helping Adam to play the game first and then switching to another game. Through this process children are learning to be considerate of others and exercising creative and shared problem solving.

In the developmental approach, social skills groups comprise children working on goals at similar developmental levels. Activities provide opportunities individualized for each child, as well as forming group engagement, goals, and identity. Facilitators balance challenges and supports, and create a safe environment in which children feel secure enough to attempt new abilities. A parent's role is to praise and encourage their child's efforts, as well as to provide opportunities for play with peers in between social skills sessions.

Coaching Parents to Help Their Child

A clinician may coach parents to help their child through a challenging behavior. The relationship begins with a plan, including goals and strategies, giving a clear understanding that the parent is to act with authority, while the clinician is in a supportive role. Without this understanding a parent may automatically defer to the clinician as the expert.

If a parent and child are interacting, the clinician may provide objective observations to help direct the parent's attention. "Uh-oh, it looks like Jimmy is getting upset that the car won't go through. I think he may need your help." The clinician can offer specific suggestions or remind the parent of strategies, as well as give encouragement: "You're doing great. Keep it up."

Even if a clinician is already interacting with the child when a behavioral outburst begins, parents can be encouraged to react and respond. Sometimes a therapist pushes the challenge a little too far. For example, in play, the therapist says, "No, my baby doesn't like peas." The child begins to topple the whole kitchen unit. The clinician would say to the parent with regret, "I think I pushed her too far. Can you please help her to recover?" This is an opportunity for learning: The clinician learns about the child's threshold of frustration, the parent learns strategies to help the child, and the child learns through a process of being helped by the parent.

> Jorge was almost in a panic. He wanted to ride the elevator again, but he had already gone two times, and the clinician and Mom had made a plan that they were setting a limit. Jorge needed to move past the elevator to the car. He protested loudly. As they physically blocked his way back to the elevator, Jorge started to breathe heavily and looked wide eyed. They tried to walk him to the car, but he dropped to the ground in a heap. Mom was somewhat embarrassed and felt helpless. She didn't know what to do or say. The clinician coached Mom, saying, "You are the most important person to him. Let him know that he is all right and that you will help him." Mom said to him, "Jorge, it's okay. Let's go. Come on, Jorge. I'll help you. Let's go." He didn't go immediately, but with Mom's assuring voice, he was eventually able to stand

and move to the car. The clinician periodically praised Mom for staying calm and for her good efforts.

Helping Takes Time, Patience, and Equanimity

An adult can help a child by slowing down the interaction to provide time for the child to create a new response or solution. An adult seeks to hold a child at just the right level of tension, neither fixing the problem nor avoiding challenges, so that a child maintains the initial motivation without becoming overwhelmed.

Kyle is stomping his feet. He can't get on the trains to stay on the track! Dad steps in to help. The therapist suggests that Dad assist just part way. "Let's see if you can do it together." Dad then proceeds to give just enough guidance that Kyle is able to work together with him, and eventually get the train back onto the track. It takes several minutes with lots of intense effort, but the reward of a shared smile is worth it.

Taylor is screeching and standing with clenched fists. An aide steps in among the children, holding up his arms with hands out, in a sign to stop. He says, "Oh no! We have a problem." All of the children stop to look. The aide gives Taylor a moment, and then Taylor says, "Give it back!" Now the problem is clear, and Taylor is using words rather than hitting.

During the process of helping a child to move up to higher levels, an adult must also sustain the capacities of earlier levels, and may need to utilize strategies from these levels. The child's ability for basic regulation and shared attention may fluctuate, and an adult may need to use strategies to support a reciprocal flow of interaction, even while encouraging the child to use higher levels of thinking. The adult's ability to remain calm and maintain steady regulation is critical. If a parent loses patience and shifts abruptly to a threat of punishment, the child's trust can be undermined.

Sasha, Peter and Hunter are building a playhouse out of large cardboard boxes. They are very busy running, climbing, and crawling through the boxes. At some point they start to grab, hit, and push. Sasha's mom comes near and says, "Whoa! What's going on here?" She gets each child to say what he is try-

ing to do, and by her sensitive listening, questioning, and reflecting is able to slow the pace of the interaction. This allows each child to better communicate his ideas and eventually agree on a new idea for the structure.

Each experience of dealing with distress together with a trusted adult contributes to a child's sense of self, the capacities for functioning within a range of emotions, and the ability to participate in shared relationships. Working at high levels of emotion is intense for both child and adult, but once completed, there is a shared sense of pride, joy, and accomplishment.

A Difficult Coaching Situation

Sometimes adults react to a child's behavior in ways that are not helpful. A parent may be distracting the child, giving mixed commands, demeaning the child, or otherwise acting in a disrespectful or even hurtful manner. Of course, professionals are aware of their duty to report truly abusive situations. Apart from that level of interaction, adults may often act out of their own desperation, misperceptions, or misguided attempts to help.

Fortunately, no single interaction is likely to cause enduring harm. Rather, it is the pattern of interactions that leads to a child's negative sense of self and escalating patterns of destructive behavior. In the moment of a challenging behavior, professionals will do their best to support a child, while at the same time maintaining a relationship of trust with a parent.

Mom is asking Victor to give her a particular car, and makes other requests in the context of building a road in play. Victor responds by ignoring the requests and becoming increasingly rigid and obstinate.

Mom is becoming frustrated and says sternly, "You better give me that now or you're not going to play computer tonight." And then, "You're acting like a brat. Do you want a time-out?" Victor seems to freeze and look sullenly at the floor. They seem to be at an impasse and the mother looks to the clinician for help. The clinician steps in and takes an active role.

For Step 1, the clinician might use statements such as, "Uh-oh. We have a problem here." "Oh my goodness, we need to figure this out." "Mom asked for the car and now she sounds unhappy." These statements are used to attune to the general level of distress. By using a low, slow, calm voice, the clinician can de-escalate the situation, while showing respect for the parent's role. The goal is to get the parent and child to slow down and begin to move up the developmental ladder together beginning with mutual attunement, emotional organization, and shared attention. If there is a relationship of trust with the clinician, then both Mom and Victor will anticipate moving forward in a positive direction.

For Step 2, to support Victor to move to Milestone 3, using purposeful gestures in interaction, the clinician moves toward Victor to support him in responding to Mom. The clinician says, "Mom wanted this one." With this high level of support, Victor only needs a small action to respond. He might just say, "No" or "Here, you give it to her." Or he might not say anything, but pick up the car and toss it toward her, or away from her. Any response moves him further into Milestone 3. Here, Victor put his hand over the desired car.

The clinician's role is to facilitate but not take over. The clinician can simultaneously coach Mom and Victor. "Oh Victor, this is hard. You don't want to give her that one." The clinician would watch and wait to see what Victor might do next, and then let him know that his words or actions are being noted and interpreted as meaningful.

"Let's see," the clinician says and gestures for Mom to come closer. "Mom, tell Victor what you are trying to do." Mom responds, "Victor, I am trying to put the three green cars together. That's why I want the green car." The clinician says, "Hmm, I wonder what we can do." Victor then hands Mom another car. Mom says, "That will work."

In this situation the objective is not necessarily to get Victor to comply, but rather to reestablish a functional and productive engagement. With practice, Mom can learn to avoid these confrontations by using strategies aligned to his functional level. Gradually their interaction can advance to sustained shared problem solving with multiple gestures in a row, and sharing ideas.

For Step 3, as Victor and Mom are now interacting and building the road and track together, there is an opportunity to fully recover. At the end of the session, the clinician can offer a simple statement such as, "We really had fun building the track today!" For some children, a more specific review may be indicated, such as, "It was really hard when Mom wanted the green car. But, you made a good trade by giving her the green truck. That was a good idea."

Later, mother and clinician would have time to reflect on this pattern of

interaction. It might be noted that the child has difficulty with motor plan-
ning and may become frustrated with trying to put track together. Through
this observation, Mom might develop a different perspective on Victor's lack
of compliance, both in this activity and others throughout the day.

Nearing Independence

A child who has gained skills in the functional developmental milestones may only need a small cue about her capability. A subtle reminder
of an adult presence, such as, "I'm watching!" or "I hear you!" can trigger
behavior within limits. A bit of encouragement, such as, "You'll be all
right," "You're getting there!" or "Keep trying" may be enough to help a
child to return to productive activity. Or an adult might want to remind
a child about resources available either in herself or others: "Remember
the rules" (already learned and mastered) or "I think there is someone
here that knows a lot about fixing things like that" or "There is a chart
over there that shows the steps."

An important part of independence is the ability to request help when
needed. By attuning to a child's experience, an adult can use a gesture or
word to affirm shared attention and availability for support. As a child
nears independence, an adult can use open-ended offers of help: "I see
you are really struggling with that. You can let me know if you need
help." Or just communicate this nonverbally by moving to be nearby.

Terence is afraid. He glances over to his teacher, who returns the look with
a reassuring nod. Terence takes a deep breath and relaxes. He has learned
to incorporate the meaning of that glance into his growing sense of self. He
unconsciously references all of the many previous experiences of regulation
and can draw upon them for self-control.

In the second step, helping, an adult can provide the appropriate level of
support through on-going and accurate assessments of a child's abilities.
In this way, children learn to function while experiencing strong feelings
and advance to higher developmental levels, within the safety of a caring
relationship.

Chapter 8

Step 3: Recover, Review, Repair

Jimmy becomes upset after he loses at kickball, and reacts by wildly throwing his gear and running off the field. After 15 minutes of individual support from Margaret, his coach, he finally calms down. Margaret says, "Whoof—that was so hard." Taking a deep breath, she models blowing out. After a moment, she asks, "Are you ready to go back to the team?" Jimmy looks down, and appears sad. They spend another 5 minutes talking before he picks up his gear and returns to be with his peers.

After a challenging behavior reaches a conclusion, an adult can help a child return to a baseline of emotional and behavioral equilibrium. He or she can be supported to review the incident, either at that time or later, and in some cases rehearse for similar situations that might arise in the future. Finally, the child is helped to repair any harm done to objects or relationships. Natural and planned consequences of actions are entwined with the interactions of help, recovery, review, and repair.

There are many benefits to supporting children to completely recover after an incident of behavioral challenge. Without full recovery, they tend to proceed through their day with irritability or sadness, difficulty attending, and perhaps continued unwanted behavior. They may be primed to erupt with the next provocation. Similarly, an adult—whether parent or clinician—can hold onto stress, anger, and resentment. A thoughtful process of recovery, review, and repair after each incident contributes to the overall strength in relationships and solidifies learning of new developmental capacities.

When to Make the Transition to Recovery

An adult must determine when to employ strategies focused on recovery. The process of helping may come to a natural conclusion and movement onward to recovery, review, and repair. In other interactions, an adult must take more leadership in shifting the focus from grappling with the problem at hand to moving on and distancing from the incident. Surprisingly, some children will make a sudden shift from despair to happiness. This behavior usually reflects the difficulty of tolerating negative feelings and a constriction in the ability to use others for support.

It is important that an adult persists in Step 2, helping, to achieve maximal learning when there is the opportunity to do so. An adult employs patience and persistence to encourage a child to keep moving up the developmental ladder as long as it is productive. As the problem-solving efforts in Step 2 reach the limits of a child's abilities, an adult can move to strategies of a lower level, so that Step 2 ends with both adult and child feeling successful, rather than a sense of failure and resignation. Not every issue may have been completely resolved but an adult accepts their joint effort to come to the best outcome possible. Then, this adult can decide to shift to strategies for closure.

Each situation is unique. In some instances, there may be valid constraints that necessitate the most rapid recovery possible. The family may be getting on an airplane or a parent may need to make an urgent phone call. In other situations, the adult simply decides that the time is not optimal for either adult or child to persist in a problem-solving interaction. There may be a confluence of stressors, and energies must be reserved for other challenges ahead. A parent or clinician may use discretion in determining how much to flex limits or how much effort to devote to shared problem solving before moving to recovery and resolution.

The timing of a transition from problem solving to recovery is also informed by an adult's knowledge of the child and their patterns of interaction. Some children become stuck and overfocused on a problem, while others may want to detach from a challenge prematurely. Sometimes a child will suddenly transition from distress to regular activities. Unfortunately, although such a recovery may appear welcome in the moment, the child is actually bypassing the critical process of being fully conscious of the experience and building capacities to deal with distress. An adult can help children refocus on the challenge and draw them into a longer period of self-reflection and awareness of their relationship with others.

There is overlap in the steps of attune, help, and recover. Adults can invite children to utilize their capacities to find acceptable solutions to their distress, including the capacity for organizing their own recovery.

Recovery

Recovery is the process of shifting from an experience of distress and the work of problem solving back to a state of calm regulation. Children are first helped to calm, and then challenged to work through their distress. When this process approaches completion, an adult may again help the child calm down and relax, but now with a focus on closure and moving on. Strategies for recovery include the following:

Provide Comfort Focused on a Relationship

A gentle touch or look, or a soft voice can express acceptance and recognition of the child's efforts at Step 2. "Okay, let's go back now" or "Okay, that's a good idea. Now, are you ready to try again?" Even if a child who does not understand the words may be soothed by the general tone of the interaction. Providing comfort does not relieve children from responsibility for their behavior, but it does convey that there is an underlying reliable foundation of care for them, even when their behavior has been unacceptable. A clinician or parent must be able to honestly forgive a child's transgressions in order to express genuine warmth, without anger or spite.

Use Sensory-Motor Supports to Help Calm

To help a child relax and transition back to previous activities, an adult can soothe a child using knowledge of their individual differences and sensory preferences. An adult may adjust the environment or provide sensory input such as jumping in place or singing a favorite tune. "Let's take a little walk and deliver these papers before we go back to class." While walking, they may climb some steps, march to a rhythm, or carry a heavy stack of papers.

Offer Questions About Readiness

An adult can guide a child by asking, "Are you okay now?" "Shall we go back?" "Are you ready?" This gives the child a chance to gather a self-appraisal and engage in a two-way exchange about readiness to move on. If the answer appears to be "no," an adult might ask, "Do you need another minute?" "I wonder what will help." Or, "I wonder how I can help you to feel ready."

Focus on a Child's Physiological State

Adults can help children be aware of how their body feels and what they might need to relax. An adult can comment on observations, such as, "Your fists are really tight," "You are sitting on the edge of your chair," "Wow, you are breathing hard," or "You look a little sweaty. Are you hot?" An adult can use general or more specific questions such as, "Are you feeling thirsty?" Some children will volunteer information, such as, "My head hurts," or can say what they need to help their physiological state, such as, "I need a cold drink" or "I need to go outside."

A child may use similes or metaphors: "I feel like I'm going to melt," "I feel like a volcano after it erupted," or "I am a hungry Tyrannosaurus." At a higher level, a child may connect physical feelings with emotions: "I am exhausted from being mad." It is helpful for an adult to be an active listener so that the child is encouraged to be reflective. An adult might note patterns of response and say, "I notice whenever you get mad, your stomach hurts." Or wonder if it hurts more or less than a previous time. Adult should provide opportunities for children to orient to their own feelings. It is not effective to simply label emotions; in fact, doing so may interrupt the important development of self-awareness.

Help a Child to Relax With Words and Gestures

An adult can help a child shift to recovery by using a simple gesture with sound effects such as, "Whoa! That was hard," while using a motion like shaking water off of hands, or blowing out noisily. Or model actions like, "Let's shake it out" and while shaking the whole body, or "Let's stomp it out" while stomping the feet, perhaps adding counting, a rhythm, or a song. If a child is scowling, grimacing, or holding tension, an adult can use a song that draws attention to each part of the face and body with a focus on relaxation, or use a mirror to help reference the signs of tension and then relaxation.

Broaden the Frame of Reference

Children in distress may be narrowly focused on their own feelings, desires, and perspective. Adults can help broaden their frame of reference to the larger environment and time frame. They can draw children's attention to distant sights and sounds, what others are doing, what they were doing before, or were planning to do. Adults can supply information, such as, "All the children are doing art now. You can go back and work on your project." Through broader awareness, children can consider their experience in the larger context with others' perspectives, and achieve a sense of relevance and balance in their experience. Rather than distraction, this places their experience in relation to others. After Pablo and Johnny scuffled, the teacher told Pablo, "Johnny went to the nurse. He needed a bandage. But he is okay. He'll be back in a few minutes." A broader focus can help a child to relax and can also lead to a process of reviewing past events.

Help Create a Plan for Transition

An adult can help begin the transition back to regular activities, perhaps by holding out a hand, or helping a child stand up. Or the adult can engage the child in making a plan, such as, "What can we do to get ready? We have 5 minutes until lunch." While providing opportunities for the child to initiate ideas, the adult might also offer some suggestions, such as, "Would you like me to go with you?" "Would you like me to sit by you when we go back?" "What will you have for lunch?" The discussion might become more elaborate with multiple steps, contingencies, and negotiations. A path to normalcy helps a child to reorient and recover.

Help a Child Resume Activities and Relationships With Grace

Adults can help children return to previous activities with a minimum of embarrassment or disgrace. Reentering a social group or activity can be facilitated so that the child experiences a minimum of negative attention or shame. The adult can protect the child's privacy by not revealing unnecessary information to others, and can help the child be accepted by modeling acceptance.

Use Symbols of Recovery

A child who has capacities for symbolic thinking can use this skill in recovery. A conclusion might include writing a note, where a child tells a peer, "I feel okay now." Or the child could indicate on a thermometer, drawing, or graph that his level of stress was back down to the bottom. A child could act out recovery symbolically, such as saying, "Camille [a doll] is ready to go back to class" or pretending to be a powerful character that is ready for a new challenge. By knowing a child's interests, an adult can encourage these types of symbolic expression.

Use Reflective and Abstract Thinking

In conversation, a child can be encouraged to talk about relative degrees of calmness and recovery, compare one experience with another, or reference a personal value about self-control.

> Ryan has been working with his therapist using a scale of 1 to 10 to describe different feelings. Now Ryan is struggling after feeling slighted in a peer interaction. As he begins to calm down, the clinician says, "I wonder how you are feeling now." Ryan says, "I'm down to a 5." The clinician responds, "Well, that's still a little high—sort of medium." "Yeah." "I wonder what else will help." "I could just go home." "Sorry, you can't go home until 3 o'clock. I wonder what else might help." "I just want to relax for a minute. Maybe I can sit in the reading corner until third period." "Okay, that's a good idea. You are finding some good ways to calm down." Ryan adds, "Yeah, I am learning to tune in to my inner peace."

Ryan is becoming very reflective. He is concerned about nonviolence and animal rights. He is learning to use his capacities for abstract thinking to form concepts that support his behavioral and emotional regulation.

Review

After working through a challenging behavior, a child may be able to reconsider what has occurred, and through this review, solidify learning, as well as arrive at a more relaxed and secure level of resolution.

Russell was angry that his mother had left the room. The clinician had inter-rupted his play and asked his mother to step out. When she returned, Russell looked down and would not talk to her. The therapist spoke to him directly, saying, "Russell, I know you didn't like it when I asked Mom to leave. Now she is back, and I won't ask her to leave again. She is going to stay here with you." Russell looked up at the stranger, and then at his mom, and was ready to continue playing.

Strategies for review include the following:

Provide Information for Clarity

It is sometimes helpful to recount the sequence of events of a difficult inter-change immediately after it ends. Reviewing can ensure that there is a shared understanding of what has occurred, and help draw a connection from ini-tial steps to the conclusion. An adult might use phrases such as, "That was a big surprise when the ball hit you in the face!" "Do you remember what you did next?" "Yes, and then Mark kicked you too." "Mike had to help you stop by holding you." Through such a review, adult and child have a chance to slowly recall each step along the way including actions and feelings, correct misperceptions, and consider various perspectives. In addition, the adult can help the child appreciate the effects of their actions on others. By the end, a child may be able to experience a more complete sense of closure.

Reflect at Higher Levels

Children may be able to postulate multiple reasons and feelings for their or others' behaviors; they may reflect on levels of intensity of feelings, or even consider behaviors in light of their own values.

Postpone the Review

An adult may judge that a child's regulation is quite fragile and anticipate that reviewing what has just happened might cause her to experience more distress. In that case, the adult may want to simply help the child recover and postpone the review to another time when the child's regulation is more stable and secure. Later, that evening or the next day, when the child is calm or rested, the adult may choose to review the key points of what occurred.

Put Behaviors in Context to Help Discern Patterns

During review, adults can help children recognize patterns in their reactions and behaviors. Adults might help them recall how they felt when something happened and then what actions they took. For example, "When Jared called you stupid, how did you feel? What did you do?" Then an adult might ask a broader question, such as, "When someone calls you names, how do you feel? What do you usually do when you feel that way?" By thinking about feelings and actions from a distant perspective, children may be able to see similarities and connections, and group like feelings and actions together.

An adult may be able to encourage children to further elaborate on the sequence of feelings and actions, both for themselves and others, and consider other possible responses. This opens the door for problem solving, planning, and negotiation. It is more effective when an adult does not rush to label emotions, make connections, or offer different options, but instead provides an opportunity for children to arrive at these ideas themselves.

Rehearse

In addition to reviewing an incident, it may be helpful to consider possible outcomes for a similar situation in the future. A conversation about hypothetical problems might occur after an event, or at a later time such as before a similar situation.

> *Johnny was throwing the ball into the basketball hoop with his dad. He was rarely successful. After six failures in a row, he lost his temper and threw the ball over the fence. The next day, he wanted to play basketball with his dad again. His dad said, "Johnny, remember what happened yesterday?" They proceeded to review the sequence of events, how they both felt, and how they had to work together to retrieve the ball and apologize to the neighbor. Dad asked with an optimistic tone, "What will happen today if the ball doesn't go in?"*

Children may be able to provide a rational scenario for their upcoming behaviors. However, they may not be able to think logically for these highly charged situations, and their responses will reflect a lower level of functioning, including magical thinking or strategies that would be ineffective. An interaction with an adult provides an opportunity to practice thinking at gradually higher levels of reflection and problem solving. Even without a thorough and rational plan, these conversations can help children modulate their emotional responses in a subsequent challenging situation.

> *In response to Dad's question, Johnny gave a series of colorful responses. They both smiled as Johnny suggested first, "I am going to shoot 10 baskets in a row!" Dad asked again: "That sounds really good, but . . . what if you don't?" Johnny said, "Then I will get a cannon and shoot the ball and make it bounce off the roof and then go in!" Dad smiled at this creative thinking. "Wow! That's quite an idea!" Dad shifted his tone and continued, "I just hope we don't have to get it out of the neighbor's yard again." Johnny looked away, and then got the ball and said, "Let's go!"*
>
> *Predictably, Johnny again had difficulty getting the ball through the hoop. They celebrated the near successes but after numerous misses, Johnny and his Dad were able to reflect on the disappointment: "This is hard, like yesterday." Johnny wanted to continue and they persisted a little longer. Finally Johnny said, "Let's play something else" and went calmly inside.*

Sometimes in rehearsal, a child will offer a response such as, "Then I will hit him really hard." Hearing this, an adult might counter, "If you hit him, then what will I do?" Or, an adult might say, "I wonder what else you might do." Through talking about their hypothetical reactions, children are often able to better control their actual responses. When a trusted adult listens to their ideas and honors their efforts, children can often tolerate more difficult emotions.

When a child has capacities for logical and reflective thinking, it is useful to have a conversation in which an adult encourages the child to think about the past and anticipate the future, including actions and feelings. The adult and child can negotiate about a problem, and discuss possible outcomes for themselves and others.

Focus on a Child's Goals

Review and rehearsal discussions might focus on goals from the child's perspective. "I wonder what you were trying to do." "I wonder how many baskets would make you feel good." Review and rehearsal, either immediate or delayed, provide opportunities to slow down events that happen quickly or simultaneously.

Repair

An important aspect of closure from a challenging behavior is taking responsibility and learning how to repair the hurt caused by one's actions. Like other aspects of growth, learning to repair occurs in gradual developmental steps, until it becomes a part of a child's character. Repair helps to restore and can even strengthen relationships as amends are made and forgiveness is received. Children who experience the full circle of contrition, repair, and pardon grow to be gracious toward others who may transgress against them.

Strategies for repair include the following:

Offer Information About the Result of Behavior

The earliest step in learning to be responsible for one's actions is to become aware of the result of one's behavior and choices. For this, an adult can draw attention to the damage caused to objects or people. Initially, children may look and listen and yet not understand the connection between their actions and the outcome; but as they learn about cause and effect through many experiences, they begin to recognize the connection between their actions and the result. Only gradually do they perceive how their actions can make someone else feel.

Natural Consequences

Natural consequences are the direct result of a child's actions. A child who breaks a toy can no longer play with that toy. A child who is late getting ready may miss the beginning of a party. If a child hits a friend, the friend will be sad and may choose not to play anymore. Children experience natural consequences for their actions throughout the day. An adult can choose whether to help resolve the consequence or let it stand. If a child spills her milk, does the parent refill the glass or say, "Sorry, no more milk for lunch"? If a toy is broken, is it replaced, or not? The answer of course depends on the situation, and parents must constantly find the balance between shielding their children from hurt feelings and disappointments, and letting them suffer the negative consequences of their behavior.

In making decisions about consequences, parents can be guided by developmental level and the child's capacity to understand the impact of their actions. At early milestones, children only know whether their actions result in feelings of pleasure or displeasure. As they develop capacities at Milestones 3 and 4, they are more aware of how their actions cause others to be happy or unhappy. At Milestones 5 and 6, they are learning concepts of right and wrong, good and bad, and can experience a more profound sense of guilt for their errant behaviors.

Consequences not only reinforce an action by their resulting benefit or detriment but can also provide a way to redeem a sense of guilt. A child can develop a sense of a justice and fairness when outcomes are commensurate with actions. A balanced approach to consequences creates security in the limits provided by an adult relationship. Relationships can also be strengthened as an adult empathizes with children's sadness as they must endure the negative feelings resulting from the effects of their actions.

Less Natural Consequences

Consequences can also be imposed to reinforce learning. A consequence, sanction, or punishment may include taking away a privilege or requiring some action to be accomplished. In order to be effective, a child must understand the relationship between the actions and the consequence. Ideally, an adult and child would create a plan and have a shared understanding about specific consequences for specific behaviors ahead of time. Such a plan can help a child accept the consequence in the moment.

Consequences may occur immediately or later. Generally, children at the earlier milestones will learn best from immediate consequences. Children with higher capacities are able to recall the behavior and make a connection to a consequence at a later time. However, the ability to make this association decreases with time. Consequences are also more effective when they are related to the offense. A child who fights over a certain toy may not be allowed to play with that toy for some period of time. However, if the child breaks the toy, and then is not permitted to engage in some other activity, it is more difficult for a child to appreciate the lesson. More powerful lessons are learned when a consequence is immediate and directly related to the offense.

Unfortunately, when consequences are delayed or unrelated, children may simply feel persecuted or may draw inaccurate conclusions about why they must suffer the punishment. Challenging behaviors may escalate if consequences are not aligned with a child's developmental capacities, or may undermine a sense of trust between adult and child. Children who feel misunderstood, shamed, or rejected can become despondent, withdrawn, anxious, irritable, or aggressive. Spanking and corporal punishment also harm the bonds of trust between adult and child. Although harsh responses may seem to achieve the desired outcome in the moment, they do not contribute in a positive way to a child's development or healthy relationships.

Mechanical Repair: Fix What Was Broken

A very straightforward way to help children recognize consequences and correct misdeeds is to repair an object that they have broken or to clean up a mess that they have made. Initially, a child may need maximal support to do a simple step such as picking something up off the floor. Gradually the complexity of the repair can expand. A child and adult may work together to clean up, or try to glue and tape a broken object. Later, a parent may state a required outcome, like, "Sweep up all the glass and make sure none is left." With experience, a child learns to anticipate possible solutions, and may need only a prompt such as, "You'd better fix it." Later, a child will be able to initiate and complete the repairs independently without any direction.

Replace What Was Damaged

When an object cannot be repaired, a child may be able to supply a substitute. This may involve creating something, relinquishing something the child owns, or earning money to buy a replacement. It is important for adults to consider proportionality in setting the expectations for such consequences. The goal is that children learn about responsibility and how they can feel proud about healing the hurt they have caused. Overly painful consequences, such as asking them to give up a prized possession, do not provide the good feelings that motivate them to take responsibility to repair their error on their own.

Apologies

An apology is a symbolic gesture to repair a relationship after a disruption. There are different stages of apology, based on a child's awareness of wrong-doing. Very young children appreciate others' feelings and may do something to comfort someone that is hurt or upset. Before long, children begin to appreciate the connection between their actions and another's feelings. Forced or coerced apologies lack the true sentiment of remorse and only serve to reinforce adult authority. Rather than insist on an apology, a parent may continue to help the child develop awareness of other's feelings.

Do a Good Deed for Others

Another form of symbolic repair is to do a good deed for others. If it is impossible to directly repair an object or relationship, children can restore their integrity by giving their time and energies to help others, perhaps in a way that relates to their challenging behavior. An adult and child could create a unique activity that the child could do to help a parent, sibling, or others, or the choices could be generic. For example, a set of activities are written on slips of paper and placed in a jar. These might say, "Do something nice for a neighbor." "Help a stranger." "Spend one hour volunteering." "Visit an elderly person." These options could be prepared ahead of time as a family activity. It is important that doing a good deed is approached with an attitude of repentance and repair, rather than as an onerous punishment. Doing a good deed supports a sense of pride and honor in belonging in relationship and community.

Benefits of Recovery, Review, and Repair

Numerous benefits are derived from taking the time for a thorough process of recovery, review and repair. By working through a challenging behavior to completion, children gain respect for others, increase self-esteem, and gain a sense of responsibility for their actions. Through innumerable instances of conflict and repair, they learn that it is possible to err and still be accepted, and become invested in building relationships. Each child's unique pattern of recovery provides that child with strategies for lifelong success in the resolution of conflicts with others.

PART III

THE LONG-TERM PLAN

Chapter 9

Creating a Plan

Jordan bites suddenly with no apparent cause.
Katie panics with any change in routine.
Gabriel erupts in anger whenever he loses a game.
Zeke draws violent pictures and has no friends.

After responding in the moment of a challenging behavior, a parent, teacher, or clinician can take time to reflect and discern patterns in a child's behavior and interactions. By recognizing common factors in these situations, and with awareness of the impact of individual differences, and the history of interactions in specific relationships, an adult can correlate the unwanted behaviors with specific areas of developmental weakness and create a plan to improve those areas.

A developmental framework is used to identify the underlying functional emotional milestones that are delayed or constricted. Rather than a narrow focus on teaching a predetermined desired response or rule for a specific situation, a developmental approach creates opportunities for children to expand their capacity to interact at gradually more advanced levels of thinking and communicating while experiencing greater intensities of emotion.

A key benefit of a long-term plan is that learning interactions can occur when a child is not at the peak of distress. Strategies can be implemented throughout the day during the natural flow of events and during play. With a focus on specific types of emotional exchanges, an adult can be more aware of opportune times to take advantage of a situation and draw out the interaction. In addition, the adult may add activities or change circumstances to offer more opportunities to practice the identified developmental capacities.

A long-term plan has two parts: (1) to deduce the pattern in challenging behavior and interactions and recognize the corresponding deficits in the functional developmental milestones that underlie the behavior, and (2) to create opportunities to practice and expand this capacity, utilizing specific strategies tailored to that child, his individual differences, and unique relationships.

Identifying the Goal Milestone

A search for patterns in challenging behavior focuses on how specific behaviors occur over a broad time frame, including examination of a child's developmental history, relationship history, and the parents' own history, thoughts, and perspectives. It is important to recognize that all human behavior is linked to emotional experience, and that a behavior that seems random always has a connection to some affective energy. Finding a pattern is the result of reviewing the behavior, when it occurs, with whom, and the sequence of events, with an interest in a child's overall emotional life.

A child's day is always full of drama, challenges, discoveries, and learning. Almost continuously, children are challenged, or challenge themselves, to conquer more, to explore, and thus to learn. Parents and other adults provide support to temper those challenges. An unwanted behavior may be the result of a mismatch between challenges and abilities in a particular moment or by creating unmanageable stress over hours or days. Stress can reach a tipping point when tiredness, hunger, or too much or too little of a particular sensory experience manifests in a behavioral breakdown. Stressors may include new fears or fantasies, unspoken disappointments, or misunderstandings. For a child with autism or developmental challenges, the signals of stress and an impending disintegration may not be obvious.

Challenging behaviors may be a marked deviation from a previous pattern. Regressions often occur after significant events in a child's life: moves, change in classroom, or other changes in the schedule. If there is a sudden change in behavior, a clinician should inquire, along with the parent, What has changed in this child's life? This may require a conversation with the classroom teacher or caregiver. A careful evaluation, with a high level of suspicion, should be done to consider possible health issues. Could the child have a hidden cause of pain—headache, earache, or toothache? Is sleep being disrupted? Unfortunately, another cause for regression is abuse. It may be emotional abuse, such as being bullied at school. At other times there may be verbal, physical, or sexual assault. In every instance, regressions must be thoroughly investigated to try and determine the cause. A thorough assessment leads to a more accurate understanding of the child and more effective intervention. Some children are able to report what is distressing to them if simply given the opportunity.

By putting problematic behaviors into a full context, a hypothesis can be formed about the possible contributing factors. Then, by utilizing the developmental framework, a clinician can identify how a behavioral challenge reflects deficits in specific milestones.

It is often possible to identify one specific developmental milestone as the priority for immediate intervention. The lowest milestone with significant constrictions may be the most critical to address, even when a child has capacities at higher milestones. While focused on one milestone, a child's development in other milestones and in sensory-motor, cognitive, or language skills may also be addressed, as interactions utilize all of a child's developmental capacities simultaneously.

Writing Short-Term Goals

Goals are always written from a positive perspective of what children will do, rather than what they will not do. For example, "Jason will remain calm during circle time at school, with his aide sitting at a distance, 4 out of 5 days per week." Knowing that Jason is often overexcited and disruptive during circle time, the behavioral challenge is implied rather than stated explicitly. Or, for Robbie, who would spit and struggle for long periods when upset, a goal might be, "Robbie will recover from distress through reciprocal interaction with his mother within 15 minutes on more than 50% of occasions."

The link between a troublesome behavior and developmental skill can also be described with the phrase, "in order to" and then describing the purpose for the goal for adaptive functioning. For example, "Katie will construct a story with a logical sequence in pretend play with beginning, middle, and end, around a theme of fear and bravery, with an adult play partner providing minimal support, in order to increase her ability to tolerate situations that provoke anxiety." Sub-objectives might include the ability to extend the play to include a variety of scary ideas, use a variety of solutions, take on various roles, and over a longer time period and to heightened levels of emotion. Progress might be documented in her response to anxiety-provoking situations in real life. Using the phrase, "in order to . . . " is a reminder to consider how the immediate explicit goals are related to long-term goals and function, even into adulthood.

Beginning with a broad stem, specific modifiers can be added to specify the feelings involved, relationships, time and place, and can include the level of support needed. Each goal should be objective and measurable in some way, often in frequency, number, or duration. The following are the broad goals and stems for goals for each Milestone.

Milestone 1: Shared Attention and Regulation

The broad goal is the ability to feel safe and secure in a wide variety of environments, and to take an interest in new experiences and in people. The ability to modulate responses to various sensory experiences, in conjunction with human interaction, creates shared attention. With mastery of this capacity, a child has a generally positive emotional tone, and can sustain attention within a broad range of levels of arousal and excitement.

- Child will attend to people and activities (in a specific environment; near or distance).
- Child will remain calm.
- Child will recover from distress.

Milestone 2: Engagement

The broad goal is the ability to form relationships based on mutual trust and affection. With mastery of this milestone, a child derives pleasure from being in special relationships and has a strong capacity for love and caring. Relationships become sources of comfort and contribute to resiliency and a capacity to tolerate distress. In combination with higher capacities, a child can experience joy in symbolic representations of love and to appreciate many forms of beauty.

- Child will participate in a shared activity, enjoying the engagement.
- Child will respond with pleasure with intentional behaviors to continue the interaction.
- Child can be comforted through interaction with care provider.
- Child will anticipate familiar games.

Milestone 3: Two-Way Communication

The broad goal is to be able to interact with purpose, to distinguish and utilize a range of different emotional gestures, to initiate interactions, to be curious and explore, and to respond in a flow of reciprocal interactions.

- Child will respond using purposeful actions, sounds, words, or gestures to indicate purposeful intentions (beyond needs).
- Child will initiate interactions by using purposeful actions, sounds, words, or gestures.
- Child will use purposeful actions, sounds, words, or gestures in reciprocal interactions to indicate intentions (while demonstrating an increasing range of emotions, including curiosity, frustration, joy, sadness, or fear).
- Child will recover from distress through back-and-forth interaction.

Milestone 4: Complex Communication

The broad goal is to be able to engage in complex, sustained interactions while reading and responding to another's emotional cues; to work toward a shared goal, to ask for help, offer help, give praise, apologize, and comfort others. The child pursues goals with persistence and celebrates accomplishments with communal pride in teamwork and collaboration.

- Child will sustain a continuous flow of co-regulated social interactions, using multiple gestures in a row.
- Child will respond with purposeful gestures or words to another's feelings (specify) within the context of a sustained social interaction.
- Child will sustain an interaction to consider options, consider others' perspectives, and effectively resolve a problem.
- Child will work toward a common goal, seeking and offering help.

Milestone 5: Symbolic Thinking

A broad goal is to be able to create and use symbolic ideas in play, art, and language to express a wide range of emotional experiences; to use symbols to express wishes, feelings, and ideas in regard to the present, past, and future.

- Child will use novel play ideas demonstrating imagination and creativity (not imitation or scripted).
- Child will engage in symbolic pretend play with others, incorporating another's ideas into the pretend play.
- Child will utilize magical solutions to problems in play.
- Child will utilize reality-based solutions to problems in play.
- Child will use words or other symbols to express feelings, wishes, and intentions.
- Child will recover from distress using symbolic or magical ideas.

Milestones 6–9: Logical, Comparative, and Abstract Thinking

A broad goal for the higher milestones is to be able to use logical, multi-causal, comparative, reflective, and abstract thinking; the ability to understand motivations and emotional consequences for self and others, to plan and predict, to form opinions, to judge right from wrong, and to discern humor, deceit, and fraud; to reflect with humility, forgive themselves and others, appreciate kindness, and be grateful.

- Child will connect two or more ideas logically in discussion or play.
- Child will respond logically to "why" questions regarding his own and others' actions.
- Child will build logically on another's play idea.
- Child will create dramas with a beginning, middle, and end (sequencing of ideas in logical order).
- Child will plan drama before enacting the ideas.
- Child will conceptualize the big picture with multiple interacting factors, rather than focusing only on details or using fragmented thinking (jumping from one idea to another).
- Child will describe details, including ascribing feelings to characters or people, in big-picture scenarios, and identify motivations.
- Child will predict feelings and actions of others (characters in pretend and in real life).
- Child will reflect logically on own feelings and others' feelings after a drama, or real-life event.
- Child will express opinions, negotiate, and compromise.

Higher-Level Thinking

- Child will describe multiple possible feelings, intentions, or perspectives as causes or consequences for an event.
- Child will describe degrees or levels of emotion in regard to an experience (self or others).
- Child will reflect using personal standards or values.

Each of these stem goals is then combined with modifiers to make it specific and measurable, as suggested in Table 1.

Emotion

Each goal can specify the emotional area of focus. With advancing skills, a child begins to organize and function across a broader range of emotions, and then utilizes emotional ideas in a symbolic way.

Liam loses a race and throws his jersey in the trash. "I'm a bad runner." Dad is unsure how to console him, while being truthful about his running skills. Liam often becomes self-critical when he does not live up to the high stan-

Table I.   Modifiers for Goals

Emotion	Context		Level of Support	Frequency
	Relationship	Location		
Calm, except when stressed—tired, hungry, ill			Intensive physical/sensory-motor support and/or intensive verbal and nonverbal support	Occasionally, intermittently 5–10% of opportunities # per hour or day or week # minutes (duration)
Calm, even when stressed—tired, hungry, ill	With • parents • familiar adults • classroom aide • teacher • siblings • one peer • two peers • a group of peers • strangers • others	• Home • School, classroom • School, lunchtime • School, recess • After-school program • Park • Store • Community • Organized sports • Other	Persistent and/or predictable support In proximity From a distance	Usually >50% of opportunities # per hour or day or week # minutes (duration)
Specific affect states: • excited/happy • angry • sad • anxious • frustrated • disappointed and/or • surprised			High affect, gestural, language, and sensorimotor supports Structure and scaffolding In proximity From a distance	Consistently 80–90% of opportunities # per hour or day or week # minutes (duration)
Specific emotional themes			Spontaneously and independently	
Full range of emotions				

dards he has set for himself. A goal is written: "Liam will be able to reflect about degrees of disappointment and sadness, in conversations with Mom and Dad, about real-life events, with predictable support, twice a week." With this focus, activities were devised to use visual representations of a rating scale that helped Liam to discern levels of distress. Dad challenged Liam to think honestly about his abilities and emotions. Liam quickly began to use this scale when reflecting on emotions, both for himself and for others' experiences.

Relationships

Goals may be defined in regard to the ability to interact within specific close relationships, or with distant relationships, adults, peers, groups, or strangers. For example, "Mary will engage in reciprocal interaction in a pleasurable game with a parent [or sibling, or peer]." "Johnny will seek help from a peer [or parent or teacher] when frustrated."

Clyde always started conversations with adults with, "What kind of car do you drive?" Clyde was fascinated by cars and enjoyed talking about them in detail, but unfortunately it often became a one-sided monologue. A goal was created: "Clyde will use big-picture thinking, involving multiple interacting factors, rather than focusing only on details, while talking with adults, with minimal support, on three out of four occasions." To accomplish this goal, Clyde and his clinician created many activities to help him increase his awareness of others' perspectives, interests, and especially feelings. Gradually, Clyde was able to connect his interest in cars to interest in other aspects of a new acquaintance. After improving his ability to think more broadly, he also was able to have more success with peer relationships, as well as academic work.

Location

Goals may specify in which location a skill will be used. Because each location presents a unique set of sensory variables, may be relatively familiar or unfamiliar. The location may include who is present, the time of day, whether it is before or after another event, or other descriptors of the environment, in addition to the type of location or a specific location.

Level of Support

Goals can describe the level of support that a child may need, from physical assistance, to intensive support at close range, to moderate or minimal cues at a distance.

> *Brady usually enjoys walking up and down several aisles before he and Mom leave the store. Today Mom is in a hurry and needs to skip this ritual. Mom says, "I know you want to stay, but today we have to go straight out the door." Typically, in this situation she would have to carry a screaming child out the door. Today, Brady protests with a look of anger and gestures to the aisles. He tries to pull Mom toward the back of the store. Mom says slowly, "Brady, not today. We're going straight to the car." Brady squirms and utters an angry whine. Mom says again, "I know it's hard to leave, but we are going now." Mom takes his hand and says, "Let's go." Brady stomps his feet going out the door.*

A goal they are working on is, "Brady will use purposeful actions, sounds, words, or gestures in reciprocal interactions with Mom to indicate intentions while feeling angry or frustrated, with intensive sensory-motor and language support, on four out of five occasions." Here, Brady and his mother have exchanged affective cues in looks, vocal tones, and actions, which have helped to modulate his intense feelings. For weeks, they have practiced using back-and-forth gestures to communicate around many smaller frustrations. Now, Mom is confident that Brady can manage his distress through their interaction.

The capacity for independent skills, such as the ability to tolerate delayed gratification or to be persistent in a solitary pursuit, are appreciated as extensions of capacities for emotional regulation initially learned through co-regulated interactions with others. Later goals might state, "Johnny will persist in problem solving independently for 10 minutes before seeking help." "Sue will play independently for 5 minutes while waiting for Mom's attention."

Recovery from distress has a similar progression: "Sam will be calmed from distress by active support from mother or father, without use of distraction, 5 out of 10 occasions." The progression from active interaction to independence is incremental, but always founded on previous success within a trusting relationship. Later, "Sam will be able to recover from distress by requesting and utilizing a self-calming technique, and will return to work independently, 50% of occasions."

Frequency

A treatment plan creates goals and benchmarks of progress toward those goals. It is usually necessary to construct a quantifiable measure of change for each goal. Because development involves complex social interactions and does not follow a linear progression but rather transformations with periods of greater disorganization and then reorganization,

Please and Thank You

Learning manners occurs at all levels of development but with different levels of meaning. The word "please" can be taught in a rote way in conjunction with a request. Similarly, "thank you" can be connected with receiving a desired object. A child also learns the meaning of these words by being the recipient of requests and thanks. After many repetitions, the words gather more meaning because of their association with particular emotional experiences. A child can then use the words to influence interactions. A child who asks plaintively, "Pleeeease" with a sorrowful expression and pleading body language may be more successful in his request. The word becomes part of a complex dynamic of balance of control within a caring relationship.

"Thank you" may simply be associated with a happy feeling at first, but with developmental growth, a child gains greater awareness of the perspective of others. Then, a child may have a deeper sense of gratitude and truly appreciate another's generosity. The ability to use polite manners in a genuine way is linked to overall development. With advancing developmental capacities, a child is able to use manners as a natural part of caring relationships. Families place different priorities on the use of these words as well as other manners associated with their family culture.

it is difficult to track progress with a specific measurable skill. However, goals can be defined with a combination of qualitative and quantitative factors, and measured in terms of quantity, frequency or duration.

Strategies for Practice

After identifying the goal milestone, a long-term plan involves creating opportunities to practice skills at the goal level with strategies that are specific to the milestone target and tailored for a specific child and family. Development occurs in small, incremental steps through a process of engagement, challenge, a child's discovery of solutions, and repeated practice.

Intervention aims for the just-right level of challenge. Children seek out and learn through novel and exciting experiences if they are not overwhelmed by anxiety or frustration. By engaging in interactions that encourage them to expand beyond their range of comfort and familiarity, they have opportunities to discover new ways to interact and learn to broaden their functional capacities. Some children have a narrow range between calm composure and overwhelming distress. The key to progress is helping a child to gradually expand this range, through closely attuned interactions and practice.

A developmental behavioral plan includes strategies to practice in interactions throughout the day, including during events of daily life, structured activities, and free play. Free play or Floortime offers an enjoyable and effective way to practice interactions across an emotional range, and achieve the just-right balance of comfort and challenge. Free, spontaneous, child-led play offers unique opportunities for a child to learn and is always an important element of the long-term plan.

Plan for Rest and Breaks

Even when engaged in pleasurable learning, children need periods of rest. Mental rest may involve physical activity or specific sensory input. It is possible to create breaks that are times of productive engagement, rather than time for self-absorption. By knowing a child's interests and sensory-motor profile, an adult can fashion interactions that are relaxing and simultaneously sustain a warm relationship.

Children also enjoy and have a right to time alone. While it is optimal to frequently engage them in interactions, it is also important to respect and encourage growing independence. When children rock alone in the corner or repetitively flick a piece of paper, it is difficult to judge whether they are experiencing pleasure or an uncomfortable compulsion. A long-term plan can attempt to make solitary activities more meaningful as well as introduce children to other activities that they may choose for relaxation, such as listening to music, reading, or exercise. As they grow into adulthood, these independent activities and privacy will contribute to overall quality of life.

Over a broader time frame, life's challenges must be balanced by calming, soothing, and nurturing exchanges. When children experience increased challenges in daily life, school, or clinical intervention, they will need additional time for relaxation and activities that utilize developmental capacities that are already strong. An adult may need to consider how to revise a schedule to create this balance, and how to provide more comforting interactions at other times of the day.

Plans for Milestone 1

Escalation

Damien is very excited by the special event in class. He screeches and pounds his legs. Suddenly, he stands up darts out the door. He pushes over little Marta, who happens to be in his way. His one-on-one aide runs after him.

Sometimes behaviors occur suddenly, with rapid escalation from zero to 100. A slight change in routine or environment may trigger huge reactions. In the moment, an adult can only attune to the extreme level of excitement or distress, and try to help the child calm down, while keeping everyone safe.

Withdrawal

Most of the time, Steve enjoys activities with his family and does well at school. Despite his diagnosis of autism, he plays in a little soccer group once a week and is learning piano. However, when Steve is overwhelmed, he curls up in a ball on the floor or crawls under a table at school, closes his eyes, and chews his shirt collar. He sometimes hums to himself and does not respond to efforts to entice him to come out.

Damien has a pattern of sudden escalation, and Steve has a pattern of withdrawal. In both extremes, the child needs practice and support to build capacities at Milestone 1. Although Steve has some higher capacities, when a child has a pattern of becoming so anxious or upset that they become self-absorbed and unable to interact, the priority is to increase capacities at Milestone 1, basic regulation and shared attention.

To build capacities for regulation and shared attention requires a commitment of time to provide consistent adult companionship throughout the day. By learning to read a child's cues, an adult is better able to support a child through smaller stresses as well as major upsets. Gradually, a child will rely on that adult to help, and the escalations will not be as often or as fast.

Strategies for Practice at Milestone 1

- Continual assessment and remediation of triggering factors where possible
- Consistent adult presence to read a child's cues and provide support
- Note signs of impending distress and act proactively
- Soothe through activities that build shared attention

Plans for Milestone 2

Success with behavioral development is founded on trust and engagement with others, created by shared experiences of pleasurable interactions. It can be very difficult for a parent to engage a child who is acting in ways that feel like rejection, or are hurtful or frankly traumatic. Yet a patient, persistent focus on discovering ways to share warmth is the basis for higher-level abilities.

Diego loves to play games on the computer. When he comes home from school, he goes directly to the computer. It is difficult for anyone to talk or interact with him while he is playing. When he has to stop, he becomes very upset, and screams loudly enough to disturb the neighbors. Diego can only be calmed by either eating a favorite food or playing a solitary electronic game. His parents cannot describe any fun activities that they currently enjoy doing together with Diego.

Diego has significant deficits in Milestone 2. A complete assessment reveals that although Diego has strong cognitive and language skills, he lacks friendships and may be somewhat depressed.

The goal for Diego is to increase the depth of warm feelings in relationships with his family and peers, and his capacity to engage in pleasurable interactions with others. The plan includes learning more about Diego's favorite games, as well as pleasurable activities that he enjoyed with his parents in the past. All available information about his interests and sensory-motor profile is used to create opportunities that might entice Diego to interact and enjoy the social engagement.

When a child engages in solitary play, it may be possible to join the play in a manner that makes it more exciting and pleasurable. By respectfully following a child's lead, an adult can add to the child's enjoyment, rather than being experienced as intrusive and disruptive. At other times, it is more successful to offer new opportunities for interaction. For example, Diego's parents might be able to stop on the way home from school to do a different activity together. As the child's repertoire of enjoyable activities increases, he will seek them out in preference over solitary play, and he is also building a warm relationship that can support him in distress.

In a typical hectic life, compounded by the special needs of a child with developmental challenges, parents might need to make a special effort to find times for relaxation with their family. A clinician can help to highlight the value of this family time, and guide them in activities that are fun and engaging, yet not stressful or demanding for a child. A family might enjoy walking together in the evening, playing games, or reading aloud.

It is the beginning of the school year, and the daily schedule and routine have all changed. Gavin always likes to wear soft clothes, and today he is insisting on wearing his pajamas to school. Mom is as stressed as Gavin about getting him to school, and is feeling a need to take charge. Gavin is refusing to change.

Sometimes a direct confrontation occurs between a child's desires and a parent's authority. The situation can escalate as a child becomes more stubborn and defiant, until even a patient parent reaches a point of anger and exasperation. Stepping back from the conflict can provide time to regain a sense of connection, and perspective on priorities.

Gavin's mom took a deep breath and decided to take another few minutes to share a warm understanding moment with Gavin. She talked about the favorite character on his pajamas and how they could read a story about him at bedtime. She then took out several acceptable clothing options and allowed him to make a choice. Eventually he went to school happily wearing sweat pants and a top that also had his favorite character.

When a child frequently escalates to high levels of anger or other distress, a parent must call upon a high level of patience and empathy to support their child. Over time, a child will come to rely on their calmness to buffer their own strong feelings.

Sometimes, a child is left alone to recover from distress, or given a sensory activity to do by themselves. A parent may feel that they are ineffective in helping their child in that moment. Some adults are so uncomfortable with a child's actions that they also withdraw or avoid interaction. They may literally stay away from home, have the child in programs all day, or simply go into another room to avoid a confrontation. However, this pattern bypasses important opportunities for building a close relationship. Often the child is unable to reach a truly satisfying resolution to the initial problem, and may simply become detached from their intent. Plans can focus on helping parents to find ways to effectively help calm their child, and increase warmth in the relationship.

In some instances, a parent makes rather dramatic and sudden shifts in approach from nurturing and patient, to demanding and threatening, and even to pleading and apologizing. A parent might avoid setting a limit and make offers, bribes, or promises. If the child does not accept these offers, the parent may get frustrated and go back to being a stern disciplinarian. A pattern of wide swings in emotional tone are exhausting for both parent and child. A treatment plan involves finding the small steps to success, while respecting parents' authority and building sensitive flexibility. By recognizing patterns of reaction to stress in both a child and parent, a clinician is able to help reframe the challenge, modify expectations, and help a parent react with patience and empathy.

Strategies for Practice at Milestone 2

- Create opportunities to interact in fun activities
- Join in a child's play and interests
- Match activities to the child's sensory-motor profile
- Set aside relaxing time to be together
- Use empathy and patience while teaching limits
- Use relationships to soothe a child in distress

Plans for Milestone 3

Mom knew Teddy only liked a particular yellow cup and was careful to always have it available. Teddy's therapist suggested, "Let's try a green cup that is almost the same." They supported Teddy through his surprise, worry, and protest, with empathetic interactions, while also maintaining an attitude that it really was okay. Parent and clinician stayed relaxed, created some playful interactions with the cup, and helped Teddy to overcome his initial worry and resistance.

When parents have worked intensively to develop a warm relationship and soothe their child through distress, it can be daunting to present a new challenge or impose a new limit. Parents may have a pattern of distracting their child from distress or accommodating the child's needs. The success in engagement is so precious and at times precarious that it is difficult to put it at risk.

It is important to recognize when a child is ready to increase their tolerance and function across a broader range of emotions. A plan at this stage includes practice communicating when feeling frustrated, angry, afraid, or sad. As adult and child move into interactions around negative feelings, they can take advantage of the frequent small degrees of drama in everyday life, as well as create new challenges to practice in therapy and play. Gradually, the child will use purposeful gestures while experiencing stronger emotions, such as when confronted with a more difficult limit.

Because a child with developmental challenges may have difficulty reading affective cues, it is helpful for a parent to use heightened affect. The caveat is that it must be genuine. A parent or clinician must be natural and congruent in facial expressions, words, vocal tone, and gestures, so that the child can perceive and understand the emotion being shared. Some children may be frightened by exaggerated affective expressions, so the degree of drama must be graded to the child.

Chloe enjoyed playing blocks with Mom, but when Chloe's block didn't balance the way she wanted, she made a sound of huge distress. She had few in-between expressions, and Mom reported that she had quite a temper. She calmed down just as quickly, but it was difficult to avoid these frequent outbursts.

Mother would typically move quickly to repair the problem. With support, she learned to use a frustrated tone, and helped Chloe to organize and sustain interaction through her distress. This is a subtle but substantive change. Through numerous such brief, attuned expressions of affect, Chloe learned to engage in reciprocal interactions that helped her organize and modulate her feelings.

An adult can note opportunities throughout the day to use affective gestures, such as "Oh no! Where is it?" "Oh no, it's gone." "Oh! What was that sound?" with matching emotional tones and gestures to build emotional range. It is not necessary to use an emotion word, such as, "That's so frustrating!" The important part of the interaction is the emotional communication. If language is used without matching emotion, the message is not only less efficacious, it can actually be confusing. Imagine saying "That's so frustrating!" in a cheerful voice and with a smile.

Mom said to Luc, "Time to put shoes on," as she placed the shoes by his feet. He didn't move. She picked up a shoe and handed it to him, saying, "Put shoes on." He took the shoe and started to put his foot in. He was having difficulty. Mom got down close, and said, "Uh, that's not going in!" He set it down and started to get up and walk away.

Mom encouraged him, saying, "You can do it. Try again," and handed him the shoe. He took it and the sequence repeated, except this time Luc protested and pushed the shoe back to her. She kept encouraging him and helped just a little. They had an animated little exchange with single words and sounds, including "Pull . . . " "Oh no," "Ahh," "Yes!" and many looks and movements. After several minutes, Mom said, "You did it!" and they shared a high-five.

Luc had succeeded not only in learning to put on his shoes, but in engaging in a reciprocal gestural dialogue, while feeling some level of distress about a new expectation. The goal of opening and closing circles of communication while experiencing a range of emotions can be included in goals for all disciplines. A plan might include a focus on specific emotions, relating to the child's life, and advance over weeks to include other emotions. A child can read books, watch videos, or use play materials to explore a specific affect. All of these activities offer opportunities for a child to engage in two-way communication using a differentiated affective range.

Strategies for Practice at Milestone 3

- Practice using negative affective gestures in frequent low-intensity interactions
- Take advantage of small dramas in daily life
- Create opportunities to practice affective gestures, such as in play or reading books, or in daily activities
- Practice specific negative emotions
- Use congruent, genuine affective expressions

Plans for Milestone 4

At Milestone 4, children begin to use more complex emotional signals to communicate and problem solve. Now, a parent can set limits through word or look and get an appropriate response. Some children have difficulty reading and understanding these social cues, and are helped by making the cues more definitive, in a way that matches their sensory profile.

> *Madeline is an active, sensory-seeking girl who loves to climb. Unfortunately, she sometimes chooses to climb trees or onto tables. Although she has good balance and motor coordination, she is very quick, and her climbing is sometimes dangerous. Madeline delights in roughhouse play and will be persistent in her appeals to play tackle with Dad, or to go to the park and swing with Mom.*

Madeline's parents want her to be able to have coregulated interactions around limit setting. The goal is to stop and come back when her parents call, and for her to discern when her parents are especially serious. Together, parents and clinicians draft a plan with different levels of intensity, ranging from a gentle call to a stern, "Stop!" and "Come now!" It is appropriate for her to respond to the gentle call with a question, or request more time, and so on. With the urgent call, she must act immediately. The plan calls for practicing multiple times each day in safe situations, initially with a lot of support.

Parents will practice how to clearly use facial expressions, gestures, and tone of voice so that their message is clear, and provide different levels of intensity. If Madeline needs physical support, it will be provided as well, as her parents patiently help her understand what is expected.

It is also recognized that Madeline is more relaxed after she has had a period of active play with strong proprioceptive and vestibular input. The plan includes a variety of appropriate ways to engage in active play that provides the needed sensory activity as well as creating more opportunities for social problem solving, such as freeze tag, and being a leader and a follower in Simon Says.

Madeline will be praised for coming when asked, but more importantly, each time is an opportunity to expand her capacity for sustained coregulated interactions with as many emotional signals as possible. By extending the interactions, she will learn to express her ideas and feelings and simultaneously decipher and modulate her behavior based on an adult's cues. Madeline may interact about her excitement and joy, confusion, anger, or sadness, and may test her limits of negotiation. Ultimately Madeline will become less impulsive because she shares her ideas and looks expectantly for feedback.

Over time, an adult can use shorthand, less overt messages as a child needs only a partial cue to read approval or disapproval. Eventually, a parent may only give a look that conveys, "You know what I am going to say." Ultimately, a child can anticipate and remember limits, even without a parent's immediate presence or command.

> *Kara is distressed by her torn paper at school and is becoming agitated. Mr. Mark, her teacher, knows that Kara tends to give up easily. He approaches and says, "Uh-oh. What's the matter?"*
>
> *Kara makes a sound of distress, "Mmmm, it tore." She is actually tearing the paper more as she is rubbing it. He says, "Wait! Let's fix it." She stops, looks up, and pushes her paper toward Mr. Mark.*
>
> *He says, "What can we do? Shall we tape it?" She nods. He adds, "Where's the tape?" and looks around with a where gesture.*
>
> *Kara looks around, sees the tape, and looks back to him; he seems not to see. She points, says, "Over there," looks at him again, and then gets the tape and brings it back, giving it to him.*
>
> *He says, "Oh, there it is!" and hands it back to her. "Here, you can do it."*
>
> *Kara struggles to cut a piece of tape, and Mr. Mark provides just a little help. She tries to place it, unsuccessfully. She crumples the tape and throws it down. "Stupid tape!"*
>
> *He says, "Oh no. That tape is so tricky! Try again. . . . Maybe it will stick this time."*
>
> *Kara places the tape successfully enough. She pauses and looks at the paper. Mr. Mark says, "Looks pretty good. Is it okay?" Kara nods and relaxes.*

Kara is beginning to use multiple gestures in a row, and sustain an interaction through distress. Mr. Mark gauged his level of help to encourage her to persist and experience success through their interaction. He might respond to other challenges with gradually less support, as Kara learns to tolerate even greater levels of frustration.

A plan to build skills at Milestone 4 includes practicing sustained interaction and coregulation in events that occur throughout the day. An adult can take advantage of things that need to be fixed, or activities with a goal, such as cooking, art, or construction activities to practice shared problem solving. If a child has an idea, even if it obviously will not be successful, an adult can allow her to try the idea and then continue problem solving together, without providing too much instruction. The adult provides just the level of support needed so that a child sustains interaction through an emotional challenge, including asking for and using help.

To support understanding, adults can express emotion with a slightly dramatic affect and provide time for a child to notice, interpret, and respond. They can create opportunities to practice, such as purposefully having a missing piece that must be found, or trying an idea that doesn't work. They can also do something unexpected like handing a child a fork instead of spoon, or putting a cup on the table upside down. An adult might wait for a child's response, and then share in the surprise: "Uh oh! That's not right," and work together to fix it. It is important, however, to keep the interactions genuine and not devolve into simple silliness.

Bobby, a 7-year-old boy with mild cognitive disability, likes to rough-house play and run outdoors with his brothers. Recently, his brothers have started building elaborate block and road constructions. Bobby wants to join their play but inevitably, they end up fighting. Bobby grabs pieces he wants and insists they must go in a certain way. His brothers say he is interfering.

Bobby is having trouble using gestures to signal his intent, reading social cues and modulating his behavior based on his brothers' cues. He is perceived as stubborn and selfish. The long-term plan includes graded opportunities to practice interactions involving reciprocal affective exchange. At first, a parent will need to join the boys, to slow down the interaction. Dad can help Bobby notice his brothers' signals, tolerate disappointment and frustration, as well as help the boys to negotiate their ideas.

Strategies for Practice at Milestone 4

- Look for opportunities for shared problem solving in daily living or in activities such as construction, games, arts and crafts, or cooking
- Extend interactions as long as possible
- Gradually increase obstacles to encourage creativity, asking for and using help
- Provide the just-right level of help to encourage the child to persist, negotiate and compromise
- Allow failures as well as successes
- Use clear, differentiated expressions of emotions and intensity
- Heighten affect to help to bolster an initial desire so the child will not abandon it
- Attend to a full range of affects
- Help peers to read the child's cues
- Consider how auditory, language, visual, and tactile cues may help a child understand affective expression

Plans for Milestone 5

When Donald is angry he clenches his fists, gets close to the person bothering him, and looks menacing. His face becomes flushed, and his look is intense. At times he grabs or pinches, but generally threatens more than acts. Donald will sometimes state what is bothering him, such as, "Don't cut in front of me!" or "I am not a geek!" Many of his peers are afraid of him.

Some children have difficulty shifting anger and aggressive feelings from action to symbols. Rather than using words to argue or complain, they still demonstrate their emotion through their bodies. A goal for Donald is to learn to express anger in a fully symbolic way, and to gain a secure sense of self so that he will be able to tolerate frustration, hurt, and disappointment without triggering a cascade of overwhelming feelings and impulsive actions. Broader coping skills can be gained through interactions that encourage Donald to be assertive and to know that he can gain support through relationships with helping adults.

Intervention can help Donald think about his actions and how they are connected to his feelings. Through reflection, he was able to describe that he did not like to "be put down." The therapist asked him to describe how he felt when that happened. He said, "Like I want to kill someone!" Gradually Donald was able to see a pattern in his feelings and actions. Later, after discussing other situations, Donald was able to label the emotion as "furious." Now he could talk about many situations that made him furious, and how he usually responded. He was liberated from acting on impulse and could consider other options for dealing with this feeling.

Keith likes fiction. He often wears a themed T-shirt to school, and when distressed, he will mumble, "To the sea!" This is usually accompanied by a dramatic ritual movement of three swings of his arm.

When anxious, a child may engage in rituals or rigid, repetitive behaviors including movements, words, or sounds. While Keith's capacity for symbolic thinking is wonderful, he will often utilize these fantasy ideas to cope with challenges in a manner that is socially unacceptable. Not only can he seem to be detached from reality, but he also seems to be stuck in a repetitious pattern of responses. By utilizing a developmental framework, it is possible to create a plan to help Keith to expand his ability to use symbolic ideas in a more interactive and effective way.

Those who know Keith well may sometimes recognize that he uses certain phrases that correspond to situations in a particular video. They then may be able to connect the meaning of the references to the circumstances of the moment. They conclude that Keith is often anxious. While he can spend hours playing with his sister or his parents at home, he becomes stressed with changes of routine and at school. The goal for Keith is to decrease his overwhelming sense of anxiety and to be able to express his concerns and request help in more appropriate ways. The plan includes daily practice in spontaneous play, in which a receptive play partner will help him elaborate on his ideas of danger, rescue, bravery, good, and evil. Through this play, Keith will strengthen Milestones 1-4, as well as explore and master strong emotional themes through the safety of the symbolic world, Milestone 5. All of his teachers and therapists will communicate about ideas developed in play, so that ideas and words that arise, such as "surprise," "scary," "brave," and the meaning of his unique symbols are shared between them all.

The plan also includes developing a consensus with all of the teachers and caregivers about how to respond in the moment. Adults will recognize that Keith is acting out of anxiety, and will use Steps 1, 2, and 3 to help him organize and process the experience in an interactive way. The adults will also try to anticipate stressful situations and provide support so that he can proactively communicate and seek help as needed. The goal is not to avoid challenges, but to match the support so that he can be successful in interactions while feeling anxious.

Strategies for Practice at Milestone 5

- Engage in conversations about feelings, so that a child can discover connections and patterns in their feelings and actions, and ultimately use labels to categorize feelings
- Engage in child-led pretend play, and challenge the child to expand emotional ideas
- Explore symbolic emotional ideas together in books, drama, and music

Plans for Milestone 6

Anna screams at her mom, "Don't give the big spoon to Eva!" Mom is surprised and perplexed by Anna's distress. She asks Anna, "Why can't Eva have it?" Anna responds, "It is the blue one!" Despite further questioning, Anna is unable to explain the reasons behind her distress.

Gregory is crying and distraught. Dad asks, "What happened?" Gregory responds, "We are racing, and Dave's truck is bigger." Dad asks, "Did Dave win the race?" Gregory answers, "I want my line closer." Dad tries to negotiate a fair racing game, but it is difficult because Gregory is so confused.

The ability to connect ideas logically happens gradually. A major insight of the developmental model is that this cognitive skill is learned first through organization and connection of emotional ideas in social interaction with others. A plan can provide opportunities for a child to practice linking feelings and thoughts in play and conversation. Over time, the child advances to make logical connections, and then consider multiple causes or feelings, compare intensity of feelings, and ultimately reflect using a personal standard.

> Mom and Dad are watching a competition show on television. Gregory comments, "That looks hard." Dad seizes the opportunity to ask, "What do you think is the hardest part?" Dad mixes questions and comments. He relates a time when he did something hard, and asks Gregory about when he might have felt that way.

Through many such discussions, Gregory becomes more adept at talking about his ideas and comparing different experiences, and even makes some insightful observations. Some children with social challenges have very good memory and analytic skills and apply those skills to decipher the social-emotional world. They may ask questions and look at people inquisitively as if they are doing a scientific analysis of emotional expressions and trying to form accurate concepts. However, in order to participate in a rich emotional interchange, they must connect facts with their own lived emotional experience.

> Joanna is a teenage girl with autism. She is very interested in boys and wants to have a boyfriend. She chooses clothes that are revealing and engages in sexually provocative behavior, such as sitting next to boys and touching their arm, or sending love notes during class. Her parents are afraid that her behavior is becoming dangerous because she is so indiscriminate in her advances.

The complex world of teen relationships, including peer pressures and a drive for independence, can be confusing and overwhelming. A specific focus on the development of higher functional emotional capacities provides a systematic format for sorting and organizing these intense feelings.

Joanna is able to connect actions and consequences for some behaviors, such as understanding that stealing in the store could send her to jail, but is not able to do so around relationships with boys. She seems not to understand how her behavior may be perceived and does not even have a clear idea about what it means to have a boyfriend. In addition to learning some basic rules about safe and appropriate behavior, Joanna will benefit from a long-term plan that will help her think logically about motivations and consequences of her actions.

Joanna enjoys music and writing songs. Her plan includes working with a music therapist, writing and discussing lyrics and music. Through a creative outlet, children can be encouraged to explore their feelings and ideas, and challenged to consider possible connections between their feelings and actions. By elaborating about her dreams and wishes, along with a trusted therapist, Joanna can establish a better understanding of reality and fantasy. Of course, she needs close supervision and guidance as she is developing these new skills.

> *Brian was approached by Connor, a classmate in the hall. Connor told him, "Can you put Carmen's lunch in the red locker?" Brian considered Connor to be a friend, and wanted to help, and so he did what Connor wanted. Later, Carmen couldn't find her lunch, and ultimately Brian got in trouble. Connor and others laughed when Brian looked foolish.*

Unfortunately, some children are victims of bullies and predators. Children can be vulnerable if they are unclear about whom to trust and then are unable to defend themselves. These children may have difficulty reading social cues and may miss the subtle meanings in language, sarcasm and humor. Through a plan to practice at all milestones, they can learn to recognize the feelings of true friendship and become better able to discern malicious intentions in others.

Some children with disabilities develop bullying behavior themselves. Sometimes, a child may provoke another child without recognizing the distress they are causing: children may imitate others actions or remarks without understanding, or they may ridicule something that is unfamiliar and makes them uncomfortable. A child may make offensive comments about another's dress or religion because they are using concrete thinking, and are unable to distinguish the actions of an individual in relation to a group identity. Their words may be an attempt to defend against feeling threatened and powerless.

At other times children seem to anticipate the battle they are creating.

Alec said he wanted the red chair. Omar heard him, and ran to sit in the red chair first. Omar would frequently boast, call names, disparage others or do things that infuriated his peers.

A child's inappropriate and offensive actions may actually be a misguided attempt at closeness and friendship. Bullying, involving manipulation and planning may indicate a more significant problem of low self-esteem and lack of secure, trusting relationships. In each situation, a professional can respond in the moment to sensitively guide the interaction, but more importantly, assess the complete profile of the child's development in order to create a meaningful plan.

Adair is a teen who spends time alone listening to music with dark themes. He often draws pictures depicting gruesome violence and death, mixed with religious symbols. He will talk about his drawings with a few people, but often sits with his head down and does not initiate conversation.

The Word "Friend"

It is important for professionals to use the word "friend" with careful consideration. Friendship is a very special relationship that is acquired over a period of time with many experiences of mutual pleasure as well as shared experiences of distress and recovery. Sometimes the word "friend" is used casually to refer to new acquaintances or classmates even though a true friendship has not been established. The misuse of the term "friend" can cause confusion for some children.

Unfortunately, children that have difficulty forming friendships may experience misunderstanding, rejection, and even bullying from peers. A professional can help a child to distinguish an act of kindness from an act with malicious intent, and when a relationship is casual or intimate. Understanding relationships is an ongoing process and begins with the earliest interactions with peers at school. Everyone can celebrate when a child develops a true friendship.

After a slow process of careful and respectful listening, a clinician develops a positive rapport with Adair. Gradually, Adair begins to talk about the ideas in his drawings. It quickly becomes apparent that he has many questions as well as misperceptions about the world, becoming an adult, death, and religion. His capacity for elaborating his ideas and logical thinking is not strong. A long-term plan has the goal of increasing a positive sense of self-identity, forming healthy relationships with people outside of his family, and increasing his capacity to form personal values.

With an attitude of openness and following the child's lead, his therapist is interested in knowing what Adair thinks and feels about the music and the images that he chooses. In the process of exploring those ideas and encouraging Adair to reflect on them, the conversation might extend to topics such as different political viewpoints or judgments about style in music or art. The discussion might surround topics of uncertainty such as religious beliefs or the unknown.

During this process, the relationships of trust with parents and therapist must be carefully nurtured, while providing boundaries to keep Adair safe. As a teenager advances towards adulthood, a therapist must be mindful about issues of privacy and confidentiality between the teen and the parents. Because the developmental approach focuses on relationships, the opinions and priorities of the parents continue to be important factors in success. The developmental framework guides this delicate balance and offers a path toward the development of strong personal values that support an attitude of care and concern toward others.

It will be a long process for Adair to reflect on the main issues in his life, but with a steady foundation of trusting relationships, there can be steady progress. A child like Adair can gradually learn to tolerate uncertainty, to respect different perspectives, and to adopt positive values. The growth is motivated by satisfaction in curiosity, discovery, creative thinking, reflection, and the joy of sharing in the interchange of ideas.

Strategies for Practice at Milestone 6

- Show respectful interest in a child's thoughts and ideas
- Build on previous levels of trust and reciprocal, coregulated interactions
- Take advantage of opportunities to discuss and reflect on feelings

- Have conversations that deepen and broaden ideas; make plans together; consider alternatives; negotiate about limits
- Use creative activities such as writing, music, poetry, art, dance, and drama as a medium to explore feelings and ideas

Intensity of Intervention

The intensity of services will depend on each child's unique needs. An advantage of working closely with parents is that they can implement strategies throughout their daily interactions and magnify the impact of intervention. The frequency and type of intervention is often dependent on funding sources, but hopefully a family can access the type and intensity of care appropriate for their child.

It is important for professionals to identify when a child needs more intensive intervention or additional help from another discipline.

Alexander had a habit of taking off all his clothes. At home, his parents and siblings were accustomed to his nakedness, but as Alex was getting older, this behavior was becoming an obstacle to having others in the home, and more of a concern that he might disrobe in a public place.

In this situation, it is important to intervene in a way that can quickly change this behavior. In addition to the obvious behavior, it is important to understand the perspective of the parents and the greater issue of setting limits.

Cathy engaged in self-injury. Her mother was alarmed and told the school-teacher. Cathy blandly admitted it, but was taciturn and provided no further thoughts about why she did it, or how she was feeling. The teacher immediately spoke with the school principal, and they arranged for individual and family counseling.

Family issues and relationships are often very complicated. Behavioral issues impact family dynamics, and family interactions often affect behavioral challenges. A professional has the responsibility to identify the level of intensity of support that a child and family may need in order to be safe and to live with dignity and hope.

Implementing the Long-Term Plan

A developmental approach provides a universal framework that parents, clinicians, and teachers can use to address a challenging behavior. Despite the best efforts to address behavioral challenges effectively in the moment, children need ongoing opportunities to promote their underlying developmental capacities. A long-term plan can identify or create situations with the just-right level of challenge, so that skills can be learned in small incremental steps toward the behavioral goals. Long-term goals encompass both moving up the developmental milestones and also the capacity to use those skills with greater stability and across contexts and feeling states.

Goals and strategies are not static, but are continually modified as the child, parents, and life events influence development, and as the child advances. There are no presumed limits on how far a child may progress, or the range and depth of their ability to relate, communicate, and think.

Chapter 10

The Use of Play

When a child has behavioral challenges, play is an important component of the long-term plan of intervention. The skills learned during play support the ability to modulate emotional responses at other times while experiencing distress. A child benefits from frequent opportunities to engage in a variety of play experiences, with the support of an adult who can provide the appropriate level of challenge.

Play is distinct from other activities because it has the basic qualities of freedom, spontaneity, and joy. A child's play is self-directed, with self-control and self-determination, or shared control with another player. Ironically, play is also balanced by self-imposed restraint, rules, and roles. The pleasure and developmental learning gained from play are the result of the interplay of freedom to explore and create, and the limits that children define for themselves, in their invented play world.

Social, interactive play creates shared understanding of the play context with a sole purpose of enjoyment. There can be playful competition, fear, or surprise—all of which are enjoyable through a dynamic affective exchange. In play with others, a child becomes involved in a cocreated experience with ongoing communication, excitement, and negotiation. Trust and warmth in relationships increase as the boundaries of safety are respected, and the play does not elicit overwhelming emotion or distress. The quality of playfulness in interactions contributes to a relationship of warmth and trust that is present and available even when not engaged in play.

Floortime is a specific type of free play, using intervention strategies corresponding to the DIR functional emotional developmental milestones (Greenspan, 1992, 2006). In Floortime play, there are no adult directives, and the only rule is that a child must not hurt people or damage property.

> Floortime should be full of surprises . . . The goal is to be a good listener and responder—to be naturally curious and interested in your child
>
> —Greenspan, 1993

The content of play ideas are generated from the child. In a stimulating environment, with an enthusiastic play partner, a child will be encouraged to take the initiative and share in pleasurable interactions. Children will challenge themselves to solve problems or will symbolically enact their ideas and concerns. A child may play out a sensory challenge that is frightening, or create a scenario that is a transparent reflection of a real-life concern.

While play ideas are child led, play experiences can also support specific developmental needs. Strategies can be directed toward helping children strengthen weak areas in functional capacities that manifest in their behavioral challenges. All play experiences using a developmental approach have common elements, including following a child's lead rather than directing the play, engaging in a sustained flow of reciprocal interaction, and challenging the child to deepen and broaden emotional intent, communication, and thinking. In play, an adult's affective expressions, genuine interest, and enthusiasm create a shared experience that is pleasurable and supportive of a child's developmental growth.

It is important to plan a play experience for the appropriate developmental level. The play might be planned to focus at a level where the child has constrictions and areas for needed growth. At the same time, the child may have some constrictions at lower levels or capacities at higher levels. The lower milestones provide the foundation for higher skills and must always be relatively secure in order to advance. By finding the level where the play is successful, adult and child form a strong relationship for moving up the developmental ladder.

The Play Environment

Play can take place anywhere and anytime. With younger children, play often occurs on the floor with toys, but play can also occur outdoors or in playful moments in the car or in a store. For older children, play may also include creative activities such as writing, art, music, drama, or simply a conversation about imaginary ideas. A play environment can be created to support a particular level of play, and can be designed to reflect a child's unique profile and interests.

A playroom should be safe and inviting, with many opportunities for exploration and initiative. The selection of play materials is critical to supporting developmental goals. Toys can be available that challenge but not overwhelm physical or cognitive abilities. Battery-operated toys and closed-ended toys such as video games are generally discouraged because they limit the range of creativity and imagination on the part of the child. Toys that offer opportunities for choice and elaboration are preferred.

Sometimes, one child will take time initially to explore the play materials available in a new environment before beginning play, whereas another will engage with the first item seen, without further exploration. The approach to play and the choice of play materials may provide insight into the child's visual-spatial awareness, attention, emotional preferences, and cognitive strategies. An adult can observe and follow the child's lead and join in either exploration or beginning play.

The choice to move from one toy to another may also provide insights about development. Children may have difficulty expanding their ideas for play with a particular toy; they may shift attention because of frustration or anxiety, or may be distracted as they notice another toy. It is important to observe and try to discern the quality of the shift in attention, rather than simply labeling it as being "all done" and put a toy away. An adult may want to try to entice the child to continue and expand the play, or at least leave the toy as an option for later play.

Many children will play with one toy, shift attention to another area, and then to another, and eventually return to the initial toy. A circuit may be created as they reach the maximum tolerance for the physical, cognitive or emotional demands associated with one toy, and shift to a more familiar or less challenging toy. In this way, they can regulate their own emotional level of challenge, as they gradually approach or recede from the more difficult interaction. It is important to keep toys out, even as a child moves on, to provide the opportunity to return and continue to expand toward mastery with those items.

A child may combine toys of different types, or use them in an unconventional way. Again, an adult can follow the child's lead and interest. Some children, especially those with poor visual-spatial skills, may scatter toys and create disarray. Here, an adult can quietly help keep a sense of order to support focus and continued productive interaction. A more formal clean-up and closure can be accomplished in conjunction with the end of playtime and transition to another event.

The following examples illustrate how play-based strategies can support a child with behavioral challenges to build needed skills, corresponding to the functional emotional developmental milestones.

Milestone 1: Shared Attention and Regulation

Carla seems to have a short attention span. She looks at toys briefly, sometimes picks one up and sets it down again, and then moves on. If Mom reads or sings a favorite song, she will stand and look for a short while. She likes to squeeze into small spaces. Often, in apparent distress, Carla will scream and throw whatever is within reach.

Carla has constrictions in Milestone 1. The goal for play would be to help Carla to gradually increase sustained shared attention and decrease moments of distress. In Floortime, everything a child does is viewed as an opportunity to join, engage, and create a sense of shared experience. It is noted that she has limited motor skills but does notice and attend to music and sounds. She also seeks out deep pressure and proprioceptive input. These clues might help to plan out play activities that combine these interests. For example, play might include music making, or dramatically reading stories, combined with proprioceptive input such as pounding on a soft drum or pushing or pulling together to make a sound or in conjunction with a sound.

All activities could be tailored to Carla's preferred level and type of sound, touch, and movement, with the overarching goal of doing activities together. Close attunement to her subtle cues can help to elucidate her individual profile, and then adjust the environment or offer activities to soothe her when distressed, as well as to gradually help her to tolerate a broader range of sensory experience. Soothing activities can be combined with human interaction as much as possible.

Daniel sees Mom's paper, grabs it quickly, and begins to wave it before his eyes. He sometimes engages in waving paper, alone, for long periods of time. He often seems unaware of people and will watch a fish tank, moving fan, or other spinning objects.

Daniel has constrictions in Milestone 1. Further assessment is needed to gather a complete understanding of his sensory and regulatory profile. It is clear that he is sensitive to visual stimulus.

The goal in play is to achieve shared attention. A plan would include activities that can combine preferred sensory experiences with awareness of another person. This may be accomplished through the introduction of novelty and stimuli that heighten interest but do not overwhelm Daniel so that he is unable to shift his focus of attention. A variety of materials might be offered, such as shakers that provide sound and visual interest, aluminum foil on a soft stick, or flashlights. An adult would closely follow Daniel's lead in exploring the items, join in the exploration, and look for opportunities to expand the play. For example, if Daniel waved the foil sticks in the light, an adult might also wave a stick and match his rhythm with an added sound effect. Mild obstacles could be created, such as blocking the movement of the stick by jumping in the way, or bumping the stick against another stick, but always in a playful way.

It may be more effective to select an alternative activity, based upon a different sensory-motor system. For example, Daniel may also enjoy the sound of a musical instrument, walking, or playing with a pet animal. Any of these activities can be expanded, while making it a shared experience.

Five children in a social skills group were playing with a bubble machine. They became more and more excited as they ran around the room popping the bubbles.

The challenge here is for an interventionist to find the right balance between enthusiasm and chaos. Through fun, shared engagement, children expand their capacity to function at higher levels of arousal, but there is a risk that a child may become overwhelmed and disengage. A professional also has a personal level of tolerance for noise, movement, and excitement. Capacities for regulation are expanded by experiences at the edge of the comfort zone, so a professional must be self-reflective and comfortable in supporting children in loosely structured, exciting play according to their needs, rather than prematurely imposing order and rule.

Strategies to Support Play at Milestone 1

In Milestone 1, the goal in play is to help a child increase the capacity for basic regulation and shared attention with another person, rather than engaging in solitary play with objects or self-absorbed or aimless activities. Through frequent supportive interactions with others, children gradually expand their capacity for regulation and shared attention during higher levels of arousal and emotional intensity. Strength at Milestone 1 is the basis for further functional emotional development. Strategies include the following:

- Watch closely and join with the child's interests, or in a way aligned with his or her individual sensory-motor profile.
- Adjust the environment to help the child feel calm and safe.
- Engage all the senses; speed up or slow down; raise or lower affect to create interest and novelty.
- Gradually challenge the child to sustain engagement across higher levels of excitement, surprise, and a full range of affect and arousal.
- Encourage shared attention by considering where your body is: Move to be near, in front of the child, or in the child's path to the desired object; continue moving as needed. Or consider staying in

one place if that helps a child to be calm and attend to you, perhaps using auditory cues.

- Eliminate extraneous sounds so that all auditory cues support shared attention.
- Create a physical space that encourages shared attention, such as a tent made with a sheet, blocking off an area, or using a large box or tunnel to limit physical and visual field.
- Engage in play involving physical body-to-body interaction.
- Incorporate preferred toys with your body, such as having the train go through your legs, or over your head, or hide an object in a pocket or behind your back.

Milestone 2: Engagement in Warm, Trusting Relationships

Ronnie shows limited interest in others. He sometimes enjoys coloring with his mother or dancing to music. When upset, Ronnie paces the floor and is difficult to console. He does not respond to questions about what he wants and does not accept any offers of help. If someone reaches out to touch him, he screams even louder. Eventually, all the adults are resigned to sitting helplessly and waiting for him to eventually calm down on his own.

Ronnie has deficits at Milestone 2. He does not know how to use the sense of connection to others in trusting relationships to be comforted in times of distress. It will be helpful to build this capacity through shared play interactions that build a warm sense of engagement.

Play at this level consists of the many idiosyncratic, personal games that are created between parent and child. A similar emotional dynamic is often present in these games, involving anticipation and then a sudden release of tension, such as, "I'm gonna get you!" or "Ready, set, go!" games. The more often the dynamic sequence is repeated, the greater the anticipation and fun. Through multiple similar games and repetitions, the child forms a sense of warmth and intimacy with that adult. Because of their relationship, the adult is then able to comfort the child when they are distressed. With an increase of these experiences the child begins to expand a sense of interest and trust to other people, with an expectation of positive feelings.

As in Milestone 1, play at Milestone 2 does not necessarily involve toys. A parent can support engagement with body-to-body play, a singing game making up silly rhyming words, or other sensory-motor play. A parent can have an attitude of playfulness throughout the day, such as singing games in the car, playful exploration during mealtimes, or fun routines around bedtime. Interactions at this level are built from emotional attunement and appreciation of a child's individual responses to sensory experience and individual interests, as well as the parent's personal way of playing with the child.

Strategies for Play at Milestone 2

The key elements of play at Milestone 2 are that an adult and child create their own intimate knowledge of each other through familiar games, and that they become able to anticipate and elicit increasing levels of excitement and pleasure. Strategies at milestone 2 include the following:

- Follow the child's lead, and build on his or her interests.
- Create microdynamics of a pleasurable rhythm of interaction, building tension and then release, such as, "Ready, set . . . go!" Or incorporate personalized versions of nursery songs or rhymes.
- Use repetition to increase predictability and familiarity, and then entice the child to continue by inserting something new and surprising.
- Use increased affect and pauses to heighten anticipation.
- Read signs of readiness for faster or slower interaction, and when a child is showing signs of stress. Match a child's availability and avoid intrusive, teasing, or overwhelming interactions.
- Carefully interpret the meaning of a child's behaviors. For example, he may turn away, which could be interpreted as disinterest, or might indicate that he is waiting for another turn. When it is unclear, adults can give the behavior a positive meaning through their response.

Milestone 3: Two-Way Reciprocal Interactions

Tom likes to play with little cars, and plays happily with Mom rolling cars down a ramp. Tom chooses a car and follows Mom's car through the bottom of the structure and up again. When her car momentarily blocks his way, he tenses his muscles and stops. He seems unable to coordinate a physical response or find the words to say. After a moment, he grabs Mom's car and continues playing alone.

Tom is able to participate in back-and-forth interactions that are fun, but not when he is distressed. Mom practiced playing with Tom using various expressions to communicate frustration, sadness, surprise and frustration that matched his experience.

Tom's car rolls off the table. Mom sees his concern and says, "Oh no! Not again!" with a slightly exaggerated dramatic flair. Tom watches closely, and does not get as upset as he might have before. For several days, Mom offers this expression and variations of it in different contexts. Tom starts to respond by mimicking both the words and the accompanying gestures. One day, Tom rolls his car off the table on purpose, and looks to Mom and together they say, "Oh no! Not again!" The next time Mom's car blocked his, he was able to say, "Oh no! Move car!"

Strategies for Play at Milestone 3

In Milestone 3, the goal in play is that a child will increase the capacity to initiate and respond in reciprocal two-way interactions, around a range of different affective experiences. Strategies include the following.

- Watch closely; find meaning, affect, and intentionality in everything a child says or does.

Nancy was running back and forth along the fence. Mr. Tom thought, let's make this a game. He got three other children to race along the fence as well. Each time they got to the end, they got a high-five and a cheer. Now Nancy had playmates, and they eventually organized themselves, without his help, so that they all gathered and started to run at the same time. Nancy was part of the group.

- Advance from doing something together, to reciprocal interactions.
- If a child is interested in a toy, find a way to be part of the play. Catch the cars and roll them back, or use your puppet to eat the food they are making. Offer choices.
- Help children do what they want to do; help create goals that expand their interests. For example, when a child is tossing things, offer a bucket or other location; when they are knocking things over, stack them back up; or make a finish line for cars rolling down a ramp.
- Building on a child's intent, challenge her to expand and extend the interaction. Hold the affective excitement longer, or increase the anticipation and drama.
- Be aware of the pace of the interaction to create a reciprocal balanced flow, in actions, gestures and language, in initiation and response. Allow ample time for a child to initiate. While being part of an exciting interaction, do not get ahead and begin to take the lead in the play. Entice the child to initiate by using clear affective cues to sustain shared attention and create appealing opportunities to interact.
- Use playful obstruction—be an obstacle for a child to negotiate, or do an act that a child will want to reverse—but always in a playful way. At first, the child may not recognize interference as playful, but when an adult can make it fun, through timing, affect, and respect, then the child will shift from barely tolerating an interaction to wanting to continue. The strategy of playful obstruction must be balanced with more time honoring a child's intent.

Mom said to Ida, "Oh my! There is a big cow in the way of the train!" Normally, Ida would quickly not tolerate anything that interfered with her train, but Mom's affect held her attention momentarily. Then Mom said, "I'll get it!" and pushed it out of the way, with a big plastic stick. Ida watched and smiled. A minute later, Mom said, "Oh look! There's another cow coming!

Here, let's move it!" She handed Ida the stick. Ida was happy to help. This was the start of play that included many different animals that impeded the train's progress, and the discovery of fun ways to help the train get through.

- Keep it fun; resist asking questions that elicit a factual or closed-ended response, such as, "What color is it?" "What is this called?" A parent is often anxious to teach facts and explicit behaviors, but a child benefits more from opportunities to lead and expand play ideas.
- Use playful interactions throughout the day that encourage a child to act: "Where is your sock?" A child may gesture, and an adult might say, "Oh! I'm sitting on it!" Or purposefully put on obviously mismatched socks, so the child will be motivated to tell you. Take advantage of little dramas that occur naturally throughout the day, to practice using affect cues around a range of emotions.
- Be animated and use a range of affects to amplify and differentiate the range of emotions. Use congruent emotional gestures, of words, expressions, tone of voice, and so on, to communicate the range and intensity of feelings being experienced. Ensure that the expressions are genuine and not overly dramatized.

Milestone 4: Coregulated Interactions and Shared Problem Solving

Claire is bossy and demanding. She is easily perturbed to extremes of emotion if her demands are not immediately met and she is not in charge. Claire likes to play dolls with her friends, but she constantly tells everyone exactly what to do. When upset, she sometimes sits with crossed arms and refuses to move or talk. At other times, she screams her demands.

Claire has difficulty working through difficulties with patience, asking for help, and adjusting her actions based on another's ideas and actions. A comprehensive assessment reveals that Claire has significant challenges with motor planning, sequencing ideas and actions, and visual-spatial awareness. While she is playing, she actually does not execute many complex actions with the dolls. And although she gives many directions, she has a hard time finding the words she wants and in understanding receptive language.

In addition to occupational therapy, speech and language therapy, educational instruction, and patient soothing when distressed, Claire will benefit from play designed to strengthen Milestone 4. An adult can be a good follower as Claire directs the play, encouraging her to sustain the interaction and then finding opportunities for shared problem solving. Following her interest in dolls, an adult might set up a playroom with toys such as a dollhouse, baby bath, food, a kitchen, bed, blankets, a doll's car, and so on. Materials may be selected that will not demand advanced motor skills and that will easily support expansion of representational play.

> *Vicky, a therapist, plays with Claire. Claire is feeding a doll. Vicky takes another doll and says, "I'm hungry!" Claire takes Vicky's doll to hold and feed it. Vicky then gets another doll and says, "Me too, can I have some?" Again, Claire takes it. Vicky sees that Claire is having difficulty positioning the three dolls, and helps. Then Vicky offers Claire another spoon and more food. Vicky comments, "Ah, the babies are so happy." Claire then directs, "They have to go to bed." Vicky helps to bring the beds near. As Lisa tries to put them in the crib, the dolls don't fit together. Vicky says, "Ugh, they don't fit!" Claire does not persist and begins to take them out. Vicky says, "Oh, they're tired. They need to sleep." Claire turns back to the crib. Vicky offers, "I can help! This can be a bed." Then they work together to fashion a bed out of pillows and blankets.*

By encouraging Claire to take the lead, Vicky has gained Claire's trust and is able to join the play. Gradually, Vicky helps to expand the range of feelings, such as frustration, that Claire can tolerate, and helps her engage in shared problem solving.

Later, an adult may challenge Claire's directives. Claire might say, "Put beans in the soup." The adult might say, "I don't like beans. I want noodle soup." Or if Claire says, "Put the doll in the car," an adult could say, "Can I just sit on the swing first?" Claire is then encouraged to either persist in promoting her idea or to invent a new idea and negotiate a compromise. In either case, she is learning to interact while feeling a heightened level of arousal.

Throughout these interactions, there are multiple exchanges of looks, vocalizations, and gestures to express pleasure, displeasure, concern, delight, frustration, anger, surprise, and so on, including using multiple gestures in a row. At Milestone 4, children are able to engage in coregulation—the continuous reading and responding to another person's affective communication to guide their interaction. Building upon the shared attention and mutual regulation of earlier milestones, they now develop a greater capacity for incorporating a broad array of different affective gestures into this dynamic exchange.

Strategies for Play at Milestone 4

In Milestone 4, the goal in play is to help children increase their capacity to sustain interaction through many emotions, using multiple gestures in a row, as well as participating in shared problem solving with a common goal. Strategies include the following:

- Offer toys or games that build on a child's interests and are representational (such as dolls with food, tea set, shopping with cash register and food, cars and trucks and road set) or that require construction and problem-solving activities with a goal (such as Lego, blocks, marbles, tool set and wood).
- Offer semistructured activities with lots of flexibility (cooking, arts, and crafts). Activities may also focus on visual-spatial problem solving (hide and seek), or auditory processing and language games (music making, or rhyming songs).
- Create problems to solve (such as, some of the cars do not fit in the tunnel).
- Act like you do not understand the child's desire, or don't know what to do, so that she persists in showing or asking.
- Take advantage of breakdowns to work out repair (a car has a broken wheel; the mast on the ship falls over; need to make a sign). Search for and use paper, tape, scissors, paint, string, and so on.
- Work together, but follow the child's ideas (even if they are bound not to be successful) rather than being directive or providing solutions. Give just enough support to sustain the interaction.
- Throughout the interaction, notice the child's feelings and interact

with rich affective gestures. Slow the interaction; hold the affect and attention to a problem, so that the child can organize his feelings and ideas.

- Encourage children to be persistent in their efforts, ask for and accept help, and gradually increase their ability to tolerate frustration, disappointment, confusion, and so on.
- Follow the child's lead. Encourage the child to direct the action by being a good follower. Ask, "Where should it go?" "Okay! Should I put it in hard or soft?"
- Don't take "no" as the end; continue to offer another idea, and encourage assertiveness. "Okay, not that one. How about this one?" "Oh, not that one either. Here, I'll put it in the reject pile. Is this one to your liking, Chief?" Perhaps offer something very different and fun.
- Promote playfulness throughout the day: "Let's see who can run to the swings first!" "Look! I can make it balance on the edge."
- Take advantage of natural opportunities for problem solving together: "Let's figure out how to carve this pumpkin. Where should we put these sticky seeds?"

Milestone 5: Using Symbolic Ideas

Manny is an active boy that loves to run and roughhouse. Although he speaks in sentences, he does not seem to understand explanations about rules, reasons for waiting, or benefit from planning ahead. He is often reprimanded and then seems confused and dejected.

In play, he gleefully uses a little figure to knock other figures off the castle wall. Then he knocks the characters off the pirate ship. Mom wishes that he would "be nice" to the people. The therapist, Sue, says, "Let's help him to be powerful." She offers Manny a little sword for his figure, and comments, "You are the mightiest of all!" She also offers the cannon to Mom to join him and help in the battle. She advises Mom's character to "Follow Manny's command!" Sue asks, "Are the guys on the castle good guys or bad guys?" Manny is not sure. Sue continues, "Okay, I can tell your man is really strong. Look out! This guy is getting up on the wall again!" Manny begins the attack anew, now directing Mom to use the cannon as well.

By helping Manny to elaborate his idea in pretend play, Manny is entering into the symbolic world. Here is a safe dominion for Manny to experience being in control and powerful. When Mom joins in on his side, he can relish her participation. Through questions and comments, the therapist can help Manny to gradually clarify the meaning of his actions. When she probes for a higher level (good guys or bad guys) and he does not know, the therapist does not provide an answer, but continues to give him opportunities to expand his own ideas. Over time, Manny may introduce a frightening or evil figure, or expand the role of the vanquished. The adults will watch closely for the introduction of new ideas and feelings, and encourage Manny to explore those ideas and begin to make connections between ideas.

The therapist will also help Mom understand why this type of play is useful, and how the themes of aggression and power are important for Manny. Pretend play is a way for Manny to act out his feelings within a range of arousal that he can control and with the security of a safe relationship. The therapist can help Mom appreciate that pretend fighting is not equivalent to bad behavior and that this play will not translate into being mean in real life; in fact, it may help Manny develop greater comfort in modulating and expressing his feelings appropriately, rather than simply feeling dejected and powerless when he lacks understanding. Through such play, Manny will gradually develop higher levels of complex and logical thinking.

Ray is a quiet boy who easily follows familiar routines and accepts changes as well, but he often reacts impulsively. Once, he grabbed someone's food in a restaurant as he walked by, and another time he pushed a child in line at the grocery store, while reaching for candy. In his academic work, he is making progress when he can memorize facts, but is unable to create an original story. He likes to draw, and fills notebooks with multiple copies of his favorite cartoon character and his favorite subject—food.

Ray has some constrictions at the lower milestones but has most deficits in Milestone 5. Ray is vulnerable to events in the moment and acts immediately on his feelings. Play can help him build a capacity to function and communicate with ideas rather than actions. The goal is for Ray to use symbols to express his ideas and to expand and elaborate his ideas using creative thinking. With this capacity, he will be able to signal his intent rather than act impulsively, and eventually be able to negotiate and reflect on his ideas.

Because Ray likes to draw, the play sessions involved creating murals together with his therapist. At first, he drew familiar cartoon-type characters and his favorite foods. In a playful way, the therapist joined in the drawing. With support, Ray was able to describe more about these characters and the significance of the details. The therapist playfully challenged him to expand and create new characters. Over time, these drawings provided a medium for Ray to begin to both symbolize and talk about his feelings and ideas, including his interest and anxiety about getting food and eating. Now, when Ray experiences strong feelings around food, he can utilize language to express his ideas and negotiate between his desires and limits.

> *Isabel was pretending about animals in the zoo. Each little animal was inside a strong fence. Then one of the animals escaped and ran out. Then the tiger and lion also escaped from their enclosures. As more animals became loose, Isabel began to use sounds and yells and fewer words to describe the action. Then she started to knock over some of the blocks and generally became disorganized and dysregulated. The therapist introduced the zookeeper, who had the power to bring the animals back home.*

In this case, the therapist was helping reinforce the idea that adults are present and available to provide safety, from physical threats but also for overwhelming feelings.

Sometimes, a child's play is provocative, such as using bathroom humor or enacting a purposely malicious act.

> *In pretend, Timmy had his dog poop in the play house, and then increased the naughty behavior by having the dog chew up a shoe. As Timmy continued to ramp up the mischief, he became somewhat agitated, and looked to the therapist to see her reaction.*
>
> *Timmy needed support to find a counter to the mischievous dog. Rather than threatening a punishment for the dog, the therapist wondered if the dog might be lonely or bored, and gestured toward some other dog figures. With Timmy's endorsement, the therapist, as another character, brought in more dogs to play.*

Here, an adult has shown through symbolic play how bad behavior can be transformed with the help of an empathetic adult. It is critical not to lead the play, but if a child is spiraling into distress, an adult can offer just the level of support needed to sustain regulation. A knowledge of the child's actual patterns of interaction can help inform the ideas suggested in play.

The Meaning of Symbols

The capacity to think in symbols is generated by a child's discovery of a way to connect many related experiences and feelings with a symbolic mode of expression. A child may use verbal or nonverbal language, act out an idea with figures or objects, or express ideas through creative writing, art, music, or dance. Close attention to a child's choice of symbols can be enlightening as they reveal the child's thoughts. It is possible to gain insight into the child's concerns by carefully tracking the ideas portrayed and the sequence of emotional themes through the course of play.

> *Alejandro is fascinated by the Titanic and he also likes volcanos. Both frequently appear in his pretend play and in his drawings.*

These are common symbols that might be interpreted to represent sudden, powerful, and frightening events. They may be chosen as favorites because they mirror the child's real-life experiences. In play, a strategy to help Alejandro to gain mastery over these feelings might include helping him act out his ideas, plan and anticipate the crash or explosion, and consider the effects on the characters. While not leading the play, an adult can help by slowing down the sequence of events and exploring the associated feelings, including fear, bravery, sadness, and kindness.

> *Thomas always chose the smallest character for himself, and used that character to battle the bad guys through all types of danger. His bravery contrasted with other moments of hiding.*

Thomas's symbolism transparently reflected how he felt small and surrounded by danger, and his perception of two options, either fighting or hiding. By joining in his play, an adult is able to help Thomas to collaborate with other helpers and gradually elaborate his ideas about other ways to conquer the dangers.

In play, it is not uncommon for children to purposefully challenge themselves to pretend about an idea, take it just so far, and then back away when the idea provokes too much anxiety. "It really wasn't a scary bear; it was just a puppy dog." Or they will completely shift attention to something different: "Let's play ball now." The extremes of feeling and thought can mirror the pattern of responses in daily events. Through play, a child can be supported to gradually modulate a greater range of responses.

Sometimes children will be wary of including a frightening symbol. They may see an alligator, snake, or fighter, and say, "I hope that alligator doesn't come over here!" Of course, the adult would want to help the child to explore those feelings. Later, an adult might say, "I wonder if that alligator is waking up!" By partnering with the child in the play scenario, such as, "Let's hide together," or "Shall we build a wall?" the child may be emboldened to incorporate the frightening idea into play. A frightening idea may be portrayed as an angry character, a strong character, or a confusing character—any feeling may create anxiety for a child.

> In play, Sean softly said, "He's dead," as he laid a little character on its side. The therapist said with some concern, "He's dead?" Sean replied, "Yes, he was bad."

By obtaining further history, it became evident that Sean was confused about being in trouble and death. By being open to a child's expressions, it is possible to become aware of these misperceptions and then help to correct them. It is always important to allow children to express their ideas, being careful not to override their thoughts with our feelings, our unease with their feelings, or our desire to protect them from painful emotions.

Strategies for Pretend Play at Milestone 5

In Milestone 5, the goal in play is to help a child use language and pretend play to symbolize emotional ideas, and expand and elaborate those ideas. Pretend play is a safe medium in which a child can explore and practice interaction around a range of emotional themes including nurturance and loss, fear and bravery, anger, aggression, competition, victory, and defeat. Through playful interaction, children organize their own internal capacity to think and communicate about these different emotional experiences, thereby becoming free from acting directly upon feelings. The following strategies support symbolic play:

- Create a play environment that encourages pretend play with props that support emotional themes: nurturance, exploration, fear, power, good, evil, and so on. Consider incorporating a child's favorite ideas from books or videos.
- Attend to both words and actions, and the feelings represented. Help children elaborate their subtle cues about ideas and feelings.
- Use language in balance with affect and action; simplify language when a child is challenged in other areas.
- Use artifice so that it is clear that play is a pretend world. Use altered voices and hold characters, especially to communicate strong emotions. Act upon a child's character, not the child himself, and have him interact with your character. Only interact with a child's body if he is clearly in costume, such as pretend role-play.
- Alternate between being a character and being a narrator that asks questions or makes comments or summary statements.
- If a child becomes repetitive, raise the affect and wonder, "What else can we do?"
- Be playful, but avoid being silly, sarcastic, or off topic. It is important to demonstrate acceptance of all of the child's emotional ideas, without ignoring, distracting, or overreacting.
- If a child mentions something off topic, or is momentarily distracted, consider bypassing or ignoring the comment and continuing with the previous idea.
- Allow a child to deepen emotional ideas. Avoid offering solutions to problems (healing the hurt man, rescuing the shipwreck) but rather help to intensify the feelings and problem so that the child might either add to the problem or suggest a solution.
- Offer structure or options as needed to help the child sustain ideas.

("Oh no, he's coming! Where can we hide?") Try to build on ideas they may have presented before.

- Maintain an attitude of genuine curiosity about a child's ideas and encourage spontaneous creativity. If a child is fascinated with facts or a particular topic, delve to find the affective significance of those facts.

Milestone 6: Logical Thinking

Denzel enjoys running in the play yard with his peers at school. However, he frequently gets into heated verbal altercations with his peers. At home he argues with his mother and rigidly insists his ideas are correct. When questioned, Denzel has a long string of complaints about how others do not follow the rules. He feels discouraged that school is so hard.

In the playroom, Denzel lays out all the houses and then with great glee starts the attack. It starts with a few smaller bombs, but as he gets more excited all the town is destroyed, and then he simply jumbles all the pieces in total chaos. Denzel plays out similar ideas of destruction over and over.

Denzel uses symbolic play to represent feelings of anger and aggression. Further assessment reveals that Denzel seeks proprioceptive and vestibular input and has poor visual-spatial awareness. He has difficulty with receptive language, especially when he is stressed. He interprets rules simplistically, and has difficulty being flexible and understanding perspective of others.

In play, Denzel can be encouraged to explore the intense feelings represented by the attack, destruction, and death. Although he presents with a gleeful expression, a sensitive professional recognizes the anxiety, anger, sadness, and confusion that underlie his actions and can gradually help to tease out these components. Through an adult joining the play and thereby slowing the action, with comments and questions, Denzel can consider the feelings and perspectives of different players. Advancement in the complexity and refinement in his play, along with discussion about his understanding of interactions at school, will help Denzel to be more tolerant and flexible around his expectations.

Marcy tends to be very anxious. She is resistant to going new places, and is sensitive to small changes. She came into the playroom cautiously. She slowly began to explore the play materials, and then started to arrange the dolls. Dad inquired about the characters' names, what they were doing, and so on, and Marcy described each character in great detail. "Leila has red hair, and her dress is the prettiest. No, this one, Polly, has the prettiest dress. She is going to wear a yellow hat that matches." Marcy placed them in the houses, but never stated what they were doing. Dad was eventually able to start interactive play by asking, "Which one can I be?" Marcy, somewhat reluctantly, gave him a dad-like figure. Using a deep voice, Dad said, "It looks like everyone is dressed so nicely. Where are we going?" Marcy said, "To a dance!" Dad said, "Yeah, a dance! I'll drive—everyone in!" Now Marcy and Dad could continue to expand the play ideas.

Some children can be overly focused on details and have difficulty expanding thinking and being open to considering new options and possibilities. Marcy was often worried about things she could not control, and then became even more rigid with a narrow focus of attention. With gentle, patient partnership, an adult can help Marcy enter into dramatic play and begin to place all the details that are meaningful to her within a bigger context. Being prettiest revealed her concern with competition and self-esteem. At the same time, she was able to suggest going to a dance, which represented an assertive exploration of something that would be very frightening for her in real life. By playing out these ideas and others, in partnership with Dad and Mom, Marcy can increase her self-confidence and begin to form broader concepts of herself and the world.

Mary is usually in a state of low arousal and is content to sit and daydream. In the schoolyard, she tends to wander aimlessly by herself. Mary appears to have intellectual deficits, but her true potential is not known. When asked questions about a story, she does not know the answer and will make seemingly random guesses. It is unclear if she has been listening. She often distracts others in class by humming. She is given constant reminders to be quiet and pay attention. In play, Mary likes puzzles and baby dolls, and will sometimes say a character is a good guy or a bad guy, although their actions do not necessarily correspond with these titles.

Play can help Mary sustain a focus of attention, engage in coregulated reciprocal communicative exchanges, and elaborate her ideas. While much of her schoolwork involves rote learning, free play will tap her interests and motivation and elicit her potential for thinking, language, and movement. With support, Mary became animated in play and generated many novel ideas. It was discovered that Mary had significant challenges with receptive language, but with gestural support and high affect, she was able to connect ideas, create logical stories, and demonstrate her innate intelligence.

Larry was being teased and bullied at school. Others called him names, pushed him, and took his lunch. Larry was often left feeling embarrassed, angry, confused, and sad.

In play Larry enacted villains, which he would hit and then shoot with pretend guns. Although he had killed them, they would revive and sneak up on his character again. For Larry, guns were a magical solution for a problem for which he had no other recourse. However, even in pretend, this was ineffective. Magical thinking is an expedient solution for frightening and overwhelming ideas. With help, Larry was able to explore his angry feelings and invent other solutions. In play, he imagined poison, and then throwing the villains in jail. Gradually, he was able to enlist others to aid his efforts. As he gained confidence to extend the play, he included feelings of sadness, betrayal and embarrassment. He was able to consider multiple perspectives and motivations of the various characters. After creating these dramas, Larry began to tell his parents more about his experiences at school.

Bullying is a complex issue. Not only did Larry need to cope with his feelings, he needed to learn whom to trust and when to be suspicious of another's intent. A long-term plan included helping him develop true friendships. At the same time, he was offered some protection at school by closer monitoring by adults and adjustments to his schedule. Gradually, Larry gained the capacity to discern genuine friendship, and gained confidence through their interactions together.

> *Andrew will be moving to a new house and everything is being packed. Just last week, his grandfather, who had spent a lot of time with him, passed away. Now, Andrew is generally irritable and is resisting getting in the car, and following daily routines.*

Play can be used to help a child to understand and cope with particular emotions and events. While difficult behaviors might be expected in this situation, play can support the recovery and even help Andrew develop increasing skills through the difficult experience. Moving, death, and loss are big concepts and need to be approached according to the developmental capacities of the child. Play might be used to enact moving from one house to another or other renditions of goodbyes and hellos. These themes might also be explored through books, including creating personalized books.

In utilizing play to support a child through trauma or when there are complex emotional dynamics within a family, it may be necessary that a mental health specialist guides the intervention. While all children experience pain and loss, professionals must consider when the needs of the child and family are beyond the boundaries of their expertise and call upon their colleagues from other disciplines.

Strategies for Play at Milestone 6

In Milestone 6, the goal in play is to help a child to elaborate emotional ideas and make connections between them, leading to sequenced, logical stories, and eventually planning and prediction of those scenarios with insight into motivations and consequences from different perspectives. At this stage, a child can build on other's ideas in a fluid exchange of sustained engagement. The challenge for an adult player is to help children whose play ideas are fragmented, jumping from one idea to another, or restricted to a narrow range of ideas to expand and connect their ideas and yet not provide all of the ideas and connections for them. It is tempting to organize a story for a child and provide logical reasoning; however, the goal is that the child will develop the capacities to organize and link thoughts on his own.

Strategies for Milestone 6 include the following:

- Within pretend play, maintain a playful atmosphere, sustaining foundational milestones of shared attention, trust, fun engagement, and sustained, coregulated interactions, while supporting creativity and imagination.
- Be part of the play as a character and introduce ideas that challenge the child to consider another perspective.
- Avoid creating a story line. Ask questions that encourage a child to think about linking events in time: "What's going to happen next?" but focus on the drama more than the plot. With an animated voice and expression say, "That monster was really scary. Now the monster is in the corner and all the animals are in the house. I wonder what the animals are going to do. . . . "
- Wonder about the how and why of events and feelings. If a child has difficulty answering, offer options but avoid answering for the child. Continue to ponder, using affect to help the child formulate a connection.
- Balance questions and comments as a narrator with being part of the action. When possible, embed questions into the character's role: "Where should I drive my truck, boss?" "Why do I have to wait?"
- Use comments to slow down and summarize events: "Wait! What just happened? I'm confused! The army is here, and now the bomb is over there."
- Link facts and actions with feelings. "It looks like the red team is really strong and brave!"
- Ask open-ended questions that probe a child's opinions. "Which army is better?" "Why is he the good guy?"
- For children who are focused on details, use summarizing statements that help them see the big picture or pattern in events. For children who describe only broad ideas, help them attend to details.
- Comment on what is not said or done, or themes that are avoided. "It seems like the scary aliens always turn into nice friends."

- Extend or amplify the child's idea; add another idea building on their affective idea.
- Do something unexpected that challenges a child to respond.
- At the end of the play, help the child to reflect: "What was the best part? The scariest part?" "Did anything like that ever happen to you?"

Play With Peers

Playful interaction with peers is an important venue for learning cooperation and coregulation. For a child with constrictions at the early milestones of building shared attention, trust, and simple reciprocity, there is no substitute for one-to-one interaction with an adult. A child may still benefit from peer experience, but will need intensive adult support to succeed. Having a few adults consistently in the role of facilitating peer interactions provides the advantage of the knowledge and trust between the child and the adults.

It is important that a professional utilize only the degree of intervention necessary, so that the adult does not unwittingly impede the child's opportunities to interact with peers. Although intensive support may be needed initially, the intensity of adult support can gradually decrease as the child gains new skills in interacting with others. The following strategies can be employed to facilitate interaction toward higher levels:

- Begin play with a focus on the lowest milestone that is a strength for all the children, which is often lower than what a particular child might be able to do with an adult. Utilize strategies for each milestone.
- If the child comes to an adult to show something or to seek help, the facilitator could encourage the child: "Show him," "Ask him," or "Tell her," directing the child to a peer. A facilitator may need to support both aspects of the conversation. "Joe, I think Martin is trying to show you something." Or "I think Martin needs some help."
- A facilitator may also help with interpretation of nonverbal gestures or behaviors and can help a child anticipate what is going to happen. "Look, Tom is coming over. I think he just wants to see

what you are doing." "Uh-oh, look at Susie's face. I think she is not happy." "When you turn your back, they think you don't want them to play." Sometimes a facilitator can provide information that is useful for the peers, such as, "If Mark doesn't hear you, you can get in front of him and say it again." Or "I think Jack ran over to the wall because he doesn't understand the rules. Maybe you can explain it to him."

- An adult can help a peer to understand what is hard for another child: "He doesn't like loud noises." "He doesn't know how to climb the slide." And how a child can help: "You can show him where to go."

- A facilitator can also promote conversation. "Mary, did you hear what Mark said?" "You can tell him, 'I didn't hear you.'" "What did you hear him say? That's not what I heard. You'd better ask him again."

- Most children are drawn to an interested, friendly, and fun adult. One strategy that takes advantage of the excitement of a playful adult is for the adult to connect a peer's interest in the adult to the child that needs support. So if a peer brings over a discovery to share, an adult might say, "Look, Mark! See what Pedro is showing us!"

- An adult can cease to be a source of information. After a child builds a sense of warm rapport with a facilitator, there will be a natural inclination to seek that person out for information. The facilitator can then encourage the child to find information either from peers or from other adults. If the child asks a direct question, the response can often be, "I don't know. Maybe you can ask someone over there," or, "Good question. I wonder who would know." Or simply, "Ask Mary what she thinks about that."

- A facilitator can help link children's ideas; sometimes they will connect ideas if they are simply prompted to say what they are doing out loud. "Mary, what are you doing?" "Making a cake." "Matt, what are you doing?" "Driving a truck." Mary may spontaneously say, "Do you want some cake?" or the adult might suggest, "Do you need the truck to deliver some flour for the cake?"

- A facilitator must resist the temptation to orchestrate behavior so that all conflicts are avoided or to expedite their resolution. A child learns by being challenged and working through those challenges. Sometimes, it is necessary to wait while children have unresolved disagreements or unsuccessful communication, in order for them to eventually find a solution. A facilitator might say, "Oh no! Sam really wants to go outside, but Tom wants to play a board game. That is sure a problem." A facilitator may have to wait while they try to arrive at a mutually agreeable plan. Sometimes a facilitator can clarify a conflict or simply slow down the interaction to help peers focus on a problem. "Paul said he was safe, and José said he was out. You guys don't agree." A facilitator may carefully grade the level of support, by holding the problem in focus or, if necessary, by offering options. With the lowest level of intervention, the peers have the greatest opportunity to form their own resolution.

- It is often helpful for a child to be told explicitly why a facilitator is there. "I am going to be coming every day after lunch to help you play with the other kids in the yard." Or, "I am going to be here to help you so that if you get mad the balls will stay in the yard and not go over the fence." Depending on the child's abilities, this explanation can be more or less complex. The relationship is always framed in a true attitude of care, concern, and respect. "I know you want to follow the rules today and I am going to help you." Children are usually aware of the adult's presence and can take pride when they are successful in achieving the shared goals.

Setting play dates involves consideration of children that have complementary skills and interests, and arranging times and activities that are likely to be successful. Friendships develop gradually over time and cannot be rushed. It is helpful that initial play dates are relatively brief, and in a neutral location, so that neither child becomes overwhelmed by the experience. Many of the strategies for handling conflict in the moment, as well as those for each milestone, apply equally in supporting peer-to-peer play interactions.

The Importance of Play

Play is essential in child development. During play, children experience powerful emotions and can exercise their highest abilities of engagement, communication, shared problem solving, reasoning, and reflection. For children with behavioral challenges, the skills learned and practiced in play can have a direct impact on how they negotiate the emotions that give rise to unwanted behaviors. In addition, the relationships nurtured and strengthened through play-based interactions provide the foundation for successful management of stressful events.

An adult can support the development of functional skills by being a play partner or facilitating peer play interactions. Play-based interventions begin by ensuring that time is dedicated to free play and by providing an appropriate play environment. An adult shares a child's interests, and then challenges her to advance to higher skills. Play is a safe context in which to explore a range of feelings and ideas, and pursue imagination, creativity, experimentation, and discovery. Not only do the skills acquired during play contribute to improvement in challenging behaviors, but pleasurable activities that are built on strengths and interests create the foundation for lifelong vocations or avocations and continued developmental learning throughout life.

Chapter **11**

The Course of Treatment

The DIR approach to intervention provides a framework for the course of treatment for behavioral challenges. A clinician begins by forming an understanding of a child's behavior in a broad developmental framework (D), along with an understanding of a child's individual differences (I) and patterns of interaction in key relationships (R). The structure of DIR then provides a clear path to guide a clinician in the work toward a child's developmental and behavioral goals.

As parents learn about the DIR framework, the important goals embedded in DIR, and how the intervention is tailored for the unique qualities of their child and family, they gain a sense of security in the clinical process. From the beginning parents can have hope for their child's success and seeing their child functioning as a warmly relating, considerate, and happy person in the future.

Over time, a clinician develops a deeper understanding of a child's developmental capacities and individual profile and a greater appreciation of parents' strengths, challenges, ideas, fears, and hopes. Parents share their ideas with a professional, participate during sessions, and utilize strategies in daily activities between sessions. Together, parents and professionals build a relationship of trust and respect as they work through difficult times and celebrate each step of success.

In a developmental approach, changes in a child's behavior and patterns of parent-child interaction occur gradually, especially at the beginning. Subtle but important changes often occur while building the foundational milestones of shared attention, trust, and engagement. A clinician can help parents appreciate the importance of these early milestones as the foundation for meaningful change.

Change in a child's behavior is not linear, but progresses with incremental successes, new challenges, and intermittent setbacks. The three elements of DIR provide the consistent principles to guide the course of treatment. While (R) refers to a child's relationships, particularly with parents, a key relationship is also formed between parents and the clinician.

Parent-Professional Collaboration

Interestingly, the relationship between parents and professional follows its own developmental trajectory over the course of treatment that mirrors the child's developmental milestones. Over time, a parent-professional relationship progresses from basic shared focus of attention to higher levels of thoughtful exchange. Advancement occurs in greater shared problem solving and more reflective discussions, and in an expanding breadth in the range of feelings addressed. Awareness of the strength or constrictions in the different dimensions of the relationship with parents can help guide a professional's intervention plan.

Milestone 1

From the initial stages of assessment, parents are invited to share in a therapeutic process through the professional's sincere interest in their concerns and perspectives. A clinician strives to provide a safe and supportive environment so that parents are comfortable talking about difficult emotional subjects. A shared focus is created as parents disclose aspects of their child's development and behavior and the family dynamics that they feel are pertinent and open for examination and reflection.

Most important at Milestone 1 is that the parents are fully involved in their child's treatment and make a commitment to regular attendance and participation. It is helpful to communicate an expectation of partnership both explicitly and through the tone of interaction. From the start it is necessary to coordinate schedules regarding the timing and frequency of sessions and establish a shared understanding about the possible duration of treatment. An ongoing interest in recognizing the parents' needs and accommodating when possible serves to nurture the parent-professional relationship.

Sometimes parents are resistant to engaging in work with their child because of a previous experience. The child may have been enrolled in a program in which a professional worked directly with her and excluded parent participation. Professionals may have unwittingly given the message that because of their qualifications parents should simply defer to them. Unfortunately, when parents relinquish this authority to a professional, it undermines their confidence and diminishes the potential impact of their daily interactions.

Some parents have difficulty being consistently available. Clinicians may become angry or resentful that parents do not seem to care or make adequate efforts to support the clinical process. A wise clinician will seek to understand the reasons why it is difficult for a parent to be fully engaged. By doing so, a clinician may not only gain useful information that may help decrease barriers to collaboration but may also form empathy and compassion for the parent's situation.

During the course of treatment, some parents become uncomfortable when they are unsuccessful in their attempts to interact with their child or with certain types of behavior in play. Parents may leave the room or simply distract themselves by becoming self-absorbed, looking bored, or by making unrelated comments, jokes, or conversation. The professional is then charged with addressing the difficulty and helping them reengage and feel successful.

Therapists often witness parents' heroic efforts to care for a child with behavioral challenges and to cope with enormous demands and stresses. Some parents struggle to obtain the basics of physical and mental health for themselves and their children and families, or struggle with a myriad of financial or work-related challenges. The ability to attend to a child's behaviors and developmental needs may be impacted by a family's abilities to meet basic necessities, intermittently or throughout the course of treatment.

In some instances parents may be physically or mentally unable to adequately nurture and parent their child. A professional may be required to take a more active role in working directly with a child, while simultaneously seeking support for the parents. Although it may not be within the scope of practice to help parents obtain social supports or medical care, it is within all professionals' role to refer a family to resources for help when a basic need is identified. Part of the therapeutic process may be to help parents recognize the need for additional support and build trust to seek out that help.

A professional is required to report any situation in which it is suspected that a child is experiencing emotional or physical abuse or neglect. A clinician then has the awesome responsibility to support both parent and child, through multiple layers of challenge in trust, anxiety, trauma, and shame. A mental health provider is best suited to provide support in such a situation, but all professionals may have some role in supporting the parent and child. Through patient and consistent care, a clinician may have the opportunity to establish a new relationship of trust, and gradually build on the strengths of love and hope that parents have for their child.

Participation in developmental relationship–based treatment is a demonstration of parents' care for their child. Parents often must sacrifice their own needs to obtain treatment and may be coping with worry and grief. A clinician may encourage parents to seek support and find time to care for themselves so that they can be more available for their child. A professional that appreciates parents' vulnerabilities and devotion to their child will respectfully build a secure base of parent-professional relationship.

Milestone 2

As a clinician proceeds with an empathetic perspective of the parental role, a relationship of trust between parent and professional is formed. The same sense of pleasure and warmth that is the goal in Milestone 2 for relationships with children also applies to the parent-professional relationship. As parents develop familiarity, comfort, and confidence in their relationship with a clinician, they become more deeply engaged in the process of working together and doing the hard work involved in changing their thoughts and actions as needed to support their child.

There are parallels between the therapist's relationship with a parent and a parent's relationship to a child. By experiencing the therapist's sensitivity and patience, parents may then be able to replicate these responses when similar emotions are aroused in interaction with their child. Some parents may not have experienced healthy trusting relationships with their own parents, spouse, or others in their life. Through reliable positive interactions with a therapist, parents may be enabled to create deeper levels of warmth, calmness, and consistency in their relationships with their child.

Some parents are prone to distrust professionals or at least harbor suspicion, especially if a previous experience with a professional has been hurtful. Some displace anger directly onto a clinician and may be generally pessimistic and skeptical about the potential of any intervention strategies. Some even seem to undermine a child's success. Here a clinician is challenged to maintain professional perspective, consider the underlying reasons for these responses, and redouble efforts at building trust by steadfastly finding a parent's strengths, active listening, and encouraging open communication.

Other parents may tend to have feelings of dependence or strive for a personal connection with a therapist. Here, a professional will vigilantly maintain boundaries and support parents to recognize their distinct roles, appropriate means of communication, and topics of discussion. Therapists may also be tempted to become a confidant or a friend to a family member; however, blurring the professional boundaries can undermine the ability to achieve the desired goals.

It is essential for a clinician to maintain an attitude of respect for a parent's experience, role, and ideas. In working with children and families, a professional is privy to personal struggles, weaknesses, and foibles as well as differences based on cultural background. It behooves a clinician to avoid critical judgments and rather identify a parent's strengths and build from those strengths. Most parents have a strong love for their child despite all of the behavioral challenges.

Milestone 3

A goal for the parent-clinician relationship is to establish a comfortable pace and rhythm of rich verbal and nonverbal exchange. Behavioral challenges evoke strong feelings in parents, who may describe joy, pride, sadness, anxiety, anger, frustration, disappointment, or more complex feelings of jealousy, embarrassment, shame, distrust, or confusion. These emotions may be expressed in a coherent manner with context and abstraction, or they may be physically expressed in visceral reactions and not be explicitly acknowledged.

Each parent has his or her own style of communication. Some adults express emotion more openly and others are more restrained. Like an adult-child relationship, in a professional-parent relationship, the professional must take greater responsibility to achieve successful communication by adapting to the style of a parent and following her lead. By carefully observing all of a parent's communicative clues, a professional can sensitively support a smooth flow of interaction that gradually increases in range and depth.

Milestone 4

Milestone 4 involves complex communication in which a parent and clinician develop their own pattern of working together and problem solving. Parents come to a session prepared to report on events with thoughts and questions. The sessions take on a routine such as discussion, play, reflection, and planning. Clinicians find a way of supporting parents through coaching, joint play, or modeling that works best for a particular parent and child. Throughout the session, parents and clinicians are able to sustain their conversations with continuous shared attention and coregulation.

Reciprocal dialogue often involves problem solving focused on actions: what to do or not do in the moment, and how to create learning experiences for a child through unstructured and semistructured play experiences. Although parents might like to begin with immediately receiving instructions about what to do to resolve a behavior, in actuality, a complete understanding of a problematic behavior and creating an effective intervention plan takes time. In urgent situations, it may be helpful for a professional to quickly offer some ideas regarding ways to handle a problem; however, giving detailed steps of correct responses to behavior is often disappointing and can actually undermine the development of an effective parent-professional collaboration.

A relationship of mutual respect and trust allows parents to tolerate uncomfortable feelings associated with disagreement, and enables them to offer ideas, listen, and engage in creating a plan. Both parents and clinician offer observations and interpretations of behavior and interactions. While they may have different perspectives, parents and professionals create a set of mutually accepted interpretations of behavior as well as shared goals. Then they work together to select priorities and propose strategies to try. Over time, parents and clinician persist through both successful and unsuccessful efforts.

Some parents and clinicians are uncomfortable when certain feelings are aroused. For example, clinicians may feel flustered when they are uncertain or confused, and react by bypassing a presenting problem or giving rigid instructions, rather than engaging in shared problem solving. Or an interaction with the clinician may cause parents to feel anxious, angry, or embarrassed, leading them to be dishonest, detached, or belligerent. Discomfort with feelings and the subsequent reaction is often a reflection of a clinician's or parent's own background and may be strong and unconscious. Hopefully, clinicians, through professional training and supervision, have self-awareness of their own tendencies. When parents and clinicians are able to persist in problem solving through the more difficult times in their relationship together, not only will treatment be successful, but parents will feel empowered, encouraged, and proud of their efforts.

Milestone 5

Not only may conversations involve decision making about actions, but parents may also describe their feelings, hopes, and fears. Just like the development of symbolic thought in a child, parents may begin by describing physical symptoms associated with emotional experience. They may report feeling knots in their stomach, headaches, or exhaustion. Later they may relate global feelings to their actions: "I feel that the only way I can cope is to stay at work longer."

Eventually, a parent may be able to identify specific feelings and fantasies without acting upon them. "I get so mad when he does that, that I want to just lock him in his room." "I am so hurt when he does that I want to just sit and cry." Parents may describe their fears for the future. "I hope he doesn't end up in jail or on the streets."

Parents can also imagine positive outcomes. "I want him to go to college and have a successful, independent life." "I think he will eventually become a graphic artist, and these outbursts will be under control." A clinician acknowledges these general or more specific expressions and encourages parents to explore and elaborate their thoughts. Sometimes, parents' fears, fantasies, and hopes are extreme and unrealistic; however, the ability to talk about these ideas leads to higher levels of reflection and planning.

Milestone 6

At Milestone 6, parents are able to reflect logically about their feelings and actions. "I was really tired and frustrated, so when he started throwing things, I just lost it. Then, I stopped myself, realized he was probably hungry, and just decided to be calm and get him something to eat." A parent may also express different intensities of feeling. "I was worried that he might be lonely, but I was more worried that he would miss out on a great experience, so I let him go."

Now parents can consider multiple perspectives and how their actions reflect their own values. "The teacher thought he was being defiant, but I thought that he was just confused, so I asked the aide to help him. To me it was more important that he understood how to do it. I wish he knew how to ask for help." These insights may lead to priorities and plans for the future.

Parents might reflect how their own past experiences affect their interactions with their child. "My dad was always distant, so I want to make an extra effort to spend time with her. I decided to cut back to part time at work, so I can be home more." Or, "Growing up, I was always in trouble. I don't want Malcolm to feel that way."

Over time, a parent and clinician develop a rapport that includes an ability to reflect on their work together. The parent might predict how a therapist will respond. "I heard your voice in my head." Or, "I thought you would disapprove, but I gave it to him. I guess I was feeling like I wasn't ready for another fight." Or, "I thought you would be proud of me." Eventually, parents may reflect abstractly about their work with a clinician. "You gave me hope, and now I really believe he is going to be all right."

The Structure of Sessions

The structure of sessions varies greatly depending on the context and role of the professional in regard to a behavioral challenge. A professional may or may not be present at the actual moment of a difficult behavior. Often, a professional is supporting overall developmental capacities during play-based sessions or semistructured activities, along with providing guidelines for managing behavior at other times.

At the beginning of each session, clinicians typically inquire about events since the previous meeting. Based on this information, they may choose to adapt or modify plans for the session. They then describe the goals and review the strategies of particular focus at that time. They may explain to the parents why certain toys are available or why the environment is arranged in a certain way. By establishing a common understanding, professional and parents are aligned as a team, and subsequent coaching can utilize abbreviated messages or cues.

As the session unfolds in a play-based intervention, a professional must attend simultaneously to both parents and child, and their interaction. The clinician balances between joining the play, coaching, and offering comments or questions. Even when playing with a child directly, the professional strives to maintain shared attention with a parent. As the clinician recognizes parents' efforts and offers observations and reflections, parents gain confidence to try new strategies as well as initiate their own ideas.

At the conclusion of a session, parents and clinician can take a moment to reflect on the play that has just occurred. The clinician may highlight key moments, including the parents' role in the interaction. By utilizing their knowledge of developmental principles, a clinician can anticipate which skills will emerge next. A clear developmental framework instills confidence and trust in the treatment process.

Parent Styles

In soliciting a parent's participation in the work of changing patterns of interaction with their child, a clinician must adapt to the many diverse learning styles of parents. Some parents desire an analytical discussion and gain confidence from acquiring systematic knowledge about child developmental milestones, individual differences, and the steps of a treatment plan. They may benefit from references to books or individual written plans and strategies. Other parents may prefer only a cursory discussion about theoretical models, but enjoy talking about specific interactions with their child. While accommodating to different styles, a clinician must ensure that all parents understand the basic goals and strategies being pursued.

Adult conversations must be balanced with guided experiences with a child. Some parents like to be coached; others insist on watching and having behavioral strategies modeled for them. Often, parents learn through several different modalities. A therapist needs to be fluent in all forms of communication, and be receptive to a parent's learning preferences.

A clinician might also be on guard for the overly compliant parent, who defers completely to the clinician and asks for explicit direction. Subservience forges a path of dependence on an authority. A clinician must strive to elicit parents' ideas and help them initiate problem solving. As progress is noted, parents may express relief, pride, and optimism as they appreciate both their child's progress and their own.

Coaching

Coaching parents during interactions with their child is a highly effective method of intervention because parents are fully engaged and a professional can provide immediate and direct observations and guidance as needed. Not only is the child learning new skills, but the parents are also gaining an understanding of how to support their child's development, which can be utilized throughout the day and whenever behavioral challenges occur.

In coaching, a clinician begins by inviting a parent to simply play with the child. Without an explicit invitation, parents may assume that their role is to observe and automatically defer to the professional. The clinician should carefully consider where they are physically in the room. If parents place themselves directly in front of the child, it implies that the child will play with them. The clinician can sit close to a parent or may be able to provide guidance from a distance.

The clinician can observe the interaction and gradually proceed by providing observations of the situation. The clinician might offer, "I see that Mark really likes the cars going down the track." If a parent is trying repeatedly to engage their child without success, a clinician might reflect, "I can see that it is really hard to get him to notice." A clinician might also reinterpret the possible meaning of behaviors.

> Gregory had significant challenges in all areas of development. He was nonverbal, and had limited ways of expressing himself in movement or gestures. He did enjoy sounds, songs, and rhythms. And he loved to sit and rock with Mom, as she recited familiar little stories or chants, along with simple movements. After a few minutes of warm interaction with Mom, Gregory would abruptly get up and walk away. She experienced this sadly as an end to their moment of connection.

> An alternative interpretation was that Gregory was now renewed and was ready to continue that engagement in another activity with more vigorous movement. In fact, Gregory did enjoy other activities with Mom, although they were more challenging to sustain. Awareness of all of his sensory-motor-language-cognitive profile, and a reinterpretation of the patterns of interaction, helped to create more opportunities for engagement.

During coaching, the clinician rarely gives absolute directions. A clinician can help parents adjust their pacing to be faster or slower, or help them to become more aware of their emotional cues, tone of voice, and use of language, and their child's responses. Sometimes the clinician may wonder aloud why a parent is trying something one way rather than another.

She may offer ideas or a toy that the parents can use to extend the play. "Uh-oh, it looks like Jimmy is getting upset that the car won't go through. I think he may need your help." "I think he is getting a little repetitive and stuck." "I wonder what we could do to help him expand his play with the cars." If needed, a more specific idea can be offered, "Here's another truck you could use." "Try going up the other ramp and see what he will do." Or, as the child is starting to throw objects around the room, "Dad, what do you think will help him to calm down?" If the clinician and parents have had conversations prior to this, they will have a shared understanding about their strategies and shared goals. Professional and parents can also share a knowing glance of pleasure when a child accomplishes a goal.

In coaching two parents, a clinician may encourage one parent to interact with the child, and receive coaching, while the other parent is given an explicit role such as watching for gestures, helping to retrieve objects, or cheering success. In this way, the second parent is engaged, but will not unconsciously compete for the child's attention. Then the clinician can indicate when the parents can switch roles.

While coaching parents, the clinician alternates between talking within the play and adult talk to the parents alone. Although children can hear what is said, it is not directed to them. Children generally can easily adapt to this two-tier form of conversation. A clinician must always ensure that the messages will not be hurtful as the child may be listening, and in fact, the child may benefit from the ideas expressed.

A stance of coaching several parties in relationship is often more difficult for a professional than intervening directly with a child. Professionals must attend to two or more individuals, and consider each perspective, as well as accounting for their own presence and actions. The role of coach requires confidence, respect, care, and humility.

Modeling

In addition to coaching, a therapist may also employ the strategy of modeling. Here, a clinician works directly with a child to try a new strategy or demonstrate a way of interacting. Modeling might include using dramatic gestures, slowing down an interaction, or demonstrating a song that might soothe an upset child. Because of the skills of a professional, modeling may be effective in the moment; however, this technique may or may not be a useful way of helping parents learn to do this on their own. In each instance, a therapist may want to discuss the strategies with parents, and provide specific guidance for them to utilize in the future. A clinician must be aware of the risk that parents may feel discouraged or less competent after watching another's success, or may choose to relinquish their role to the professional.

Role-Play

Another technique of intervention is role-play. Here a clinician practices a particular strategy directly with a parent. The parent can role-play as the child, with the clinician acting as the parent. With role-play, a parent can directly experience different types of interactions. Then roles can be reversed for the parent to practice techniques to the clinician. Similarly, two parents can role-play with each other, with a clinician as coach.

It is often useful to practice using more dramatic expressions of affect. Some parents tend to use subtle expressions, and their child may have difficulty attending and discerning these cues. However, it is also important that affective expressions are sincere and not melodramatic. Practice can help parents become more aware of their own use of affective expression and learn to use modulated vocal tones, facial expressions, and gestures. Some adults are more or less comfortable with acting in this way, but it can be a powerful method for developing self-awareness and for gaining the perspective of a child.

Partnering

Parents can be encouraged to partner with their child as a team against a clinician in play. Having a parent as a partner increases feelings of closeness and enables the child to engage in more intense interactions. For example, as a clinician playfully sneaks up to surprise, a parent can exchange looks with a child and hint, "Let's go hide over there!" While building on the child's affect, the adult can help a child sustain an interaction.

With a parent partnering with a child, a clinician can challenge with a higher level of affect, such as pretending to be a very menacing big bad wolf. The parent and child can then work together to combat the threat. A heightened level of drama can elicit an increased level of interest and problem solving. Through the safety of a partner, the child can tolerate more excitement and anxiety and act with courage and confidence.

Or, if a parent is challenging a child in a way that may be overwhelming, the clinician can suggest, "I'll help you! What shall we do?" The clinician can then encourage the child to maintain engagement. When two parents interact with their child together, they can also partner to support expansion of the play with a shared focus.

Supporting Parental Authority

A clinician supports parents' authority with their child, while also helping a parent and child to better communicate their feelings and intent. Sometimes a parent may set an expectation that seems to be too high or too low. Here, the clinician guides the interaction in a way in which both child and parent are learning how to interact more successfully.

Taylor, who had some capacities up to Milestone 3, had a habit of running his hands over nearby surfaces, including walls, desks, or even other people's hair, clothes, or stockings. At the end of one session, they were standing and the adults were talking by the door. Mom said to her son, "Taylor, stop touching that wall and come stand by me!" The clinician, Maya, thought that Taylor probably would not be able to stop with that command because he was tired and bored.

Taylor did not come to Mom and continued to run his fingers over the nearby chairs. Maya wanted to support Mom's parenting role while helping her to adjust her expectations about the level of support Taylor would need to be successful.

Maya moved close to Taylor and with a serious expression said, "Taylor, your mom wants you to stop touching things right now." Taylor looked at her, but continued. Then, turning to Mom, Maya said, "Mom, what is the plan? What are you going to do next?" She knew that Taylor was listening. Mom said, "When we leave, we are going home." Maya said, "Taylor, did you hear?" She gestured for Mom to tell him directly. Mom came close and said in a calmer voice, "Taylor, we are going home because it's time for dinner." Taylor looked at her, put his hand down, and then looked at the door. Maya quickly reinforced Mom's plan: "Bye, Taylor. See you next time!"

Here the clinician was able to support the limits set by a parent, while at the same time helping the child to be successful. Through many such interactions, parents learn strategies while also attuning to their child's needs for support.

Over time, parents learn to expect to be both challenged and supported. As in any kind of intense work, the relationship between parents and clinician can become strained at times. A parent may feel criticized by the coaching and respond by withdrawing, or may become argumentative. The clinician then must take the responsibility to address the issue. Sometimes, parents and clinician may go into another room briefly to clarify what is happening and come to a consensus on the goals and strategies going forward. Many children can tolerate a few moments on their own, or another adult can assist by staying with them.

Additional Meetings

The clinician is constantly balancing how precious time is allocated between discussion and direct interaction with the child. Parents' concerns are always a priority. Sessions may be added to attend to urgent concerns as well as to gather information on life events, review treatment plans and strategies, and network with other team members.

In discussion, parents and clinicians have time to recount interactions in more detail and reflect on different perspectives. Additional modes of communication, whether notes, e-mail, or phone calls, can be used between sessions or if a parent cannot attend. If multiple caregivers or professionals are involved, it is essential that all share in active multidirectional correspondence. If a professional must work with a child directly, without a caregiver, then it it becomes especially urgent to have good communication with parents.

Practice Between Sessions

Practice is an important aspect of learning any new skill. Children need many opportunities to practice and advance their underlying developmental capacities. At the end of each intervention session, the clinician can discuss ways for parents to help the child practice emerging skills, both in play and in daily interactions. Floortime play is an important component in a long-term plan. As challenges increase in school, social interactions, or life events, it becomes even more important to set aside time for play and to increase the time for adult-supported play.

D: Using the Developmental Milestones to Guide Treatment

There are two general directional forces for developmental growth: toward higher milestone capacities and toward broader capacities at each milestone. Growth proceeds in both directions simultaneously. During intervention activities, strategies may be designed to support one direction or the other, while at the same time always following the child's lead and taking advantage of opportunities to support progress toward emerging skills in either direction. Plans for addressing behavior in the moment and the long-term plan also proceed concurrently. As a child advances in developmental capacities, the response in the moment reflects these new skills.

In play-based intervention, it is especially important that parents have an understanding of how behaviors fit into an underlying developmental framework, and that clinicians consistently reference goals and strategies related to the milestones. While play is inherently joyful, play-based intervention also includes challenging a child to explore uncomfortable feelings and persist in problem solving. If strategies and goals are not understood, parent, child, and clinician may all have fun in play, but the child may not achieve any significant developmental progress.

Moving up the Milestones

Wayne has a hard time playing board games. He is happy as long as he is ahead, but often disregards the rules when he falls behind. Playing a board game with his brothers usually ends in yelling and anger. Wayne has strengths at Milestones 1, 2, and 3 and has goals to advance in shared problem solving and coregulation capacities at Milestone 4. As part of the assessment, the clinician has questions about Wayne's ability to understand rules, due to either challenges in receptive language or concept formation. When there is an argument, everyone talks quickly, which may make it even more difficult for Wayne to understand. A consultation with a speech and language pathologist has been requested and it was recommended to provide additional visual cues to support the play.

The plan is for a clinician or parent to practice playing with Wayne, together with his more patient older brother. At first they will play other sports games that involved a loose form of competition, then advance to short board games with many chances to win, and then competitive games that are more challenging. Initially, Wayne and his brother may play as a team against Mom. They may also allow Wayne some latitude with the rules, while they gradually challenge him to enjoy higher levels of anticipation and tolerate disappointment within the play. The focus will be on an animated exchange of affective cues while having fun, to build Wayne's capacities at Milestone 4.

A key ingredient for successful change is to present a level of challenge that is just above the child's current skill level. For many children, the range between the level of challenge that promotes progress and the level that is overwhelming is very narrow. Parents and clinicians often work on the cusp of dysregulation as they strive to find the just-right level of challenge.

Molly loved to dress up as a princess. Sometimes, she would use a magic wand to change animals from one type to another. Everyone enjoyed her creativity, and she even invented new names for animals. Dad pretended to be a sorcerer with magic powers to change animals as well. However, when he changed a kitty into a snake, she became so upset that she couldn't speak and suddenly kicked over the play structure. It took some time to re-engage and support her to create a solution for the evil sorcerer.

Working to Broaden the Range of a Developmental Milestone

The focus of intervention may be to strengthen a child's capacities at a particular milestone, so that he can function using those abilities with more people, in more contexts, and in particular, while experiencing a broader array of emotions.

Ricky had volatile behavior. In play, he was very interested in a popular fictional world with powerful aliens and opposing armies of alien creatures. He collected the figures and liked to spend time arranging them all carefully, and then staging an attack between two groups. Actually, it was the only play that interested him. He became animated with genuine pleasure when talking about these characters. He was very tied to the facts and details sur-

rounding the fictional world, and it was difficult to elicit an original idea, or to extend any of the play ideas.

Although Ricky had constrictions in regulation, an area of focus of intervention was to broaden his capacities at Milestone 5, symbolic thinking, as this in turn would support his regulation. When considering the affective themes of his play, it became apparent that there were elements of aggression, power, and danger; however, those feelings were represented in a somewhat superficial way.

In play, Ricky was gradually challenged to elaborate and go deeper into the feelings represented. Ricky often rushed through an idea or changed the subject to a safer topic. Gradually, he increased his capacity to sustain interaction when fighting the evil figures and being powerful against danger. While intervention strategies were also proceeding outside of play, his symbolic play advanced to include a wide range of themes including nurturance and friendship, as he became a hero and protector. Over time, Ricky's volatile behavior diminished and he was successful in school and at home.

Moving to Lower Milestones: Setbacks and Regressions

There are times when goals and strategies must move to lower developmental milestones. A setback or regression in behavior may occur after a particular event, or when a number of smaller stresses accumulate and overwhelm a child's abilities to adapt. Elevated expectations for learning or behavior naturally cause stress, especially if they coincide in several venues. Challenges are expected around changes in routine, such as the start or end of school, a move to a new home, vacation, illness, or the birth of a sibling. Regressions may occur after a wide range of events in family life such as a sibling moving away, rearrangement of furniture, or the death of a pet. Less obvious stresses may include changes to or from daylight saving time, changes in sleeping or mealtime schedules, or a new student in class. In particular, it is important to consider that an underlying health issue may be triggering a change in behavior.

Philip was back to an old behavior of hitting. Mom was very angry when he hit her, and even more so when he hit his new baby brother. She had just gone back to work and was tired and overwhelmed. She spoke sternly to Philip and explained how hitting hurt.

Of course, in this situation, it is easy to empathize with both Philip and Mom. When there is a regression, a clinician can help to identify the stressors and help to align expectations. Philip cannot be allowed to hit but may need additional support to address his feelings of distress, using strategies corresponding to the early milestones of warmth and reciprocity, rather than appealing to logical reasoning.

Darren had been toilet trained, but had regressed and was now back in diapers. Recently, he was found taking off his diapers and smearing feces on the walls. After cleaning up, his parents had been advised to place him alone in his room, without any toys, for 30 minutes. After any repeat of this behavior, he was placed in his room for a longer period of time. Unfortunately, this approach did not diminish the behavior—in fact, it escalated.

An assessment revealed that Darren had some capacities at Milestones 1, 2, and 3. He was not yet able to sustain coregulated interactions and had no language or other evidence of symbolic thinking. In addition, the assessment uncovered several new stressors in Darren's life. He was in a new school placement and his favorite aide was no longer working with him. He was frequently placed in a time-out area at school.

Intervention began with addressing the support needed at school, and focused on strengthening the early milestones. A treatment plan included close supervision to prevent opportunities for smearing, and more support overall. Darren needed to develop a trusting relationship with an adult so that he could gradually advance his capacities to communicate and have purposeful interactions.

Sometimes a child's progress seems to be stalled as he replays a similar idea over and over, draws the same image repeatedly, or frequently talks about the same issue. These ideas and images usually represent an overwhelming feeling, and the child is attempting to utilize these outlets to gain some control or mastery of these disturbing emotions. It is helpful to consider the relationship between the preferred ideas and real-life experience. Play-based intervention and changes in daily life work in tandem to support progress.

At times, challenging behaviors may actually be developmental progress, even when they seem to be a regression. Development naturally goes through periods of upheaval and challenge, followed by reconsolidation and organization at a higher level. The typical obstinacy and negativity of a 2-year-old is a reflection of a burgeoning sense of self-determination and independence. While an occasional tantrum in a toddler is expected, when a child reaches a similar stage of independence at a later chronological age, it can be more difficult to appreciate as progress. For a child who has been spitting, striking out, and showing other primal signs of rage, a change to crying in sadness is also an advance. Whenever there is regression or an obstacle to progress, a thorough reassessment may help to identify the cause.

I: Individual Differences and Working With a Team

An important aspect of understanding behavioral challenges is to recognize how individual differences in sensory processing, motor skills, language, and health contribute to behavior. Over the course of treatment, clinicians must continuously consider how these differences may support or be a barrier to progress. Individual differences are not static, and a child's array of abilities or deficits may have different impacts at different times.

Several professionals are often involved in children's development. It is always helpful for those professionals to collaborate, along with the parents, in a team effort. Although adults may have distinctly different areas of expertise and responsibility, and may even work from divergent theoretical models, it is still beneficial to share impressions and coordinate efforts.

Ongoing communication between professionals allows greater understanding of a child's behavior in day-to-day events, as well as overall developmental capacities. Various professionals may be able to address skills that complement each other's goals, or decide to divide goals to avoid presenting conflicting or confusing strategies or recommendations to children or parents. To facilitate communication, consent for disclosure of information and confidentiality may be reviewed periodically with the parents.

During the course of treatment, clinicians may identify an aspect of a child's behavior or family interaction that is beyond their area of expertise. It then becomes important to consider the assistance of a mental health professional, such as a psychiatrist, psychologist, marriage and family therapist, or social worker. A mental health professional can help parents to understand and address strong feelings and reactions.

Clara was overwhelmed with emotion at her 3-year-old son's aggressive themes in play. With the support of a mental health professional, she was able to draw connections to her past. As a girl, Clara had witnessed her father being physically aggressive toward her mother. With support she was able to gain perspective and support her son to explore and elaborate his aggressive themes and advance to healthy competition.

It is helpful for all professionals to be aware of indicators that a consultation is indicated and be familiar with the range of disciplinary specialists. A situation may call for consultation with an occupational therapist, physical therapist, speech and language pathologist, registered dietician, physician, mental health specialist, law enforcement, child protective services, educational specialist, music therapist, art therapist, or other child development specialist.

In some situations, medical care is indicated to help with the biological differences that lead to behavior. In addition to general health issues, the triggers to consider the use of psychotropic medication usually involve uncontrolled and dangerous aggression, destructive behavior, or self-injurious behavior. A consultation for medication is also indicated when there is a possibility of mental illness including depression, obsessive-compulsive disorder, or mood or thought disorder, or if there is a possibility of seizures, gastrointestinal problems, or other health problems.

With dangerous behaviors, a family may need to consider additional levels of supportive care, including in-home or out-of-home care, on either a temporary or permanent basis. A professional working with a child may be in a position to broach this topic with the parents, or seek out a referral to do so. In the case that emergency plans need to be implemented to keep the child and others safe, all members of the team should be informed and assist as appropriate.

Intervention in the School Setting

Teachers often find it challenging to connect with parents around a child's behavioral challenges. In order to meet, teachers and administrators may need to accommodate parents' schedules. Various alternatives may need to be considered to establish consistent communication.

Communication must be two-way so that teachers are aware of a child's experiences at home, and parents must know about the child's day at school. By sharing histories, priorities, goals, and strategies, professionals can gain a more complete understanding of a child and can create a plan for intervention that has the best possibility for success.

A teacher instructs and supervises a group of children. Yet when a challenging behavior occurs, a child inevitably requires individual attention. It is helpful to designate a particular adult to form a relationship with the child, and then to be the person to interact when needed. Through gaining an in-depth knowledge of a child and the treatment strategies, and by building a trusting relationship, this adult is best able to support a child's behavior and advancement. If a classroom aide is assigned this role, it is imperative to have the proper training, and that the assignment is consistent over time in order to support the development of a strong relationship with the child.

R: Patterns of Relationship During the Course of Treatment

A child's relationship with the parents is the primary context of developmental intervention. Advances in developmental capacities are a reflection of progress in this relationship. Parenting is a journey of parents and child growing together. Each parent-child relationship is unique; however, three challenging patterns of interaction may become evident during the course of treatment: directing the child through challenges, avoiding challenges, and expectations that are above the child's current capacities.

Pattern of Directing the Child

Sometimes it is difficult for parents to watch their child struggle with a problem or fail to perform. They may be so anxious for their child to accomplish a task that they are compelled to give instructions or jump in and help. Here a clinician can help by making a plan ahead of time about how to encourage the child's initiative and then signaling the parent at a key moment. A clinician might use a raised finger, or a touch on a parent's arm, or a verbal cue: "Let's see if Johnny can figure it out." At these coaching moments, it is important that the parent sustain shared attention and not completely withdraw. The parent can be encouraged to continue the engagement and communicate interest and attunement, perhaps saying, "Ah, that isn't going in!" "You are really trying hard." A clinician can help parents appreciate their child's efforts and initiative.

Todd entered the playroom, which had a variety of toys available. Todd picked up a car and rolled it back and forth. Mom picked up another car and rolled it toward him. Then she said, "Follow me!" She rolled her car up the ramp. She continued, "Come this way. Let's go to the store." Todd followed her down the ramp, and then stopped. Mom tried to organize the story, "The store is over here and we can buy groceries and then make dinner." But, Mom sensed she had lost his attention. She knew he liked colors and said, "My car is red. What color is your car?" He answered, "Green." She continued, "And how many wheels does it have?" He didn't answer. She said, "Let's count: 1, 2, 3, 4." After a little while, Todd said, "I want to go."

The interventionist wanted to increase the sense of engagement and fun in the play. In her eagerness for playing together, Mom had inadvertently taken over and diminished the possibilities for Todd to explore and initiate his own ideas. The interventionist cued Mom to remember to observe and follow his interests. The interventionist suggested that Mom invite him back to play, and then simply make sound effects to match his movements with the car. He smiled when hearing her deep "zoom-zoom." Before long, they were re-engaged and Todd was having fun doing different movements with the cars, to elicit different funny sound effects from Mom.

Pattern of Avoiding Challenges

Some parents, consciously or unconsciously, seek to protect their child from distress by avoiding challenges. Parents may have the habit of asking the child's permission rather than setting a limit. They may avoid situations that may be stressful, or even deceive their child about events that could arouse painful feelings. In some situations, the parents have difficulty dealing with negative feelings such as sadness, anger, or fear, and avoid these feelings themselves. This pattern of interaction can create a barrier to progress and parents can be helped to find a balance between protecting a child and offering the just-right level of challenge for progress.

Stephanie's parents liked to have fun. In play sessions they were constantly joking, teasing, and being silly. At the same time, Stephanie was often not fully engaged in the interaction. Many of the comments were at an adult level, and Stephanie was more of an observer, as she continued to play on her own. The clinician recognized that the parents were not fully successful in their attempts to get Stephanie's attention. The pattern of joking and banter helped to fill in the gaps in their engagement. By sensitive coaching, she was able to help the parents attune to Stephanie's subtle cues and maintain their focus on her, even though it was difficult.

Eileen was fascinated by elevators. This became problematic because she would always want to push the buttons and ride. If this behavior was thwarted, she could be very loud and push anyone in her way. Mom was unable to physically restrain her and was resigned to avoiding any buildings with elevators. In fact, they usually stayed home. With help, Eileen and her mother worked on building a relationship with capacities at Milestones 1–4. They learned to sustain interactions, even when Eileen was sad, disappointed, or angry, and learned coregulation around limits. After she had developed these skills, elevators were introduced in pretend play. Finally, the concepts learned in play-based interactions allowed Eileen to bypass elevators and meet other challenges with Mom's support.

Pattern of High Expectations

A parent's expectations for successful behavior in new contexts, or under stressful conditions, may not be met. A goal to sit quietly in church for an hour or to end a repetitive behavior may not be realistic. A clinician can help a parent appreciate the facets of a situation that may be creating additional challenge, and outline the incremental steps as well as supports needed to reach a goal.

Not infrequently, a child has a mixed pattern of abilities that create an illusion of higher abilities than he actually possesses. The child may be very bright, learn quickly, and have advanced vocabulary and fund of knowledge. At the same time, that child may have a limited understanding of social cues and have significant constrictions at each of the developmental milestones. A parent may engage in conversations about news of the day or other adult-level concerns, assuming that the child will benefit from this type of interaction. Unfortunately, without sufficient functional emotional development, the child may be unable to gain perspective on these ideas, and become irritable or anxious. Here, a clinician can guide the parents to focus on strengthening the lower milestones and limit expectations for success at higher levels until those skills have been attained.

Brandon often embarrassed his parents with his rude comments. When given a gift of a model car, he responded, "I don't like cars." He was quick to tattle on other children that did not follow the rules, and would even correct adults. His logic was usually correct, but he lacked a sense of social perspective. His parents tried diligently to explain how his actions made others feel.

In pretend play, Brandon began by dictating the rules, and controlling the play so that others were only allowed to watch. Very gradually, by using strategies aligned with early milestones, Brandon developed trust and enjoyment in playing with the clinician and his parents. Although this took time, he then had the foundation to gradually advance up the milestones, and eventually developed friendships and a very sensitive attunement to others' feelings.

Continuous Assessment and Reassessment

Implementing a treatment plan involves continual reassessment, expanding insights, and periodic updates to the plan. Parents' involvement can be strengthened by reviewing and building on their priorities, interests, and strengths. If parents seem to lose enthusiasm, a professional must seek to reengage their participation by gaining a greater appreciation for their perspective and ideas. Reassessment may include review of their past experiences. As the child matures, each adult will find that his or her strengths and interests align to greater or lesser degree with those of the child. When two parents work in concert, these differences provide a rich network of supportive interactions.

When encountering obstacles to progress:

- When a child is not progressing as expected, it is wise to do a complete reassessment. Often, such a review will reveal the barriers to progress.
- When challenges increase, a child needs additional support, such as extra Floortime play sessions with parents.
- If a child is not successful, then goals should drop down to build the child's capacities at the lower levels.
- When progress slows, consider obtaining outside consultation with another discipline.
- When evaluating a treatment plan, a clinician can use the help of reflective supervision.

Reflective Supervision

Reflective supervision is a type of confidential, ongoing supervision that encourages professionals to openly discuss their thoughts and feelings about their work and then to draw connections between current experiences, previous work, and their own personal history. In addition to the traditional role of supervision in tracking progress and planning goals, activities, and treatment strategies, reflective supervision helps therapists gain insights that support their professional role, including increasing awareness of their own biases or particular sensitivities.

Every person is more or less comfortable with certain emotions and behaviors. In a professional role with families, situations may evoke strong feelings for clinicians because of their similarity to past personal experiences. Perhaps a clinician is also a parent and has dealt with a difficult behavior that is similar to the client's. Or a parent's response in some way reminds clinicians of their own parents and their feelings as a child. By recognizing and discussing these sensitivities, the clinician is less inclined to form inaccurate impressions or exaggerated responses and can better recognize when outside consultation is indicated.

A clinician's personal history can also help them to be especially sensitive and helpful to a child or family with a familiar challenge. Reflective supervision may provide guidance and reinforcement of professional boundaries when situations become especially personal.

Reflective supervision may simply be a time for professionals to acknowledge sadness about a child and family they are helping, or to celebrate hard-won success. The open nature of reflective supervision allows discussions to connect current and past, personal and professional, in recognition of the complex interplay of emotions in developmental relationship-based therapy. Ideally, every clinician has the opportunity to engage in a form of reflective supervision with a clinical supervisor or respected colleague.

Completing Treatment

In a developmental relationship-based approach, the ending point of treatment is not always clear. Because there are always new challenges, the resolution of a particular behavior is not the end of guiding and supporting a child's development. The broad benchmark for the completion of treatment is that the child's behaviors are no longer disruptive to daily life and parents have gained the skills and confidence to support their child's continuing growth on their own.

It is best if the end of treatment can be planned. Unfortunately, the length of treatment may be determined by many factors in addition to a family's progress. Often the period of treatment is dictated by a funding source. Or treatment may end because the family is moving away or a change in schedule precludes continuing therapy. The clinician and family must then alter goals and strategies to maximize the benefit of their time together.

Parents may choose to end treatment abruptly because some issue has made them too uncomfortable to continue. The clinician's offers of help may be declined. Parents may always be encouraged to consider other resources for continued support, and a clinician may help with referrals.

Ending a therapy relationship can elicit mixed emotions for both families and professionals. The child and professional usually have developed a warm relationship. Parents and clinician have created a form of intimacy. The last session can engender a mixture of celebration and sadness at the parting, or other feelings of anger, rejection, or anxiety on the part of parent, child, or clinician. Sometimes, powerful feelings are surprising and confusing. Clinicians can use supervision to gain perspective and support to respond to these feelings in themselves or others.

Tangible symbols of closure can assist with the termination. A goodbye session can be planned that involves some type of celebration and remembrance. Depending on the age and abilities of the child, some level of explanation of the ending can be provided, ranging from a simple goodbye card to a more expansive conversation about the child's new abilities and growth. Parents and clinicians may benefit from a private session without the child to recount their journey together.

Although completion of treatment has its own challenges, it also offers opportunities for growth. As children advance in school and through different treatments, many adults will take part in their life. Through the experience of developing a warm and trusting relationship with another adult, and then, with the support of their parents, coping with the sadness of separation and loss, children strengthen bonds with their parents and increase their capacity for successfully negotiating a complex emotional experience. Parents as well may benefit from the successful completion of treatment and find renewed hope and confidence in their knowledge of their child and appreciation of their progress together.

References

Ainsworth, M., Bell, S. M., & Stayton, D. (1974). Infant-mother attachment and social development: Socialization as a product of reciprocal responsiveness to signals. In M. Richards (Ed.), *The integration of the child into a social world.* Cambridge: Cambridge University Press.

Aldred, C., Green, J., & Adams, C. (2004). A new social communication intervention for children with autism: A pilot randomized controlled treatment study suggesting effectiveness. *Journal of Child Psychology and Psychiatry, 45*(8), 1420–1430.

Axline, V. M. (1947). *Play therapy, the inner dynamics of childhood.* Oxford: Houghton Mifflin.

American Psychological Association (2005). *Policy statement on evidence-based practice in psychology.* Retrieved from http://www.apa.org/practice/guide-lines/evidence-based-statement.aspx

American Speech-Language-Hearing Association. (2005). *Evidence-based practice in communication disorders* [Position Statement]. Retrieved from http://www.asha.org/policy/PS2005-00221/

Ayres, A. J. (1970). *Sensory integration and the child.* Los Angeles: Western Psychological Services.

Bauminger, N., & Kasari, C. (2000). Loneliness and friendship in high-functioning children with autism. *Child Development, 71*(2), 447–456.

Bowlby, J. (1951). *Maternal care and mental health.* World Health Organization Monograph Series, no. 51. Geneva: World Health Organization.

Bowlby, J. (1999). *Attachment: Attachment and loss* (Vol. 1, 2nd ed). New York: Basic Books. (Original work published 1969)

Brazelton, T. B. & Nugent, J. K. (1995). *The neonatal behavioral assessment scale (NBAS)* (3rd ed.). London: Mac Keith Press. (Original work published 1973)

Bruner, J. (1990). *Acts of meaning: Four lectures on mind and culture.* Jerusalem-Harvard Lectures. Cambridge, MA: Harvard University Press.

Buysse, V., Winton, P., Rous, B., Epstein, D., & Lim, C. (2012, March). Evidence-based practice: Foundations for the Connect 5-step learning cycle in professional development. *Zero to Three*, 25–29.

Cameron, W. B. (1963). *Informal sociology: A casual introduction to sociological thinking*. New York: Random House.

Carr, E. G., Dunlap, G., Horner, R. H., Koegel, R. L., Turnbull, A. P, Sailor, W., Anderson, J. L., Albin, R. W., Koegel, L. K., & Fox, L. (2002). Positive behavior support: Evolution of an applied science. *Journal of Positive Behavior Interventions, 4*(1), 4–16, 20.

Casenhiser, D., Binns, A., McGill, F., Morderer, O., & Shanker, S. (2014). Measuring and supporting language function for children with autism: Evidence from a randomized control trial of a social-interaction-based therapy. *Journal of Autism and Developmental Disorders*. Advance online publication. doi:10.1007/s10803-014-2242-3

Casenhiser, D., Shanker, S., & Stieben, J. (2011). Learning through interaction in children with autism: Preliminary data from a social-communication-based intervention. *Autism*, 1–22. Advance online publication. doi:10.1177/1362361311422052

Erikson, E. H. (1963). *Childhood and society* (2nd ed.). New York: W. W. Norton.

Fogel, A. (1993). *Developing through relationships: Origins of communication, self and culture*. Chicago: University of Chicago Press.

Freud, A. (1965). Normality and pathology in childhood: Assessments of development. In *The writings of Anna Freud*, Vol. 6. New York: International Universities Press.

Freud, S. (1960). The ego and the id. In J. Strachey (Ed.), *The standard edition of the complete psychological works of Sigmund Freud*. New York: W. W. Norton. (Original work published 1923)

Gernsbacher, M. A. (2006). Toward a behavior of reciprocity. *Journal of Developmental Processes, 1*, 139–152.

Green, J., Charman, T., McConachie, H., Aldred, C., Slonims, V., Howlin, O., Le Couteur, A., Leadbitter, K., Hudry, K., Byford, S., Barrett, B., Temple, K., MacDonald, W., Pickles, A., & the PACT Consortium. (2010). Parent mediated communication-focused treatment in children with autism (PACT): A randomized controlled trial. *Lancet, 375*, 2152–2160. doi:10.1016/SO140-6736(10)605787-9

Greenspan, S. I. (1979). *Intelligence and adaptation: An integration of psychoanalytic and Piagetian developmental psychology*. New York: International Universities Press.

Greenspan, S. I. (1992). *Infancy and early childhood: The practice of clinical assessment and intervention with emotional and developmental challenges*. Madison, CT: International Universities Press.

Greenspan, S. I. (1997). *Developmentally based psychotherapy.* Madison, CT: International Universities Press.

Greenspan, S. I. (2001). The affect diathesis hypothesis: The role of emotions in the core deficit in autism and in the development of intelligence and social skills. *Journal of Developmental and Learning Disorders, 5*(1), 1–45.

Greenspan, S. I. (2005). Social-emotional subtest. In N. Bayley, *The Bayley scales of infant and toddler development* (3rd ed.). San Antonio, TX: Psychological Corporation.

Greenspan, S. I., & Shanker, S. G. (2004). *The first idea: How symbols, language, and intelligence evolved from our primate ancestors to modern humans.* New York: Da Capo.

Greenspan, S. I., & Wieder, S. (1997). Developmental patterns and outcomes in infants and children with disorders in relating and communicating: A chart review of 200 cases of children with autistic spectrum diagnoses. *Journal of Developmental and Learning Disorders, 1,* 87–141.

Greenspan, S. I., & Wieder, S. (1998). *The child with special needs: Encouraging intellectual and emotional growth.* New York: Da Capo.

Greenspan, S. I., & Wieder, S. (2005). Can children with autism master the core deficits and become empathetic, creative and reflective? A ten to fifteen-year follow-up of a subgroup of children with autism spectrum disorders (ASD) who received a comprehensive Developmental, Individual-difference, Relationship-based (DIR) approach. *Journal of Developmental and Learning Disorders, 9,* 43–61.

Greenspan, S. I., & Wieder, S. (2006). *Engaging autism.* New York: Da Capo.

Greenspan, S. I., Wieder, S., & DeGangi, G. (2001). *The functional emotional assessment scale (FEAS) for infancy and early childhood: Clinical and research applications.* Bethesda, MD: Interdisciplinary Council on Developmental and Learning Disorders.

Horner, R. H., Carr, E. G., Strain, P. S., Todd, A. W., & Reed, H. K. (2002). Problem behavior interventions for young children with autism: A research synthesis. *Journal of Autism and Developmental Disorders, 32*(5), 423–446.

Kohlberg, L. (1981). *The philosophy of moral development: Moral stages and the idea of justice.* Essays on Moral Development, Vol. 1. New York: Harper and Row.

Kohlberg, L. (1984). *The psychology of moral development: The nature and validity of moral stages.* Essays on Moral Development, Vol. 2. New York: Harper and Row.

Liao, S., Hwang, Y., Chen, Y., Lee, P., Chen, S., & Lin, L. (2014). Home-based DIR/Floortime intervention program for preschoolers with autism spectrum disorders: Preliminary findings. *Physical and Occupational Therapy in Pediatrics, 34*(4), 356–367.

Lovaas, O. I. (1987). Behavioral treatment and normal educational and intellectual functioning in young autistic children. *Journal of Consulting and Clinical Psychology, 55*(1), 3–9.

Magiati, I., Tay, X. W., & Howlin, P. (2012). Early comprehensive behaviorally based interventions for children with autism spectrum disorders: A summary of findings from recent reviews and meta-analyses. *Neuropsychiatry, 2*(6), 543–570.

Mahler, M. S. (1975). *The psychological birth of the human infant: Symbiosis and individuation.* New York: Basic Books.

Mahoney, G., & Perales, F. (2003).Using relationship-focused intervention to enhance the social-emotional functioning of young children with autism spectrum disorders. *Topics in Early Childhood Special Education, 23*(2), 74–86.

Mahoney, G., & Perales, F. (2005). Relationship focused early intervention with children with pervasive developmental disorders and other disabilities: A comparative study. *Journal of Developmental and Behavioral Pediatrics, 26*(2), 77–85.

Maslow, A. H. (2014). *Toward a psychology of being.* Reprint, Floyd, VA: Sublime Books. (Original work published 1962)

Mazefsky, C. A., Pelphrey, K. A., & Dahl, R. E. (2012). The need for a broader approach to emotion regulation research in autism. *Child Development Perspectives, 6*(1), 92–97.

Mazurek, M. O. (2014). Loneliness, friendship, and well-being in adults with autism spectrum disorders. *Autism, 18*(3), 223–232.

Opie, I. (1997). "Hickory, dickory, dock." In *The Oxford dictionary of nursery rhymes* (2nd ed., p. 244). Oxford: Oxford University Press.

Pajareya, K., & Nopmaneejumruslers, K. (2011). A pilot randomized controlled trial of DIR/Floortime parent training intervention for pre-school children with autistic spectrum disorders. *Autism, 15*(2), 1–15.

Pavlov, I. P. (2012). *Conditioned reflexes.* Reprint, Mineola, NY: Dover. (Original work published 1927)

Piaget, J. (1952). *The origins of intelligence in children.* New York: International Universities Press.

Prizant, B. M. (2011, Fall). Straight talk about autism: The use and misuse of evidence-based practice; implications for persons with ASD. *Autism Spectrum Quarterly,* 43–49.

Rogers, C. R. (1961). *On becoming a person: A therapist's view of psychotherapy.* New York: Houghton Mifflin.

Rogers, S. J., & Vismara, L. A. (2008). Evidence-based comprehensive treatments for early autism. *Journal of Clinical Child and Adolescent Psychology, 37*(1), 8–38.

Salt, J., Schemilt, J., Sellars, V., Boyd, S., Coulson, T., & McCool, S. (2002).

The Scottish Centre for autism preschool treatment program II: The results of a controlled treatment study. *Autism, 6*(1), 33–46.

Schreibman, L., Dawson, G., Stahmer, A. C., Landa, R., Rogers, S. J., McGee, G. G., Kasari, C., Ingersoll, B., Kaiser, A. P., Bruinsma, Y., McNerney, E., Wetherby, A., & Halladay, A. (2015). Naturalistic developmental behavioral interventions: Empirically validated treatments for autism spectrum disorder. *Journal of Autism and Developmental Disorders*, 1–18.

Shedler, J. (2010). The efficacy of psychodynamic psychotherapy. *American Psychologist, 65*(2), 98–109.

Siller, M., Hutman, T., & Sigman, M. (2013). A parent-mediated intervention to increase responsive parental behaviors and child communication in children with ASD: A randomized, clinical trial. *Journal of Autism and Developmental Disorders, 43*(3), 540–550.

Siller, M., & Sigman, M. (2002). The behaviors of parents of children with autism predict the subsequent development of their children's communication. *Journal of Autism and Developmental Disorders, 32*(2), 77–89.

Siller, M., Swanson, M., Gerber, A., Hutman, T., & Sigman, M. (2014). A parent-mediated intervention that targets responsive parental behaviors increases attachment behaviors in children with ASD: Results from a randomized clinical trial. *Journal of Autism and Developmental Disorders, 44*, 1720–1732.

Skinner, B. F. (1953). *Science and human behavior.* New York: Free Press.

Solomon, R., Necheles, J., Ferch, C., & Bruckman, D. (2007). Pilot study of a parent-training program for young children with autism: The Play Project home consultation program. *Autism, 11*(3), 205–224.

Solomon, R., Van Egeren, L., Mahoney, G., Quon-Huber, M., & Zimmerman, P. (2014). Play Project home consultation intervention program for young children with autism spectrum disorders: A randomized controlled trial. *Journal of Developmental and Behavioral Pediatrics, 35*(8), 475–485.

Stern, D. N. (2000). *The interpersonal world of the infant: A view from psychoanalysis and developmental psychology.* New York: Basic Books. (Original work published 1985)

Vygotsky, L. S. (1978). *Mind in society: The development of higher psychological processes.* M. Cole, V. John-Steiner, S. Scribner, & E. Souberman (Eds.). Cambridge, MA: Harvard University Press.

Watson, J. B. (1925). *Behaviorism.* New York: W. W. Norton.

Weitlauf, A. S., McPheeters, M. L., Peters, B., Sathe, N., Travis, R., Aiello, R., Williamson, E., Veenstra-VanderWeele, J., Krishnaswami, S., Jerome, R., & Warren, Z. (2014). Therapies for children with autism spectrum disorder: Behavioral interventions update. *Comparative Effectiveness Review*, No. 137. Agency for Healthcare Research and Quality, Publication No. 14-EHC036-EF.

Winnicott, D. W. (2005). *Playing and reality* (2nd ed.). New York: Routledge. (Original work published 1971)

Young, J., Corea, C., Kimani, J., & Mandell, D. (2010). *Autism spectrum disorders (ASDs) services: Final report on environmental scan, autism spectrum disorders services project*. Columbia, MD: IMPAQ International.

Index